T5-AGM-792

SEEKING THE HIGHEST GOOD:
SOCIAL SERVICE AND GENDER AT
THE UNIVERS Y OF TORO'NTC '888–1937

In the summer of 1910, the University of Toronto opened its settlement house in one of Toronto's crowded manufacturing districts. The university's first active response to social problems in the city beyond its grounds, University Settlement (modelled on Toynbee Hall) was a conscious attempt by its advocates to apply the social views of British idealism to the problems generated by poverty. It was also the product of a philosophy that held that the study of social problems would lead to their solution.

In *Seeking the Highest Good*, Sara Burke provides an appraisal of the social thought of a succession of influential academics at the university, from W.J. Ashley, the first professor of political economy, and his successor, James Mavor, to the social philosopher E.J. Urwick – the men who forged and preserved into the late 1930s the distinctive 'Toronto ideal.' Uniting the idealist reform impulse with empirical social analysis, the 'ideal' determined the framework for the university's participation in voluntary and professional social services and provided the basis for the curriculum of the Department of Social Service in 1914.

Burke describes how the supporters of the Toronto ideal became involved in an ongoing struggle to defend their authority against the challenges presented by the female-dominated profession of social work. Burke reveals that, although women far outnumbered men on the staff of University Settlement and in the enrolment of the Department of Social Service by the 1920s, their lack of access to power in the university meant that their participation in social service was devalued by the rest of the academic community.

Burke's study uncovers the process by which the ethical beliefs of British idealism became meaningful for a large number of students, faculty, and alumni, and how, once popularized, they became incorporated into the institutional structure of the university.

(Studies in Gender and History)

SARA Z. BURKE is a postdoctoral fellow in the Department of History at the University of Waterloo, and winner of the John Bullen Prize for best doctoral thesis, awarded by the Canadian Historical Association.

STUDIES IN GENDER AND HISTORY

General Editors: Franca Iacovetta and Craig Heron

SARA Z. BURKE

Seeking the Highest Good: Social Service and Gender at the University of Toronto 1888–1937

UNIVERSITY OF TORONTO PRESS
Toronto Buffalo London

BRESCIA COLLEGE
LIBRARY
65232

© University of Toronto Press Incorporated 1996
Toronto Buffalo London
Printed in Canada

ISBN 0-8020-0782-1 (cloth)
ISBN 0-8020-7146-5 (paper)

Printed on acid-free paper

Canadian Cataloguing in Publication Data

Burke, Sara Z. (Sara Zena), 1963–
  Seeking the highest good : social service and gender at the University of
  Toronto, 1888–1937

(Studies in gender and history)
Includes bibliographical references.
ISBN 0-8020-0782-1 (bound)
ISBN 0-8020-7146-5 (pbk.)

  1. University of Toronto, Dept. of Social Service – History.
  2. University Settlement (Toronto, Ont.) – History.
  3. Social service – Ontario – Toronto – History.
  4. Sex role – Ontario – Toronto – History.
  I. Title.   II. Series.

LE3.T52 1996   361.9713'541   C95-933076-1

This book has been published with the help of a grant from the Humanities and
Social Sciences Federation of Canada, using funds provided by the Social Sciences
and Humanities Research Council of Canada.

University of Toronto Press acknowledges the financial assistance to its publishing
program of the Canada Council and the Ontario Arts Council.

FOR BRUCE AND ANNA

Find the highest good by serving your fellows
through your intellect, your wealth, your position,
or whatever talent you may possess.

Robert A. Falconer (1910)

Contents

Acknowledgments

Throughout the various stages of researching and writing this book, many people have generously given me their knowledge and time. Most of my research was conducted at the University of Toronto Archives, and I am thankful to Harold Averill, Marnee Gamble, Lorraine O'Donnell, Rick Stapleton, Legring Ulanday, and Garron Wells for their help. Tory Tronrud, the archivist of the Thunder Bay Historical Museum Society, graciously responded to my inquiry for material relating to J.M. Shaver. I would also like to thank the staffs of the Archives of Ontario, the City of Toronto Archives, the Baldwin Room of the Metropolitan Toronto Central Library, the National Archives of Canada, the Thomas Fisher Rare Book Library, and the United Church / Victoria University Archives. My research was funded by support from the Department of History at Carleton University and by a doctoral fellowship from the Social Sciences and Humanities Research Council of Canada. An earlier form of chapter 3 appeared as an article published in the *Journal of the Canadian Historical Association* NS 4 (1993).

This book started life as a doctoral dissertation at Carleton University, and I am grateful to my thesis supervisor, A.B. McKillop, for his insightful criticisms and good-humoured encouragement as the project evolved from a graduate paper. I wish to thank the members of my examining committee, Marilyn Barber, Ramsay Cook, Deborah Gorham, and Gale Wills, for the opportunity to incorporate their comments into subsequent revisions of the manuscript. I also thank Rob Ferguson, Gerry Hallowell, and John St James at University of Toronto Press.

I am indebted to my family for all the support I have received, and would particularly like to thank my father for reading the manuscript and offering his invaluable advice. To Bruce, I owe more than I can adequately express. With his realism and clear thinking, he managed to talk me through any difficulty. This book is dedicated to him, and to our daughter Anna.

W.J. Ashley

James Mavor

The "Futurist" Number

Dr. N. J. Ware, *Superintendent.*

University Settlement
Review

467 Adelaide St. West

Pamphlet announcing the appointment of Norman J. Ware to University Settlement, 1913

University Settlement, 1914

University Settlement, 1914

District office for Toronto's Department of Health, University Settlement, 1915

Class executive of the Department of Social Service, 1915–16 (left to right: Dorothy W. Eddis, Stella Ireland, Jeanette M. Rathbun, Hannah G. Matheson)

The original Social Service Building on Queen's Park Crescent, 1923

Agnes C. McGregor

R.M. MacIver   E.J. Urwick

SEEKING THE HIGHEST GOOD

Introduction

In the fall of 1910, the president of the University of Toronto, Robert A. Falconer, urged his audience of students and faculty to break down the barriers created by wealth, social position, and intellectual training, and to carry the advantages of education to those who lacked them. 'Find the highest good by serving your fellows,' he advised, 'through your intellect, your wealth, your position, or whatever talent you may possess.'[1] That winter, a young theology student and his bride decided to act on Falconer's entreaty by living in a small semi-detached house on Adelaide Street West, in the centre of one of Toronto's crowded manufacturing districts. The building had been chosen to house University Settlement, and the student, J.M. Shaver, had been appointed the new agency's resident secretary.

The members of the university were by no means alone in their concern over the social effects of industrialization and urban poverty. By the 1880s, there had been a noticeable shift of Canada's population into urban centres, and observers had started to worry that a large number of families in Toronto and Montreal – and also in such smaller cities as Quebec, Halifax, and Winnipeg – were precariously dependent on industrial wages. Investigators confirmed these fears. In 1887 the Royal Commission on the Relations of Labour and Capital had revealed that most industrial workers lived in poverty owing to low wages or unemployment, that their housing was inadequate, and that their working conditions were dangerous. In 1896, the businessman Herbert B. Ames had surveyed a working-class district of Montreal, and also had concluded that insufficient employment forced many families into chronic poverty.[2]

Since the late nineteenth century, reformers and church leaders had anxiously watched the growth of Canada's cities, and the belief that this new country would soon possess slums equal to those in London or New York had sparked a variety of reform efforts. In the areas of child welfare and public health, Canadian reformers had reacted to reports of a declining birth rate and rising infant mortality by challenging the established wisdom of *laissez-faire*, and a number of private agencies had been formed to lobby for preventative government legislation. For some critics, the problem of urban poverty had as much a moral as an economic significance, and the evils of the slum, with its seemingly unlimited degree of crime and vice, had raised possibilities of moral dissipation on a national scale.[3] Among Canadian Protestants, the social gospel had inspired an interest in social reform that broadened the traditional focus of their evangelism, and, after 1890, the Presbyterian and Methodist churches had taken the lead in proliferating city missions throughout Canada.

By the first decade of the twentieth century, the causes of urban poverty had become a central topic of debate, and schemes for social and moral renewal preoccupied reformers from a wide section of middle-class opinion. At the heart of this debate lay the question of state responsibility. The example of early welfare legislation in Britain, which by 1911 included plans for old-age pensions and unemployment insurance, drew attention to the almost complete lack of initiative taken by Canadian governments at either the provincial or the federal level. In Canada, however, responsibility for social welfare traditionally rested on the private sector; ideally it relied on the individual and the family, or, if necessary, on voluntary charitable organizations that administered both private and public funds. While this tradition would increasingly come under attack from reformers, policy makers, and social workers, government intervention in public welfare would remain limited until the period of reconstruction following the Second World War.[4]

The actions of J.M. Shaver and other students at the University of Toronto constituted only one aspect of a reform climate that prompted Canadians to apply a number of different solutions to the problem of urban poverty. This book explores a response to this perceived crisis that, if not unique in its ideological origins, gained an identity entirely distinct to the university and its own intellectual traditions. The study attempts to answer a specific question: Why did the University of Toronto choose settlement work as its first active response to the social problems in the city beyond its grounds? It is the central assertion of this book that in responding to Falconer's injunction to seek the 'highest good' through service, students and faculty at the university were primarily influenced by a dominant social ethic, a complex mixture of moral and scientific intentions that I have termed the 'Toronto ideal.' During the fifty years that preceded the Second World War, the Toronto ideal established the framework for the university's participation in social service. It was incorporated into the policy of University Settlement in 1910, and, by providing the basis for the curriculum of the Department of Social Service in 1914, it was also instrumental in shaping the academic nature of both social work and sociology at the University of Toronto. This social ethic was encapsulated neatly in another address by Robert Falconer, in which he stressed that scientific training must be combined with 'the humanitarian side' for effective social service. 'President Falconer Gives Advice to Students,' the *Toronto Mail* later reported: 'Join Science and Sentiment.'[5]

The Toronto ideal had its origins in a school of British social thought emanating from Oxford University, which since the 1870s had linked the moral incentive of philosophical idealism to the empirical study of society. At Oxford, the idealist philosopher T.H. Green taught his students that their primary obligation was to realize their 'higher selves' through service to others. Green believed that the effects of industrialization had destroyed the natural ties of interdependence that traditionally held society together, and that social reform could only be brought about by the reestablishment of local community. Once members of different classes had come into personal contact with one another, the poor would have access to, and be influenced by, the elevating culture of their educated neighbours. Through the work of the historical economist Arnold Toynbee, Green's ethical teachings became relevant to a group of young British economists, who believed that their empirical research could be applied to solve the social problems produced by industrialization. These economists used empirical or 'scientific' methodology to gather factual information that, they believed, could then be applied to satisfy moral purposes; ultimately, the study of social problems would lead to their solution. They trusted that facts on social conditions needed only to be harnessed to the moral energy derived from idealism to bring about social reform. The social thought of Green and Toynbee was, in its implications, essentially collectivist; their followers justified new areas of state intervention by the assertion that the government had a primary responsibility to promote the common good. To this extent, the political theories of the idealists, led by Green, exerted a profound influence on the formation of British liberal welfare legislation between 1907 and 1911. The teachings of Green and Toynbee also were influential in the development of British social work, inspiring the original settlement house, Toynbee Hall, in 1884, and shaping the curriculum of the first British program in social-work education, the London School of Sociology and Social Economics, in 1903.

The authority of the Toronto ideal was sustained by arguments that were not distinct to the Canadian situation, and that previously had been applied by British social critics and reformers to conditions in their own country. The acceptance of these arguments by academics at the University of Toronto ensured that once the university turned its attention to the question of social reform, it would attempt to emulate the actions of those at Oxford. Like Toynbee Hall and the London School of Sociology, Toronto's University Settlement and Department of Social Service were projects that tried to incorporate the social thought of T.H. Green and Arnold Toynbee into a practical organizational structure. The opinions explored in this study therefore fall into the category of ideas and assumptions that lie between formal systems of thought and the world of social action. The Toronto ideal served as this kind of link, forming a bridge between the ethical beliefs of British idealism, as they were articulated by an elite group of academics, and the creation of a distinct type of social service that had meaning for a significant section of the university community. As an intellectual history, this book examines the tenuous relationship between social thought and social reform, aiming to discover the process by which theory meets reality, and an idea becomes realized in collective action.

The following chapters focus on the social thought of a succession of influential academics at the University of Toronto, faculty members who, it is argued, were responsible for establishing the moral and scientific ascendency of the Toronto ideal. The approach is partly biographical, and the chapters are structured chronologically, beginning with the appointment of W.J. Ashley as the first professor of political economy in 1888 and ending in 1937 with the retirement of the social philosopher E.J. Urwick. Since this approach necessarily is determined by those who left the records – the male faculty members who held positions of authority in the university, and who articulated their views in addresses and publications – it raises the question of class and, more significantly, the issue of gender. Most of the academics discussed here belonged to the British middle classes; all certainly shared a middle-class perception of the social problems that they addressed. The reforms and solutions they advocated were shaped by these views, with little or no reference to the values of those they sought to benefit. My purpose here is not to assess the economic or social effectiveness of the reforms promoted by a few Toronto academics, but instead to uncover the process by which these ideas became meaningful for a large number of students, faculty, and alumni, and how, once popularized, they became incorporated into the institutional structure of the university. Although the dominance of the Toronto ideal was sustained until the late 1930s, its supporters were involved in an ongoing struggle to defend their authority from the challenges presented by professional social work. As this struggle remained confined within the boundaries of middle-class thought and action, the contest was propelled not by the dynamics of class, but by the conflict of gender.

Since the 1980s, new studies, particularly in the area of nineteenth-century British history, have explored the power relationships between men and women and have searched for the shifting historical meanings by which the relative categories of gender are determined. Influenced by poststructuralist theory, these studies have concluded that both femininity and masculinity are socially constructed concepts, and that each is defined in relation to the other.[6] At the University of Toronto, the construction of gender roles in social service allowed the reform interests of men and women to be both segregated and placed in contention. The Toronto ideal created a model of service that challenged the professional social work of university women in two significant ways. First of all, it elevated the superior importance of the university's young men by conveying the belief that, as society's future leaders in politics and business, they alone could bring the force of their education to bear upon Canada's social problems. Male students were taught that their manhood could best be exercised through the duties of active citizenship. Direct social service was seen primarily as a temporary way for men to gain first-hand knowledge of social problems, knowledge that, when analysed empirically, could be utilized to improve social conditions. Second, the Toronto ideal valued social service as an explicitly moral activity that ultimately benefited those who gave their services as much as it did those who received them. The teachings of British idealism supported an expansion of state responsibility, yet the vision of public welfare that it promoted relied on the self-negating voluntarism of its male citizens.

Although women at first were excluded from participating equally in the activities officially sanctioned by their university, female undergraduates and alumnae cultivated their own independent interest in social service and, after 1900, relied on the emerging profession of social work for authority. The early numerical dominance of women in social work was accelerated by the First World War, and by the 1920s women far outnumbered men both on the staff of University Settlement and in the enrolment of the Department of Social Service. Yet women's lack of access to sources of power in the university meant that their participation in social service remained devalued by the rest of the academic community. In the records, their activities often suggest no more than a silent dissension from the views endorsed by Toronto's leading male academics. While female social workers would increasingly base their claim to professional status on the possession of technical skills suited to welfare administration, the Toronto ideal would continue to regard social service as an expression of moral fulfilment, a realization of the 'highest good' that was exemplified by the disinterested male volunteer.

1

British Roots: Arnold Toynbee, W.J. Ashley, and the New Political Economy, 1888–1892

For young men attending the University of Toronto in the late nineteenth century, the creation of the Department of Political Economy in 1888 was an important step in the formulation of an ethic that would place them at the very centre of their college's new ambitions for social reform. Through the teachings of the first professor of political economy, W.J. Ashley, male students at Toronto were exposed to currents of social thought that earlier in the decade had prompted young men from Oxford and Cambridge to regard the alleviation of Britain's poverty as their own particular responsibility. The urgency of this responsibility was conveyed in the compelling arguments of an influential group of intellectuals and reformers, who turned to the idealist philosopher T.H. Green for explanations, and who looked to the economist Arnold Toynbee for inspiration. Like all idealists, Green and Toynbee were optimistic, secure in the conviction that progress was an inevitable result of human evolution. Following Toynbee's lead, many young British economists like Ashley became determined that empirical research could be applied to solve the social problems produced by industrialization. Armed with an idealist faith in social improvement, men from the ancient universities became confident that their class and gender required them to play a unique role in hastening the reformation of British society. Similarly, at the University of Toronto the idealist ethic encouraged a generation of young men to turn their attention to the practical problems of Canadian life. By doing so, it helped to transform the university's perception of masculinity, a view that until the late 1880s had been defined by the competitive and sporting preoccupations of its male undergraduates.

British Idealism and the University Settlement Movement

The establishment of Toynbee Hall in 1884 was one of the most significant of the many efforts at social reform that proliferated in Britain during the last quarter of the nineteenth century. Although the Victorian conscience had long been alive to the social criticism of Thomas Carlyle, John Ruskin, and Matthew Arnold, by the 1870s a vast section of the middle and upper classes began to criticize the fact that poverty was so widespread in Britain's emerging democracy. To use Beatrice Webb's famous phrase, 'a new consciousness of sin' had grown up among the privileged classes, inspiring a particularly intense reaction in philanthropic and academic circles.[1] One of the founders of Toynbee Hall, Henrietta Barnett, conveyed this sense of guilt with characteristic bluntness while addressing a meeting of the London Charity Organisation Society in 1884. 'Which of us,' Barnett challenged, 'having once seen a Whitechapel alley at five o'clock on an August afternoon, and realizing all it means, besides physical discomfort, could go and enjoy our afternoon tea, daintily spread on the shady lawn, and not ask himself difficult questions about his own responsibility – while one man has so much and another so little?'[2] The fervent, almost obsessive concern with 'outcast London' culminated in a flurry of reform activity during the early 1880s, and students at Oxford and Cambridge, among others, were inspired to take social action.

By the late 1870s, a strong tradition of public service had developed in the two universities, and was epitomized by the earnest young men coming out of Balliol College, Oxford. This spirit of disinterested service was inspired by the manly public-school ideal cultivated in the 1830s by Thomas Arnold at Rugby, and later mythologized as 'muscular Christianity' in the novels of the Christian Socialists, Charles Kingsley and Thomas Hughes. At Balliol, the emergence of a distinct ethic was largely due to the leadership of the college's master, Benjamin Jowett. For Jowett, the purpose of a university was to instil into undergraduates a sense of duty and purpose and, by doing so, to train them to take a leading role in the future of their country. During the 1860s and 1870s, Jowett's vision shaped the identity of his college, contrasting sharply with the insular pursuit of scholarship encouraged by Mark Pattison, the rector of Lincoln.[3] Jowett's insistence on duty was given its stirring imperative, however, by the most prominent of Balliol's tutors, the philosopher T.H. Green.

At a time when the religious faith of many students was being challenged by scientific research and biblical criticism, Green offered an alternative Christian theology, based on idealist metaphysics, that stressed the importance of an outward demonstration of good works over an inner search for salvation. He taught that it was every man's primary obligation to foster his 'higher self' through service to others. Only by realizing this higher self could a man communicate with God, the God that, Green believed, was immanent within all men. Through both his teaching and his personal example, he asserted the importance of citizenship in maintaining an integrated community, and the necessity for men of the educated classes to combat such disintegrating forces as poverty and ignorance. For Green, the reintegration of community could only be brought about by the formation of bonds of personal connection between those who were advantaged in society and those who were in need of service. The Balliol ethic was directed ultimately at the reformation of social and political life, and the principal intellectuals of the College – Jowett, Green, and the historical economist Arnold Toynbee – all looked to a rejuvenated British liberalism to bring about that transformation.[4]

Green's message gained acceptance far beyond the academic community in which he lived, and perhaps was disseminated most widely in the novels of the nineteenth-century writer Mary Arnold Ward. Although known to the public only by her married name, Mrs Humphry Ward, she was born into the distinguished Arnold family, whose surname would become synonymous with high-minded Victorian morality. Her position as a granddaughter of Thomas Arnold of Rugby, and a niece of the poet Matthew Arnold, gave her a privileged opportunity to cultivate a wide range of acquaintances in British intellectual life. In 1872, Mary Arnold married T. Humphry Ward, then a fellow of Brasenose College, and became part of 'young married Oxford,' self-consciously up-to-date with Liberty gowns and William Morris wallpapers. This society was shaped by the ethos emerging from Balliol. Like others, Mary Ward was captivated by the exhortations of Jowett, Green, and Toynbee to lead 'a useful life.' 'Their minds were full,' she remembered, 'of the "condition of the people" question, of temperance, housing, wages, electoral reform; and ... by the help of the weapons of thought and teaching, they regarded themselves as the natural allies of the Liberal party which was striving for these things through politics and Parliament.'[5] The idealism of Green and Toynbee had a significant impact on Ward's intellectual development, and she herself would later play a decisive role in mythologizing their thought through her more famous novels. Both men appeared as heroic characters in her writings: Green was portrayed as the magnetic Oxford tutor Henry Grey in *Robert Elsmere* (1888), and Toynbee gained saintly status as the doomed Edward Hallin in *Marcella* (1894). In each book, Ward offered idealist remedies for what she saw as the contemporary religious and social crisis. The novels were tremendously popular in Britain and North America, with *Robert Elsmere* selling over 240,000 copies and *Marcella* over 100,000.[6] Writing from his home in Toronto shortly after the publication of *Robert Elsmere*, the historian and journalist Goldwin Smith (a close friend of the Arnold family at Oxford during the 1860s) assured Mary Ward that she was making a stir 'even in this sequestered nook of the theological world.'[7]

The fame of Ward's books was due in part to the appeal of Green's humanistic creed for a middle-class public anxious to alleviate the 'class-consciousness of sin.' In the early 1880s, this public found its prophet in Arnold Toynbee. When he died in 1883 at the age of thirty, Toynbee had published little, and his reputation rested almost entirely on the personal influence he had exerted since 1878 as a tutor at Balliol, and as a public lecturer. While an undergraduate in the 1870s, Toynbee had absorbed the Balliol ethic, and his study of economic history was the direct result of his interest in social reform. Like his own tutor T.H. Green, Toynbee based his hope for social betterment on the belief that the classes could be united by a shared sense of citizenship. Lecturing in the north of England and in London, Toynbee told his listeners – many of whom were working class – that the lowest levels of society needed to be taught the same standard of citizenship exhibited by the highest, and that state-supported education and housing would be the means of achieving this goal. In an address that he delivered in 1881, Toynbee claimed that labour legislation and education already were breaking down the barriers thrown up by industrialization. 'We are all now, workmen as well as employers,' he urged, 'inhabitants of a larger world, no longer members of a single class, but fellow-citizens of one great people.'[8] Although Toynbee's optimistic rhetoric generally sparked little enthusiasm from the working-class members of his audience, his words had an exhilarating effect on the growing number of young middle-class men who were drawn to him.[9]

T.H. Green and Arnold Toynbee inspired Oxford men to devote their lives to elevating the working classes, but it was Henrietta and Samuel Barnett who provided a practical plan by which the idealist impulse could be brought to life. During the 1870s, Samuel Barnett was the minister of St Jude's parish in Whitechapel, an impoverished section of London soon to become notorious for the 'Jack the Ripper' murders. After 1875, the Barnetts began visiting Oxford regularly, partly to see old friends from Samuel's undergraduate days at Wadham College and partly to interest university men in their work. Among the group of young men who eventually gathered around them was Arnold Toynbee. 'In the evenings we used to drop quietly down the river with two or three earnest men,' Henrietta Barnett later recalled, 'or sit long and late in our lodgings in the Turl, and discuss the mighty problems of poverty and the people.'[10] The Barnetts invited these men to visit Whitechapel: many came to spend a few weeks, while some stayed longer, taking lodgings in the area after they left Oxford. The actual experience of 'settling' among the poor had a strong appeal for those schooled by Green to seek out their higher selves, and a growing number of university men spent periods of time living in the East End. Shortly before his sudden death from meningitis in

March 1883, Toynbee tried to explain this appeal to a largely working-class (and hostile) London audience. For Toynbee, the act of settling fulfilled his desire to redress the sins of his class, involving as it did both a clear opportunity for service and the need for conscious self-sacrifice. 'We students, we would help you if we could,' he declared. 'We are willing to give up something much dearer than fame and social position. We are willing to give up the life we care for, the life with books and with those we love.'[11]

The settling experiment of the late 1870s became increasingly popular as the poverty crisis in London's slums gained notoriety, and in November 1883 Samuel Barnett travelled to Oxford with a plan for a permanent 'settlement' of university men in Whitechapel. In October public opinion had been shocked by the anonymous publication of a sensationalist pamphlet, *The Bitter Cry of Outcast London*, which had claimed to expose overcrowding and incest among the city's poorest inhabitants. Barnett's timing was perfect: he offered the students a practical scheme for social action just as they were being roused by the pamphlet's graphic images of social degeneration. Through bringing educated men to live within sight of the poor, Barnett argued, the artificial isolation of the classes would be broken down and the creation of a community unified by common interests would become possible. 'Not until the habits of the rich are changed,' Barnett warned, 'and they are again content to breathe the same air and walk the same streets as the poor, will East London be "saved."'[12] Like Green and Toynbee, Barnett believed that male university graduates had a distinct role to play in the re-establishment of community, as they could best bring the influence of their class to bear on social problems and provide the civic leadership necessary to initiate local reforms. The desolation of the East End, in his opinion, resulted not merely from physical poverty, but from the complete absence of cultural stimulation. Above all else, university men could share with the poor their own knowledge – their enjoyment and appreciation of art, literature, and music. 'Culture spreads by contact,' Barnett would write in 1905. 'The friendship of one man of knowledge and one man of industry may go but a small way to bring together the Universities and the working classes, but it is such friendship which prepares the way for the understanding which underlies co-operation.'[13]

By February 1884, a committee had been established to take action on Barnett's plan. It seemed appropriate to many that the Toynbee Memorial Fund at Oxford should provide the financial backing for the construction of the settlement. Although most of the energy for the project came from Oxford, and from Balliol in particular, the settlement idea soon received additional support among the male students at Cambridge University. Modelled on buildings at the two universities, Toynbee Hall was designed to resemble a residential college – complete with a quadrangle – which would stand as a physical reminder of the culture it represented.[14] In January 1885, the new settlement house was officially opened under the wardenship of Samuel Barnett. It was a position he would hold until 1906, and for the next twenty years the policy of Toynbee Hall would be shaped by the force of Barnett's personal convictions. During his long tenure as warden, Barnett ensured that Toynbee Hall remained a community of men. His wife Henrietta was the sole exception.

From the beginning the settlement idea had gained support as a movement that ought to appeal directly, and exclusively, to university men. The idealism that infused Toynbee Hall conveyed an ethic that was inherently masculine. Under Samuel Barnett's influence the ideals of citizenship and service were upheld as the highest expressions of manliness. The Balliol ethic assumed that the future of Britain depended on the unselfish dedication of educated, middle-class men, who would automatically, by virtue of their class and gender, take up key positions in public life. The most vital element of the original movement, in fact, was the belief that the problems of poverty needed to be addressed by men rather than by women. Since the 1860s, charitable work in the East End had been carried out mainly by middle-class women, volunteering their time to act as rent collectors for the housing reformer Octavia Hill, or as visitors for the Charity Organisation Society.[15] It was the perception of the Barnetts and their circle that reform efforts would always remain marginalized unless slum conditions could be brought to the attention of the men destined to wield economic and political influence. Henrietta Barnett herself put it succinctly: 'If men, cultivated young thinking men, could only know of those things they would be altered.'[16] Throughout the late 1880s and 1890s, Toynbee Hall flourished in its role as a kind of residential college in the East End, where successive generations of university men gave lectures on literature or philosophy, or served on the local poor-law board, before going on to pursue their careers in civil service, religion, politics, or law. As settlement houses spread throughout Britain, however, women seeking professional training in social work began to outnumber the kind of 'young thinking men' attracted to Toynbee Hall.[17] In Samuel Barnett's view, this development threatened the usefulness of the movement in the most fundamental way, by possibly discouraging the involvement of those who moved in the masculine world of power. In 1897, he complained in a letter to his brother that a meeting of settlement workers ('a striking lot over whom the Toynbee Hall men towered') had included a large number of women. 'The women were many – too many, I think, for the movement,' he wrote. After quoting from this letter in her memoir of 1918, Henrietta Barnett tried to explain her husband's comment: 'The novelty of Toynbee was not so much that men lived among the poor, but that young and brilliant men had chosen to serve them in ways based on thought. It was the fear that men, still shy in their new role, would retire if the movement was captured by women that made Canon Barnett anxious to keep the Settlement movement primarily for men.'[18]

During the 1880s and 1890s, the figure of Arnold Toynbee increasingly came to symbolize the complex mixture of manly purity, moral certitude, and self-negation that lay at the heart of the Balliol ethic and the reform movement it produced. Henrietta Barnett later claimed that it would have been more appropriate to name Toynbee Hall after one of the earlier East End 'settlers' than after Arnold Toynbee. She pointed out that although Toynbee had been a 'loved and welcome visitor,' in no sense had he been a true settler, like the handful of men who actually took permanent lodgings in the 1860s and 1870s.[19] For most of his contemporaries, however, the association of Toynbee with the original settlement house went far beyond the simple fact that his memorial fund supported the project. After his death, the name and character of Arnold Toynbee became imbued with meaning for a growing number of admirers. Toynbee's manliness, his exceptional nobility of character, and his martyrdom to the idealist cause of social union were images that continually appeared in memoirs and biographies.[20] In a lecture at Toynbee Hall in 1894, for example, the imperial statesman Alfred Milner described his late friend in typical terms: 'He had a noble and striking countenance, combining the charm of boyish freshness with the serene dignity of a thoughtful manhood – a face of almost Greek regularity of feature.' Toynbee's death, according to Milner, was the consequence of his exhaustive round of lecturing to working-class audiences. 'If ever a man wore himself out in the service of mankind, it was Toynbee,' he asserted.[21] In a remarkably similar passage published that same year, Mary Ward echoed Milner when she introduced her Toynbee character, Edward Hallin, in the novel *Marcella*. 'To many a Trinity man in after life,' Ward wrote, 'the memory of his slight figure and fair head, of the eager slightly parted mouth, of the eyes glowing with some inward vision ... standing amid his seated and often dissentient auditors, came back vivid and ineffaceable as only youth can make the image of its prophets.'[22] Like Arnold Toynbee, Edward Hallin collapses from the stress of public speaking and dies shortly afterward. Hallin's martyrdom is explicit: on his deathbed the character despairs of ever bringing working men to accept his message of brotherhood and class cooperation.

In 1888, the idealist ethic that had inspired Toynbee Hall became incorporated into the curriculum of the University of Toronto, when one of Toynbee's closest followers, W.J. Ashley, was appointed professor of political economy and constitutional history. By the late 1880s, it was beginning to be perceived at Toronto that the university could perform a much broader public role. As at Oxford, male students began to be schooled as future leaders in their country's economic and political life. It was hoped that the new Department of Political Economy, in particular, would help prepare young men to take up these key positions, and therefore establish important contacts between academia and the worlds of business and politics. Ashley's authority would be decisive: by injecting the empirical study of political economy with the moral convictions of idealism, he inspired male Toronto students to seek a public career, providing an outlet for their ambition while satisfying their growing sense of social responsibility.

The Social Thought of W.J. Ashley

W.J. Ashley arrived in Toronto at the beginning of an important period of growth for the provincial university, in which not only the campus itself was to expand but the university's mission, as understood by its faculty and students, was to undergo radical change. Under the Federation Act of 1887 a new Faculty of Arts was created, replacing University College as the central teaching body of the university. With the entrance of Victoria College into federation in 1890, the University of Toronto was restructured into a complex alliance of partially independent institutions under the dominant control of the University Senate and Council. In addition to the Faculty of Arts, the federation included the Faculty of Medicine, University College, Victoria College, St Michael's College, and the two theological colleges, Knox and Wycliffe.[23] Physically, the university was also experiencing a period of rapid development. The Romanesque building of University College – which the novelist Anthony Trollope had described in 1861, shortly after its completion, as 'a manly, noble structure'[24] – still dominated the park-like campus in the northern part of the city. Yet during Ashley's four-year tenure in Toronto, several buildings were under construction, including the Biology Building started in 1887, Wycliffe College in 1888, and Victoria College in 1889. University College itself was under reconstruction after 1890, because of a devastating Valentine's Day fire that left only the residence wing in the west of the building untouched. Although the university lost much to the fire, in particular its museum and library, the restoration of the south and east wings allowed the main building to be modernized. This included some badly needed renovations to provide female undergraduates (who had first been admitted to University College in 1884) with their own reading room and a 'retiring room' with a new lavatory.[25]

The establishment of the Department of Political Economy in 1888 was regarded by many to be an especially valuable addition to the Faculty of Arts. The considerable excitement surrounding Ashley's appointment extended far beyond the university community, as indicated by the wide range of people who braved the unfavourable November weather to hear his inaugural address.[26] While giving his convocation address in October 1888, the president of the University of Toronto, Daniel Wilson, expressed his belief that the study of political economy would convey a new sense of civic responsibility, by equipping students to deal with contemporary social problems.[27] A more explicit statement of Wilson's rationale was given by the provincial minister of education, G.W. Ross, two years after the creation of the department. 'I was then organizing a department of political science,' Ross reflected in 1890, 'in the earnest hope that I would be able to afford to the undergraduates of our University a comprehensive course of training in economics and political philosophy, which would fit them for dealing with the many social and constitutional problems which require particular attention in a rapidly expanding country like Canada.'[28] Both Wilson and Ross assumed that Toronto's male graduates needed this training because they would, naturally, acquire influential positions within the public and private sectors.

The broadening conception of the university's role was reflected in a change among male undergraduates at Toronto during the 1890s, as the more aggressive aspects of student life were altered to incorporate a growing appreciation of the manliness of moral sincerity. The campus behaviour of Toronto men in the late 1870s and 1880s has been nostalgically portrayed by W.J. Loudon in his series *Studies of Student Life*. In Loudon's memories of the 'Golden Age,' male students – women are largely invisible – are preoccupied by poker games and 'hazing'; they have little time for studying or attending lectures, and even less interest in the problems of the world beyond the university.[29] Loudon's images of a rough and disorderly student body are borne out to a great extent by other reminiscences of the period, and also by the routine discussion of student disturbances in the minutes of the University College Council and the Literary and Scientific Society.[30] By the late 1880s, however, the unruly elements of student life had begun to coexist with a more serious attitude, which was represented in many Toronto men by a heightened sense of moral purpose. This attitude did not displace, but rather developed alongside, the rowdy aspects of campus life, and moral earnestness became incorporated into a broader definition of manly behav-

iour. One of the more prominent students at this time, William Lyon Mackenzie King, for example, could report in his diary in October 1894 that he had
participated in a brawl brought on by the hustling of freshmen by seniors,
and had distinguished himself by throwing down the college registrar three
times. Yet in another entry that same month, King could describe with equal
satisfaction his work as the convenor of the city-missions committee for the
Young Men's Christian Association on campus.[31]

W.J. Ashley therefore took up his new position at the University of Toronto at a time when both students and faculty were already reassessing their
wider role in society; a time, most importantly, when the academic community was in a mood to be receptive to the moral influence that he would exert.
With the appointment of the twenty-eight-year-old Ashley, the study of
political economy at Toronto was established in line with the new inductive
and historical school of economics, which aggressively turned its attention to
the problems of modern society. Ashley himself had anticipated that some
would be offended by his views on social reform. Thus, he perhaps was
relieved that, owing to poor acoustics, his inaugural lecture was lost to many
of the prominent citizens who packed into Convocation Hall on 9 November
1888. Although Ashley was able to report in a letter that his lecture was
received politely, he added that he would only gradually learn what people
really thought.[32] It is not surprising that he expected a mixed reaction. The
creation of a chair in political economy had long been entangled in party politics, and had sparked considerable debate in the student newspaper, *The Varsity*, over the issue of hiring Canadian candidates. Ashley was British, but his
lack of political affiliation in Ontario made him to some extent a neutral
choice.[33] The contentious nature of Ashley's opinions, however, went much
deeper than questions of political partisanship, as his views fundamentally
challenged the *laissez-faire* economic principle that was sacred to many nineteenth-century Canadians.

An undergraduate at Balliol from 1878 to 1881, during the height of T.H.
Green's influence, Ashley was drawn to the study of economic history by his
interest in social conditions. After taking his degree with first-class honours
in history, he stayed on at Oxford, supporting himself as a private tutor,
while studying political economy under Arnold Toynbee's direction. By the
time Ashley came to Toronto, he was known quite openly as 'Toynbee's dis-
ciple,' a reputation that gave him considerable prestige as the Toynbee myth
gained strength in the 1890s.[34] Ashley's allegiance to Toynbee as an economist was reinforced by his own admiration of those aspects of his teacher's
memory that quickly became romanticized. Moreover, as one of Toynbee's
most prominent students, Ashley himself contributed to the formulation of

the myth. Reviewing a new biography of Toynbee by F.C. Montague in 1889, Ashley added his personal reminiscence of hearing Toynbee lecture in Oxford on the industrial revolution. He remembered 'how that slim, graceful figure seemed to tremble and his hands were nervously strained together, as he tried to make us realize how vast and awful a revolution it had been.' Ashley then contrasted this scene in Balliol Hall with one in a 'dingy room in a miserable tavern.' 'The sensitive and over-wrought scholar presented himself for the suffrages of his fellow-citizens,' he recalled, 'and told them how much might be done even with our existing social machinery, if those who guided it did but understand of what it was capable.'[35] The reciprocal relation of fact and fiction in the process of myth making is indicated by the similarity of Ashley's memories to Mary Ward's description of Edward Hallin, which appeared in her novel *Marcella* five years later. In 1900, his original review of Montague's book was republished in a collection of essays. Commenting on the review in his new preface, Ashley compared Montague's biography to Ward's novel: 'From what I have said of Toynbee it will be seen that in my judgment the genius of Mrs. Humphry Ward had succeeded better in realising the sort of man he was than some of those who stood nearer to him in his lifetime.'[36] This blending of the real with the legendary Toynbee in Ashley's perception is also evident in an account recorded by Mackenzie King, who became one of Ashley's graduate students at Harvard University. Having long been fascinated by the Toynbee cult during his undergraduate years at Toronto, in 1897, soon after he arrived at Harvard, King eagerly questioned Ashley about Arnold Toynbee. 'He merely said that he was one of the characters in *Marcella*,' King reported in his diary.[37]

Looking back in 1907 on the development of modern political economy, Ashley tried to convey the extent of the intellectual debt he owed to Arnold Toynbee, describing him as the first to reveal 'how the historical method could be applied to the interpretation of actual conditions.'[38] He believed that Toynbee's concentration on the economic history of the eighteenth and nineteenth centuries grew directly out of his eager desire to address the problems of the present. In his opinion, the chief value of Toynbee's *Industrial Revolution*, which Ashley himself helped to edit and publish in 1884, 'lay in its showing how impartial investigation of the past could be combined with ardent enthusiasm for social improvement.'[39] Ashley's own insistence on an applied political economy, which justified its pursuit by confronting modern problems, was shaped largely by the guidance he received during the two years before Toynbee's death.

Like many British scholars of his generation, Ashley perceived the democratic state to be in a position of crisis, where political power was falling to an ignorant and discontented majority. As an economist, he turned away impatiently from what he called the 'neat little body of compendious "laws" and maxims' belonging to the old political economy, and sought instead to make sense of industrial development. In company with other young historical economists following Toynbee's lead, Ashley attacked the supremacy of the classical Ricardian school, rejecting as fruitless the deductive method that presupposed fixed abstract laws of economic behaviour. These laws had been used for half a century to argue, in Ashley's words, that 'everything in the industrial world was for the best,' and that improvement through state legislation and trade unions was pointless.[40] For the new economists, the democratic crisis created by the enlarged franchise undermined the value of Ricardian economics. Rather than force reality to conform to economic theory, they followed the inductive, or empirical, method and only generalized after direct observation of fact.[41]

The new political economy was above all to be an applied science – a discipline that could prove its utility by addressing the problems of industrial society. As Ashley explained in his inaugural lecture, all the younger economists shared a general assumption that could be simply stated: 'a Political Economy is possible which shall be of real value to society.' Although the historical economists advocated the use of empirical or 'scientific' methodology, their common belief that research should be directed towards social betterment necessarily prevented them from maintaining the scientists' supposedly detached position. The impossibility of separating 'what *is*' from 'what *should be*,' Ashley argued, required the economist to adopt some standard of reference. For Ashley, that standard lay not in individual morality but in the collective well-being of society. 'The final test in any matter,' he claimed, 'must be the welfare of the State.' While not recommending the absolute extension of state legislation, the new economists utterly dismissed the *laissez-faire* principle, believing instead that the state had a positive duty to further society's collective as well as individual concerns. As Ashley boldly told his Toronto audience, 'the state can justly claim, in the interest of the common good, to modify individual rights.'[42]

For most young economists, this endorsement of collectivism and state intervention was rooted in an assumption – derived from idealism – that the state was an institution that should promote a sense of community and citizenship among all classes. By the end of the nineteenth century, the political theories of the British idealists, led by Green, had deeply influenced liberal thought, justifying new areas of state interference. The rejection of *laissez-faire* by the historical school of political economy was, in this sense, part of a much wider movement that altered traditional British liberalism, and that, by 1911, had produced the legislative beginnings of the welfare state. Although Ashley's insistence on the need for government intervention may well have worried some of the listeners to his inaugural address, the convictions of Toronto's first professor of political economy remained within the sphere of 'New Liberal' political thought then emerging in Britain.[43] Throughout his life, Ashley consistently described himself as an 'evolutionary socialist,' but by this he did not intend to convey an affinity with the socialist movement. Writing in 1886 to his future wife, Margaret Hill, Ashley outlined the major points of his economic faith, stating that he disagreed with the socialists on several key issues. He particularly resisted their emphasis on rapid and violent change, urging instead the gradual evolution of society through such 'educating' influences as 'trade unions, co-operation, wisely-administered poor law, [and] sanitary aid.'[44] The collectivist elements of Ashley's social thought connected him, not to the socialist movement, but to the group of reformers centred at Toynbee Hall.

Ashley's historical perspective convinced him that mankind was constantly progressing upward towards a higher level of social development, and that the role of the reformer therefore was to 'hasten and assist the transition.' This idea is evident in the first part of his *Introduction to English Economic History and Theory*, published in 1888, in which he argues that the English manor had evolved steadily, and had not been the revival of an earlier and degenerated cooperative system of farming. His views on social change were mainly determined by his acceptance of the idealist belief that the individual existed morally only in relation to the larger community. In an article of 1912, Ashley explained that the work of social service must be 'guided and restrained by the thought of the social bond – the thought of society as an organism or body of interconnected relations.'[45] During his four years at Toronto, Ashley openly supported organized labour. In January 1892 he gave a characteristic public lecture on 'Methods of Industrial Peace.' According to *The Varsity*, which reported on the speech at length, Ashley explained that individual reformers should not try to alter the course of events; they should, however, be prepared to utilize the forces of change once they discovered their direction. He regarded trade unionism as just such a 'spontaneous and inevitable development,' marking it as the 'strongest evolution of the period.'[46] This emphasis on slow progress over violent conflict allowed Ashley, without alienating the more conservative elements of public opinion, to follow Toynbee's lead in advocating reform. By 1890 the chancellor of the university, Edward Blake, was able to report that the new Department of Political Economy had been favourably received, even among the bankers of Toronto.[47]

W.J. Ashley's form of evolutionary socialism closely resembled the kind of gradual state intervention that was promoted by Samuel and Henrietta Barnett under the name of 'practicable socialism.' By the early 1880s, the Barnetts had become disillusioned with the system of poor relief in the East End, which since 1869 had been regulated according to the strict 'scientific' principles of the Charity Organisation Society. Although they had worked with the Charity Organisation Society throughout the 1870s, the Barnetts became impatient with its distinction between 'deserving' and 'non-deserving' poor, a distinction that rooted the cause of poverty in the moral weakness of the individual. In 1883, Samuel Barnett published an article entitled 'Practicable Socialism' in which he maintained that even the most respectable working man could at best only provide for the necessities of life, leaving no margin for pleasure, medical aid, or old age. The only remedy, he asserted, was for the state to provide improved housing, education, medical treatment, and old-age pensions. Samuel Barnett's recommendation of state intervention, however, was as qualified as that of Ashley: the change must evolve naturally without requiring a violent adjustment of the social system. 'All real progress must be by growth,' Barnett wrote, 'the new must be a development of the old, and not a branch added on from another root.'[48] This shift towards 'practicable socialism' signified an important stage in the development of British welfare policy, offering as it did a middle ground between secular socialism and the older tradition of moral reform. Beatrice Webb recalled: 'The breakaway of Samuel and Henrietta Barnett ... from the narrow and continuously hardening dogma of the Charity Organisation Society sent a thrill through the philanthropic world of London.'[49]

The evolutionary approach to social change presupposed that the nature of human society was essentially moral, and that all developments ultimately would contribute to the good of mankind. For Samuel Barnett and W.J. Ashley, this conviction was grounded in their faith in the immanence of Christ, as both accepted the idealist tenet that God was present within men and women, and could be reached only by living in the midst of humanity. Although Barnett never challenged the fundamental doctrines of his church, by the late 1870s his experiences in the East End had led him to adopt an immanentist position similar to that of T.H. Green.[50] Ashley, by contrast, came to this opinion after completely rejecting the evangelical tradition of his childhood. In 1886, Ashley explained to Margaret Hill that he was one of those who had been led to abandon all the belief with which he had started, but that the very questioning that had destroyed his faith had eventually convinced him that unbelief was equally deficient. Ashley's need for an explanation induced him to seek a spirituality that did not require him to accept the supernatural elements of orthodox Christianity. Like so many others of his generation, he found reassurance in idealism. 'If we suppose a prompting, inspiring, indwelling something which brings about moral growth,' Ashley wrote in 1886, 'we can hardly help believing that this Something must itself be moral.' For Ashley, the existence of an ultimate good in human society was represented by 'the Christ of the Christian Church,' an historical Christ who had become for him 'the highest example of Good in man.'[51]

Ashley's loss of belief, and his gradual acceptance of a modified form of Christianity based on immanentism, was a pattern disturbingly familiar to many late Victorians. In 1888, Mary Ward captured the religious anxieties of the period in her novel *Robert Elsmere*. Much of the book's power came from the fact that Ward herself had experienced Elsmere's struggle to reconcile belief with the revelations of biblical criticism. Like Ashley, Mary Ward eventually developed a religious position that regarded the historical Christ as proof of the potential for ultimate good inherent to the human race.[52] As Ward's novel illustrated, this new faith demanded a practical demonstration of social commitment. At the University of Toronto, Ashley would attempt to inspire his young students to seek out their higher selves by offering the benefits of their education to those less fortunate in society.

Establishing the Department of Political Economy

When he took up his appointment at Toronto in the fall of 1888, W.J. Ashley was given complete control over the curriculum of the new Department of Political Economy.[53] In keeping with his own training, he conceived the study of economics to have a significance far beyond its direct academic value. Even if the student went no further with his research, the subject at the very least would improve his character by enlarging his outlook and, as Ashley expressed it in 1893, 'save him from the Philistinism of the market-place.'[54] This confidence is displayed in a letter Ashley wrote to Mackenzie King in 1906, thanking his former graduate student for a copy of King's recently published memoir *The Secret of Heroism*. A tribute to King's late friend Henry Albert Harper, the book was suffused by the idealism the two had shared as undergraduates. In his letter to King, Ashley attributed the origins of what he called Harper's 'high-minded life' to his experience as a student of political economy at Toronto. 'Among the things I aimed at in drawing up the curriculum,' Ashley wrote,

& I am bewildered now to think how young I then was, only 28, and what a free hand I had – was to bring students into touch with some of the really great minds of the

world. This was especially the case with the Political Philosophy. And all my experience at Harvard confirmed me in the belief that it was better to get men to read Plato
& Aristotle & Locke & Rousseau than to turn them on to a brand new 'Sociology.' I
can't help imagining that Harper's loftiness of thought was due in some measure to
his intercourse with the great masters of political speculation in the ordinary course
of his college work.[55]

Like T.H. Green, whose *Lectures on the Principles of Political Obligation* was
required reading for students in Toronto's 'Political Philosophy' course, Ashley believed that young men should first be taught to appreciate their
responsibility to the state, and in this way become educated in the duties of
citizenship. This perspective is evident also in the fourth-year 'Economic
Seminary,' modelled on the German seminar system, that he introduced in
the Easter term of 1889. The seminar addressed questions of both economic
theory and history, generally placing the discussion of modern issues, such
as poor relief or the prohibition of alcohol, next to examinations of the political thought of the 'great masters.' In a typical essay of 1890, one student
used Green's work to approach the subject of 'State Interference with Trade,'
basing his argument on an exploration of the relations of the individual to
the state.[56]

The moral training that Ashley's students were to receive through their
contact with political theory was to be combined with empirical research into
modern social problems. In 1889, Ashley initiated a series of studies on
Canadian conditions, believing that more knowledge on such subjects as local
government, agriculture, and urban development was crucial to the future of
the Dominion. Between 1889 and 1892 three essays by students from Ashley's 'Economic Seminary' were published under his editorship as *Toronto
University Studies in Political Science*: 'The Ontario Township,' 'Municipal
Monopolies and Their Management,' and 'The Conditions of Female Labour
in Ontario.' In his first introduction, Ashley explained that two ideas lay
behind the movement for a new political science: first, that the state could be
studied with impartiality, and second, that 'knowledge thus acquired by scientific observation and analysis will be of practical use.' Reiterating the views
that he had outlined in his inaugural address the year before, Ashley rejected
the old belief that a body of abstract principles existed that could illuminate
real life. Since the ultimate goal of political science was to bring about
reform, further development must 'take the direction of the discovery by the
methods of history, of statistics and observation, of the main facts of the
political and economic world around us.'[57]

In June 1892, Ashley accepted a professorship in economic history at Harvard University. His resignation caused some anxiety among officials at the University of Toronto. 'It would be worse than the fire,' President Wilson reflected in his diary, considering the gloomy possibility that Ashley would soon be followed to the United States by another influential Toronto scholar, James Mark Baldwin.[58] Ashley had given the Department of Political Economy a high standing in the university, and there was fear that no successor would be able to maintain this prestige. Even though the politically troublesome issue of hiring Canadian candidates was revived, Ashley's reputation at Toronto was such that the position was eventually filled by a British political economist of his own choosing, James Mavor.[59] Although Ashley had only recently come to know Mavor personally, as he explained in a letter to G.W. Ross in August, he was convinced Mavor was the best man for the job. Stressing Mavor's training under the idealist philosopher Edward Caird, and his ability to publish, Ashley argued that no other candidate possessed the same experience and high reputation in the field. 'On turning over Mr. Mavor's writings, and on talking to him and learning what manner of man he is,' Ashley maintained, 'it does seem to me an almost unhoped-for opportunity to get a really first rate Economist, and I should be greatly vexed if the opportunity could not be taken advantage of.'[60] In October 1892, James Mavor was appointed professor of political economy, and soon after his arrival in Canada, Ashley wrote to him from Harvard to express his satisfaction, rejoicing, he claimed, both for Mavor's sake, and for the sake of the University of Toronto.[61]

Like Ashley, James Mavor had many acquaintances among leading reformers and academics in Britain. His correspondence is sprinkled with letters from such familiar names as Sidney Webb, William Morris, and Patrick Geddes. Mavor liked to mention his connections, and he quickly gained an enduring reputation for pretension and name-dropping. One faculty member in his department, Vincent Bladen, remembered Mavor as a 'poseur' and a 'collector of personalities' – an observation that is to some extent borne out by Mavor's autobiography of 1923, *My Windows on the Street of the World*.[62] Mavor's enthusiasm for collecting famous people, however, helped get him the chair at Toronto. When Ashley recommended him in 1892, Mavor had only recently switched from journalism to academia. Although he studied at the University of Glasgow during the 1870s, he did not possess a university degree. Mavor's most valuable qualification at that time was the fact that he was well known in the close world of British intellectuals. As his references reveal, a wide range of prominent academics and public men were willing to testify to his ability.[63]

Mavor had made his reputation as a political economist in Glasgow in the

1880s. During that decade, the city was particularly distressed by the long depression that affected most of Britain. While working as a journalist, Mavor had witnessed the destitution of many working-class families. He became drawn to the investigation of social conditions, gaining an opportunity to study slum life closely through his membership in the philanthropic Kyrle Society. As Mavor explained in his autobiography, the goal of the Kyrle Society was similar in spirit to that of the settlement movement, 'having for its general object promotion of sympathetic relations between the well-to-do and the struggling, not by means of charitable doles, but by means of instruction and advice.' By the late 1880s, the Kyrle Society had started taking over the proprietorship of various slum tenements and, according to methods introduced by Octavia Hill in London, had attempted to improve both the moral and physical welfare of the occupants. Although Mavor learned much from his participation in this society, he came to believe that its ameliorative efforts, however worthy, were limited and superficial. He later maintained that all such approaches to social reform were flawed because they rested on the assumption that middle-class knowledge could be imposed onto the working class to bring about its moral and physical elevation. Comparing the settlement houses to the Russian *V Narod* movement of the 1870s, Mavor pointed out that both idealized the 'toiling masses' and ignored the fact that the working class had its own knowledge and code of conduct. 'The idea that they should be induced or compelled to adopt another kind of knowledge and other manners,' Mavor wrote, 'depends upon the presumption of the superiority of the latter kind of knowledge and manners, and therefore both movements handicapped themselves at the outset.'[64]

Seeking a more penetrating approach to reform, in 1884 Mavor briefly joined the new Social Democratic Federation. He soon was repulsed by what he saw as the authoritarian tendencies of Marxism, and was among those who followed William Morris in December 1884 when he split from the Federation to form the Socialist League. Mavor had been attracted to the socialists because he believed that they were one of the few British groups thinking seriously about social questions, but by 1886 he had become disillusioned with the internal politics of the League and began gradually to detach himself from the movement.[65] Mavor's interest in political economy initially had been sparked by his concern over social conditions; after 1886 he increasingly came to regard its study as a more satisfying alternative to either socialism or the hierarchical reform efforts of the middle class. His political thought was complex and often contradictory, and historians have attempted to make sense of his shift towards capitalism in later life by referring to a corresponding change in his interests away from social reform and towards economic research.[66] This view of Mavor's career, however, underestimates the fact that Mavor, like Ashley, believed his work in political economy to have a moral foundation and continued to regard social improvement as the ultimate outcome of empirical study. Although Mavor did not share Ashley's admiration for the Toynbee spirit, both men wished to use political economy to realize moral purposes. Mavor rejected the class-based aspect of the settlement movement, but he never repudiated the ethical impulse that had inspired it. Remembering his professor at Glasgow, Edward Caird, who himself had studied under T.H. Green at Balliol, Mavor claimed that Caird's influence on all his students 'was thoroughly wholesome in a mental and moral sense.' 'He deepened their view of individual and social obligation and assisted them towards estimating the relative importance of the elements which compose the total of life.'[67]

Mavor too had been drawn to the inductive school by his conviction that traditional Ricardian theory was incapable of dealing with the critical problems of modern society. 'The professional economists,' he recalled in his autobiography, 'were ... calmly reciting the economic litany as if the economic world had a kind of spiritual existence remote from the world of daily experience.'[68] In an address to an archdeaconry conference in Cobourg, Ontario, in November 1900, Mavor insisted that the role of the political economist was crucial in facilitating social progress. Asserting the historical school's main principle, he first denied that political economy could be expected to provide a definite policy that was applicable under any conditions. Instead, Mavor argued, the discipline allowed people to understand those conditions. By doing so, it indirectly influenced the empirical judgements upon which they based their public and private conduct. He then maintained that the study of political economy improved the moral sensibilities of the student, and eventually produced a better citizen. 'If we realize that after all the chief end is the building up of good character,' he told his audience, 'that this is at once, the most intellectual as well as the most economical process we shall be doing well by ourselves and by mankind.'[69]

The curriculum of the Department of Political Economy, as it was designed by Ashley and maintained by Mavor for twenty years, continued to aim at producing cultured male citizens. The 'Political Philosophy' course thrived under Mavor's rule, and honours students were still expected to come to terms with Ashley's 'great masters.'[70] The honours course in political economy retained its broad focus, in contrast to the increasing specialization taking place in other areas of the university. When Mavor organized the department's first diploma course in commerce in 1901, rather than choosing a technically oriented program on the American model, he selected a liberal-arts curriculum based on the British system, which schooled young men for the top level of commercial enterprises. The scholarly research initiated by Ashley became the primary focus of the department, as Mavor believed that social scientists could provide both government and business with expert guidance on economic policy. Mavor himself conducted a wide range of studies on such subjects as government telephones in Manitoba, the Ontario Hydro-Electric Commission, European immigration, and wheat production in the Canadian north-west. Between 1897 and 1906, he also directed a ground-breaking survey of living conditions among wage earners in Toronto, collecting revealing statistics on the fragility of family budgets.[71]

The Department of Political Economy soon became prominent in the university, and throughout the 1890s and early 1900s, it attracted some of the most talented students to emerge from Toronto. As Daniel Wilson and G.W. Ross had anticipated, the department did in fact produce a generation of graduates who gained significant positions in politics and the civil service. In addition to Mackenzie King, whose career is well known, these graduates included Hamar Greenwood, last British chief secretary for Ireland; S.J. McLean, assistant chief commissioner of the Board of Railway Commissioners for Canada; and S.A. Cudmore, chief general statistician at the Dominion Bureau of Statistics.[72] Trained to apply their skills as political economists to the solution of contemporary problems, these men also shared an identifiable series of assumptions, derived from idealism, concerning the duty of the individual to the state. Both McLean and Cudmore spent periods of time teaching political economy at Toronto. Along with other like-minded young faculty members, they were responsible for ensuring the endurance of the social ethic first introduced by W.J. Ashley.

Unlike the male students at Oxford and Cambridge, however, the Toronto graduates of the 1890s did not attempt to reform society by taking a personal role in social service. Although young men at Toronto were inspired by the idealist message to apply their knowledge to problems of poverty, their new sense of moral responsibility did not lead them to undertake any immediate plans for social action. It was not until 1910, over twenty years after Ashley's appointment, that men at the university finally united behind the formation of University Settlement, their own 'Toynbee Hall' in Toronto. Male students responded intellectually to the appeal of idealism, but for years any collective impulse towards social action was constrained and redirected by the continued authority on campus of evangelical Christianity.

2

Evangelism and the Limits of Social Action

In his convocation address of 1889, the president of the University of Toronto, Daniel Wilson, praised the city mission work of the university Young Men's Christian Association (YMCA). He claimed that such 'high aims and noble endeavors' were manifestations of the same spirit that had prompted young men from the British universities to follow Arnold Toynbee into the 'haunts of wretchedness and degradation.' 'Estimating rightly their own privileges,' Wilson affirmed, 'their sympathies have gone forth on behalf of the heathen outcasts of the east end of London; and the pariahs of long-neglected city wastes in Glasgow and Edinburgh.' In Wilson's view, the settlement movement did not spring from a new social imperative, but rather was evidence of a 'remarkable revival' of the religious element in British undergraduate life, and, as such, was comparable to the evangelical mission work sponsored by the university YMCA. By showing their growing interest in Toronto's outcast population, he explained, students at the University of Toronto were following their British counterparts in rekindling the Christian incentive.[1]

Daniel Wilson's comments are revealing. After 1888, students and faculty at Toronto became increasingly aware of the social-reform movement spreading from the British universities. In the Department of Political Economy, undergraduates like William Lyon Mackenzie King were required to assimilate the idealist assumptions instilled into the curriculum. Yet while such students were influenced by the idealist ethic, they were able to reconcile their new awareness of social obligation to the older tenets of evangelical Christianity. On the level of popular ideology, the message of idealism initially was absorbed into a much more nebulous understanding of moral responsibility that looked back for authority to the evangelical Protestantism of the mid-nineteenth century. Despite the growing importance of the social gospel among Canadian Protestants, during the 1890s the university YMCA resisted the view that its city mission work should reach beyond spiritual upliftment to more material forms of aid. For male undergraduates at this time, the duty of personal service was interpreted through the lens of an earlier tradition of evangelism. Until the first decade of the new century, the desire to serve was channelled into the limited mission work of the university YMCA, and direct forms of social action remained confined by the association's adherence to its original evangelical mandate.

The YMCA and City Mission Work

During the final decades of the nineteenth century, Canadian religious leaders and reformers conducted an urgent campaign to arouse the public conscience to what they believed were the growing moral and social problems of the industrialized city. Influenced by the social gospel emanating from the United States, many Canadian Protestants came to believe that their churches' older evangelical concern with individual salvation could coexist with an enthusiasm for social redemption on a grand scale. For those who adopted this broader perception of evangelism, the social problems created by urban expansion and industrialization required a new approach, and such activities as mass meetings and city missionary work took on a more prominent role in Protestant life.[2] In 1902 and 1907 respectively, the Methodist and Presbyterian churches established departments of moral and social reform; in 1909 the two cooperated in forming the Moral and Social Reform Council of Canada (renamed the Social Service Council of Canada in 1914). After 1890, Toronto's Protestant churches took the lead in proliferating city missions and other reform agencies throughout the city. While some church members attempted to incorporate social-work methodology, and particularly casework technique, into the policy of these agencies, more traditional evangelical goals often were embedded into the structure of their social service.[3] By the turn of the century, the settlement movement had expanded throughout Britain and the United States. In Canada, the settlement idea appealed to many reformers working within the churches, and the activities of many city missions gradually began to overlap with those of a social settlement. The Methodist Fred Victor Mission in Toronto, for example, by 1906 had sewing classes, a savings bank, and a gymnasium in addition to its gospel classes and temperance meetings.[4] Through their emphasis on Christian charity and spiritual conversion, however, the city missions or 'church settlements' differed fundamentally from either the university settlements modelled on Toynbee Hall or centres of sociological investigation such as Hull House in Chicago.

The inclusion of social-gospel priorities into evangelical thinking would become evident in the decision of the Presbyterian church to establish a chain of settlement houses throughout Canada. In November 1910, a special committee of the Presbyterian Board of Moral and Social Reform and Evangelism recommended that the church open its own settlements in major Canadian cities, arguing that it was important to distinguish between a religious settlement and a social settlement. 'What is contemplated,' the committee reported, 'is a *Church Settlement*, not only to carry on the ordinary activities of a "Settlement," but also a positive, definite, aggressive, evangelistic propaganda. The work must all be correlated under one leadership and work to one great aim and purpose – to Christianize, definitely and consciously to put the Spirit of Christ into the lives of men, and to bring men into conscious and confessed relationship to Him.'[5] In 1912, St Christopher House was opened in Toronto to act as the training headquarters and 'mother house' of the new Presbyterian network of settlements.

While there were many Protestants who found evangelical motives to be compatible with the social gospel, the strength of the reform movement by the turn of the century would become a growing source of tension in Canadian Protestantism.[6] For some Presbyterians, the overtly evangelical position of their church's Board of Moral and Social Reform conflicted with the educational aims of settlement work. Ethel Dodds Parker, who was head worker at St Christopher House from 1917 to 1921, remembered what she called 'the tug between evangelical and social Christianity'; the struggle between those who advocated evangelism and rescue work, and those, influenced by the social gospel, who stressed social prevention. Parker claimed that while St Christopher House managed to incorporate both evangelical and social-reform objectives into its program, the staff members knew, as she put it, that they were involved 'in an implicitly religious activity.'[7]

At the time of W.J. Ashley's appointment in 1888, the University of Toronto's participation in direct forms of social service was determined by the evangelical mandate of the student YMCA. During the 1880s, the same heightened moral awareness that offered such fertile ground for Ashley's teachings became expressed by the importance of the YMCA among undergraduates. The Toronto YMCA was the first student branch in Canada, originating in the fall of 1871 as a series of weekly prayer meetings held by a group of undergraduates. At a meeting in March 1873, the students formed themselves into the University College YMCA, recording into their constitution that their object was 'the promotion of spiritual interests among the Students of this College.' As its constitution indicated, the student YMCA was similar to other branches established in cities throughout Canada. The membership was predominantly evangelical, and its attention was focused on encouraging young men to earn their own redemption through an intense and personal experience of Christ's forgiveness.[8] By the late 1880s, the university YMCA also had become an integral part of secular campus life. In 1887 the student executive decided that it was necessary to raise money to support a full-time secretary to coordinate such activities as inspecting boarding houses, providing receptions for students, and looking after the arrangements of the YMCA building that had been built on campus in 1885.[9] The YMCA was eagerly supported by President Wilson, who was described by one contemporary as a 'zealous churchman.'[10] Wilson believed the YMCA to be a vital factor in the moral training of undergraduates, providing, he asserted in his convocation address of 1888, 'the courage which sustained them in nobility of aim and purity of life.'[11]

During its first fifteen years at Toronto, the YMCA was concerned primarily with promoting evangelism within the undergraduate community. By the late 1880s, however, the student YMCA was starting to extend its operations beyond the campus, responding in a tentative way to the new evangelical influences that were then revitalizing Protestantism across Canada. Under the supervision of the general religious work committee, the university YMCA made its first steps into the missionary field, supplying student teachers three times a week for the Toronto Newsboys' Home and sending volunteers to visit the General Hospital on Sunday afternoons. At its annual meeting in April 1889, the executive suggested a more extensive effort, recommending to the members 'that some mission work be undertaken in the city next fall.'[12]

In December 1890, the YMCA executive was given a thoughtful report on mission work by the convenor of the new city-mission committee, E.A. Henry. Henry was the first convenor to attempt to articulate the student YMCA's position on city missions, and his report reveals that even at the earliest stages of its involvement, the association's members were divided over the role they would play in social service. Stating that the undertakings of the committee so far consisted of weekly visits to the Newsboys' Home, Henry went on to describe the discussion that had ensued among committee members over the purpose of their work. The previous year, he reported, the visits of the students had been devoted almost exclusively to 'entertainment,' in the form of readings, Bible stories, hymns, and college songs. During their meetings, the committee members had decided that this kind of simple amusement was not enough, and that it was necessary to provide also 'more solid instruction,' such as practical teaching in arithmetic or geography. Henry concluded his report with the recommendation that the students try to convey to the boys that a 'higher life' existed, and he indicated that this might be accomplished by the means of both spiritual upliftment and practical instruction.[13]

The city mission committee's suggestion that the undergraduates adopt a more educative approach to reform, however, was rejected by other members of the university YMCA. In his next annual report for 1890-1, E.A. Henry outlined the activities of the committee at the Newsboys' Home, but at no point did he refer to any effort at practical teaching. The students entertained the boys with readings, college songs, Bible stories, and hymns, Henry claimed, 'not forgetting to drop here and there as many words as possible of an uplifting and helpful kind, in the hope that they might find a lodgment in the mind and prove an inspiration to worthier living.'[14] Like other Protestant organizations, the YMCA attracted members who embraced the broader view of evangelism promoted by the social gospel, but for the majority of its members the association existed primarily for the pursuit of spiritual interests. In the university YMCA, therefore, the tension between old and new approaches to evangelism was resolved by a sustained loyalty to mid-nineteenth-century evangelism.[15] For nearly twenty years, this loyalty would be expressed in its city mission work by a concentration on sin as a cause of poverty, and conversion as its remedy.

'More Like Unto Christ': Mackenzie King and the Myth of Arnold Toynbee

Just as many Protestants found themselves able to espouse simultaneously the goals of social reform and evangelism, students at Toronto could pursue an interest in idealism without having to deny their own wish for Christ's redemption. Since the 1880s, the thought of T.H. Green had been formally represented at Toronto in the teachings of the philosopher George Paxton Young. Young was an honoured member of the university, and in a tribute to him after his death in 1889, Daniel Wilson claimed that Young had 'exercised an elevating influence on all with whom he was brought in contact.' Young's position was eventually filled in 1891 by one of his own students, the idealist philosopher James Gibson Hume, who ensured that Green's views would remain integral to the study of ethics at Toronto.[16] While British idealism thus existed in the university as a coherent system of thought, taught by Hume and George John Blewett at Victoria College, as a popular ethic it was able to reach a much wider audience without necessarily requiring a sustained intellectual commitment to its social principles. An undergraduate in the Department of Political Economy from 1891 to 1895, William Lyon Mackenzie King was powerfully influenced by the moral atmosphere established by W.J. Ashley. His infatuation with the idealized figure of Arnold Toynbee was chiefly responsible for determining his subsequent choice of career. Yet King's intense response to the views of Toynbee and his followers did not require him to act on, or even to fully comprehend, the more complex meaning conveyed by ethical idealism. His experiences of settlement work only served to strengthen his earlier need for personal redemption.

Mackenzie King attended the University of Toronto at a time of intellectual change and administrative instability. Daniel Wilson died shortly after Ashley's departure in the summer of 1892, and, following some political manoeuvring, James Loudon assumed the presidency of the university. Although they often clashed personally, Loudon shared James Mavor's commitment to Canadian research. In 1875, Loudon had been appointed professor of mathematics and physics at Toronto, and in his inaugural lecture had bravely asserted the primacy of the scientific method over metaphysical or religious opinion. 'Truth, whether religious or scientific,' he had stated, 'will most assuredly persist unto the end; and we who believe most firmly in the truths of Christianity ought to be the last to fear the progress of research.'[17] During Ashley's four years at Toronto, Loudon had considered him to be 'a valuable ally,' and he had deeply regretted the university's loss of Ashley to Harvard in 1892. Like both Ashley and Mavor, Loudon recognized the need for information on what were distinctly Canadian conditions. In his position as president from 1892 to 1906, he strongly encouraged faculty members to conduct independent research. In his convocation address of 1898, Loudon maintained that the university should not simply be a transmitter of knowledge, but rather should fulfil its highest function by adding 'to the sum of human science.' He concluded: 'The student who makes a real contribution to the advancement of knowledge, does as much or more for his country than the man who discovers a gold mine.'[18]

Responding eagerly to the stimulus provided by James Mavor and James Loudon, students of political economy in the 1890s adopted a more outspoken position on contemporary political issues. By the middle of the decade, however, this assertiveness had led them to take a prominence in undergraduate politics that was far from welcome to the administration or faculty. In the 1894–5 academic year, an agitation involving the Political Science Club culminated in a university-wide student strike, organized and led by two of the department's more notable students, Mackenzie King and Hamar Greenwood.[19] In November 1891, the senior students had formed a Political Science Society, with W.J. Ashley as their president, to discuss economic and constitutional questions. After Ashley's departure, the Political Science Club had taken an overtly political approach, and its members had started to raise more sensitive issues. In the fall of 1894, the university council had attempted to suppress two addresses scheduled by the club: one on 'The Labour Question' by the agnostic labour leader Alfred Jury, and the other on 'Practical Socialism' by the theosophist and journalist T. Phillips Thompson.[20] In defiance of the Council, Greenwood, who was then the club's president, had arranged for the addresses to take place off campus, and in January 1895 over four hundred undergraduates had packed into Toronto's Forum Hall to hear Jury and Thompson. As reported in the *Toronto World*, the students had displayed their usual bewildering mixed behaviour, singing and shouting raucously before the lectures and then settling down earnestly to hear the speakers. 'The addresses were listened to by the students in profound silence,' the World had noted, 'and many of those present took notes.'[21]

After this episode, relations between the undergraduates and the administration had remained, as the minister of education put it, 'somewhat strained.' Increased hostility towards the university authorities had been sparked in February 1895, when an associate professor in University College, William Dale, had been dismissed from his position for publicly criticizing the chancellor of the university, Edward Blake. In a letter to the *Toronto Globe*, Dale had accused Blake of using improper influence to secure the appointment of George M. Wrong, his son-in-law, to the newly established chair of history. The students immediately had sided with Dale (Mackenzie King thought Dale's letter was 'splendid'), and in a mass meeting they had resolved to boycott all lectures at the university until his reinstatement was considered.[22] Although the strike was viewed by some observers as merely an extreme example of the disorderly behaviour that had plagued the university for years, the students themselves regarded it as a just crusade against nepotism and wrongful dismissal.[23] To the undergraduate leaders, William Dale was a martyr, sacrificing his position to reveal political corruption; to President Loudon, who had a habit of making enemies, Dale was at the top of a 'list of bastards.'[24]

The central role played by the political economy students in this disturbance draws attention to a conflict that was inherent to the moral training they received at Toronto. Their ambition was cultivated by the exhortation that they regard themselves as potential leaders in economic and political life, yet at the same time they were expected to assimilate the self-denying ethic transmitted in the idealist writings on the curriculum. In this respect, Mackenzie King was typical of his generation at Toronto: throughout his undergraduate years, he was engaged in a constant struggle to reconcile his ambition to succeed in the world with his impulse towards self-sacrifice. This struggle has been linked to King's sense of destiny and to his early conviction that he alone had been chosen to continue his grandfather's fight against oppression.[25] The conflict in King's personality, however, can also be viewed as the product of his training in political economy at the University of Toronto. Idealism appealed strongly to King, and was easily incorporated into his already heightened awareness of Christian responsibility – an awareness that had originated in the Presbyterian influences of his childhood, and had been strengthened by his fondness for the moral teachings of Thomas Carlyle and Charles Kingsley. Reading the works of Arnold Toynbee and W.J. Ashley, and attending James Mavor's lectures, King became consumed with the idea that he could contribute to social reform by pursuing a career in economic research. 'I feel more anxious than ever to work at Economics most thoroughly,' he wrote in his diary in April 1895, 'and seek to learn all I can of the masses, the labouring classes and the poor, to understand their needs and desires and how to alleviate them, and better their condition.'[26]

While so many others were drawn to philosophical idealism through a crisis in faith, King seems to have been attracted to the idealist ethic as a reaffirmation of his own confidence that Christianity could bridge the gap between rich and poor. In December 1895 King presided at a meeting of Toronto working men, and in his closing remarks asserted that social reform would provide a better resolution to the labour question than *laissez-faire*, anarchism, or socialism. Echoing Toynbee, he argued that education and the enlightenment of the masses would be able to accomplish more permanent good, and he added his belief that social reform would ultimately be brought about through the actualization of the Christian incentive. 'I closed with a strong reference to religion, the poor man as he is in sight of God etc.,' he wrote in his diary. Later that month, while addressing the Socialist Labour Party in Toronto on 'Arnold Toynbee and the Industrial Revolution in England,' King again stressed his view that religion was the secret to Toynbee's work. King's understanding of this work relied less on an intellectual sympathy than on an increasingly intense spiritual identification with the mythologized elements of Toynbee's life. After reading F.C. Montague's biography in March 1895, King had become fascinated by the image of Toynbee and the Balliol ethos he represented. That December he listened to a lecturer describe university life at Oxford, and noted in his diary: 'The reference he made to Toynbee, brought all the blood to my face in a rush. I felt it almost as a personal reference.'[27]

By the time King completed his undergraduate program at Toronto in 1895, his original goal of becoming a minister had been replaced by a desire to be a professor of political economy. A career in economics seemed to offer both an appropriate outlet for his ambition and a means of fulfilling his interest in social improvement.[28] This choice, however, did not accommodate his fervent need for spiritual redemption. As an undergraduate, he had gravitated into the sphere of the university YMCA. By the beginning of his third year, he was regularly attending association meetings and spending his Sundays visiting the Sick Children's Hospital. In April 1894 he was appointed convenor of the city-missions committee for the following year, vowing in his diary to try his best 'to do good work.' Despite his growing interest in social problems, King's activities as convenor followed the same pattern established by his predecessors; in his diary he only mentioned offering spiritual counsel and advice over 'moral matters.'[29]

While King became attracted to the settlement idea through his interest in Arnold Toynbee, his interpretation of the movement's philosophy relied on an evangelical understanding of redemption, and in practice differed very little from the approach to missionary work he had learned in the YMCA. For King, settlement work was a means through which he himself might seek spiritual salvation, and it was perhaps inevitable that he would be disappointed with the reality of residence in a settlement house. Deciding to leave Toronto to attend the new University of Chicago in 1896, he was excited by what he believed would be an opportunity to realize more fully a life of self-negation and service. Chicago was appealing to King, not only because of what he wished to gain from its university, but because the city was home to the most famous pioneer of the American settlement movement, Jane Addams, who had founded Hull House in 1889. 'It will be such a release to get into a higher plane of thought & action in I hope a more spiritual life,' he wrote shortly before leaving for Chicago. He concluded anxiously, however: 'I hope the settlement idea will prove what I imagine it to be. Even should it mean bare floor & walls I would gladly welcome it, if it develops character & makes me useful to others, less a slave to self.' In the 1890s, Hull House was an active neighbourhood centre, where a largely female staff of sociologists and social workers devoted themselves to conducting educational classes and to gathering statistical information. Soon after his arrival in Chicago, King was accepted as a resident of Hull House, yet he left the settlement after only a few months. He was disillusioned with settlement life, and questioned whether the work he had done for the neighbourhood was actually worth the sacrifice it demanded of his graduate studies. King continued to admire Jane Addams (recording in July 1897 that he found her Christ-like), but he was unable to fulfil his own spiritual needs by participating in the busy program of Hull House.[30]

In 1897, King moved to Harvard University to continue his graduate work, and there his enthusiasm for the image of Arnold Toynbee was reinforced by his contact with Toynbee's student W.J. Ashley. In the fall of 1899 King visited Britain, and on Ashley's recommendation was elected a resident of the Passmore Edwards Settlement in London. King was better pleased with this settlement. After describing his room in some detail, he concluded in his diary that it was 'a most delightful place.'[31] In sharp contrast to the squalor of the slums that enveloped Hull House, the Passmore Edwards Settlement was situated in the predominantly middle-class area of Bloomsbury near the University of London. Here King was able to experience at first hand the most faithful translation of Green's ideals into practice, as unlike Hull House or even Toynbee Hall itself, the Passmore Edwards Settlement was the most direct attempt to manifest the teachings of T.H. Green. The settlement had been modelled on a plan first proposed by Mary Ward in her influential novel of 1888, *Robert Elsmere*. Ward had envisioned a house in East London that would offer both social organization and religious comfort for those who – like herself – could no longer accept the miraculous elements of Christian theology. Her concept of a 'New Brotherhood of Christ' was explicitly derived from Green's idealism: a modern alternative to Christianity inspired by the historic Christ and based on the immanentistic position that God existed within all humanity.[32] Afterwards describing the origins of the Passmore Edwards Settlement, which evolved from the University Hall Settlement, Mary Ward claimed in her autobiography that Robert Elsmere's New Brotherhood had become a 'realised dream.' 'To show that the faith of Green ... was a faith that would wear and work,' she recalled, 'to provide a home for the new learning of a New Reformation, and a practical outlet for its enthusiasm of humanity – were the chief aims in the mind of those of us who in 1890 founded the University Hall Settlement in London.'[33] Although Ward's settlement would follow Toynbee Hall in taking up educational activities, its principal aim, according to a circular issued in 1890, was to encourage 'an improved popular teaching of the Bible and the history of religion in order to show the adaptability of the faith of the past to the needs of the present.'[34]

King's residency at the Passmore Edwards Settlement allowed him access to the people who lived in the world to which Toynbee himself had belonged. He was taken up by Mary Ward, and while staying at her large country house at Tring in Hertfordshire, briefly glimpsed the life of Britain's intellectual elite. On his way to Tring for a visit in November 1899, King was emotionally moved reading an essay by T.H. Green. He noted later that he agreed with Green's message that God was revealed in human life. Shortly afterward, King visited Arnold Toynbee's sister, Gertrude Toynbee, who had been devoted to her brother and had done much to sanctify his name – she told King that their old nurse used to say they were 'more like lovers.' Following his first meeting with Gertrude Toynbee, King was overwhelmed by his relative proximity to the man he thought of only in sacred terms. 'It was *real*,' he recorded in his diary, concluding his account of the visit with the observation: 'I seem to have come too suddenly upon what I believed I could never have done.' His brush with the 'real' Toynbee made King agonize over his own unworthiness, and he ended his diary entry with a prayer in which Toynbee and Christ became synonymous. 'Take oh God my life, purge me of my impurities,' he wrote, 'and make me as one of thy chosen servants, more like Toynbee was, more like unto Christ!'[35]

Although King found the British settlement house more congenial to the collection of spiritual aspirations he had called his 'Toynbee ideals,' even his experiences at the ideological heart of the movement did not significantly alter his perception of the idealist ethic. For King, an evangelical need for Christ's forgiveness had become inseparable from the message of idealism, filtered as it was through the popular writings of Mary Ward and the mythologizing of Toynbee's life promoted by his sister and the whole idealist circle. Simply residing at the Passmore Edwards Settlement was therefore enough for him: King did not visit Toynbee Hall until he had lived in London nearly five months, and then was unimpressed, noting dispassionately that 'there was not much to see.'[36]

In May 1898, King had mused over the idea of writing a sketch of Toynbee's life and dedicating the book to his friend Henry Albert Harper.[37] Instead of a life of Toynbee, however, what King eventually wrote in 1906 was a memoir of Harper, which in its structure and content was a sincere, if tacit, homage to the influence of Arnold Toynbee. In December 1901, Harper had drowned in the Ottawa River in an unsuccessful attempt to rescue a young woman who had fallen through the ice. In *The Secret of Heroism*, King modelled the story of his late friend's life on the pattern of martyrdom that during the 1890s had defined the myth of Toynbee. For King, Harper and Toynbee shared the essential qualities he had always admired, possessing the same manly nobility and spirit of self-sacrifice. Beginning with an account of Harper's futile attempt to save the woman's life, King went on to trace the development of character that had led Harper to that point of extreme heroism. By including quotations from Harper's journal and other writings, *The Secret of Heroism* also reveals the extent to which Harper himself shared his friend's enthusiastic but ultimately limited acceptance of the goals of idealism. Like King, Harper was inspired by Toynbee's message to use his skills as an economist to serve the public good, but he displayed little inclination to participate in forms of service that required a direct and personal commitment to social action.

Harper completed his honours work in political economy in 1895. In the years following his graduation, his ambition to succeed was combined with an equally powerful aspiration for public service. In his views on social change Harper was optimistic, and following Green's teachings, he placed great value on the importance of active citizenship and the duty of the individual. 'The ultimate solution of industrial problems,' he wrote in a letter, 'lies with the people at large, and all will be well if citizens will but discharge the duties of their citizenship.' Harper believed that in the case of the educated man the responsibilities of citizenship were particularly binding. Commenting in one article on Arnold Toynbee's claim that the great danger of democratic upheaval was the intellectuals' estrangement from the leaders of the people, Harper argued that the men who seriously studied social and economic problems should not allow themselves to be indifferent to the political system. He wrote: 'Surely a peculiar obligation to see that men think rightly and act sanely, devolves upon those whose vantage ground should enable them to distinguish what is genuine.' Although at first he did attempt to help 'the deserving poor' by forming a charitable society to chop firewood, Harper believed he could best realize what he called 'the high ideal of my existence' by applying the empirical skills he had learned as an undergraduate to the achievement of a larger moral purpose. While working as a journalist in 1898, Harper was excited by being given the opportunity to conduct an inquiry into the conditions of various working-class trades. 'I need not say that I am pleased,' he concluded, and explained: 'I have at once an opportunity of examining into the industrial and sociological conditions of the city and province, and possibly of doing good to my fellow men as the result of these observations.'[38]

After reading *The Secret of Heroism* in 1906, W.J. Ashley chose to regard the book as evidence of his own success in instilling idealism into the curriculum at Toronto. 'I will confess,' he wrote to King, 'that the circumstance that Harper was a Toronto graduate gave his story a special interest; & may I, without being too self-centred, add that it has moved me greatly to think that he was a graduate of the Dept. of Pol. Sci.?'[39] Yet while Ashley was quite justified in making this comment in terms of his own goals for the department, the memoir reveals that Harper himself found it difficult to demonstrate his commitment to idealism beyond expressing a somewhat vague desire to do good for humanity. Like that of King, Harper's understanding of the possibility of social service was confined by the evangelical climate of his undergraduate experience. As his diary entries show, King's reactions to the settlement movement in America and Britain depended on a complicated need for spiritual redemption that became projected onto – but not substantially altered by – the mythology surrounding Toynbee's life and death. Throughout the 1890s, the limits of social action at Toronto were defined by the university's evangelical tradition, and male undergraduates drawn to serve the poor did not look further than the narrow city mission work of the YMCA. At the same time, the very fact that idealism adapted so easily to Toronto's moral environment ensured its own survival. Quite unwittingly, graduates of the 1890s like King and Harper were weakening their university's ties to evangelism. Long before male students would expand those boundaries, however, female students and alumnae would quietly take the initiative in the area of social service. Even though the university would place a growing emphasis on the social utility of its male undergraduates, after 1900 university women's groups would begin to develop a program of service that drew its inspiration, not from evangelism or idealism, but from the profession of social work emerging in the United States.

3

Science and Sentiment: Constructing the Gender of Service, 1900–1910

University Settlement opened in the summer of 1910 as an entirely masculine enterprise. Operated by a male resident staff that included a Methodist minister, a medical student, and an undergraduate football star, it was intended to provide male students from the university with their first real opportunity for volunteer social service. The activities mainly consisted of football and gymnasium classes conducted by popular university athletes, and were designed to exert a manly influence on the large number of neighbourhood boys who, it was assumed, would otherwise be amusing themselves in the streets. *University of Toronto Monthly* noted approvingly in February 1911: 'The influence of a leader in good clean sport, and recognised star of the champion football team of Canada contributed quite perceptibly to the moral upbuilding of these boys' lives. It is remarkable what an inspiration such a college man really is to them.'[1] During the first year of the settlement's program, university women were given no chance to participate either as resident staff members or as volunteers, and there were no classes organized for girls or women from the district. Apart from the resident secretary's wife (who, like Henrietta Barnett at Toynbee Hall, lived and worked in the settlement house), women were excluded from any kind of involvement in the project that was to be the university's first official endorsement of social action.[2]

This exclusion is particularly significant in light of the fact that by 1910 settlement houses in both Britain and the United States had become closely identified with the new female-dominated profession of social work. Since the turn of the century, women's organizations at the university had been aware of developments in American social work, and had been showing a keen interest in supporting the growth of the settlement movement in Toronto. While male undergraduates had been limiting service to the YMCA city-mission committee, the university's female societies and associations had been slowly extending their contacts in the field of social work. Why, then, did social service become defined as a masculine venture at the University of Toronto at precisely the time when social work was gaining momentum in Canada as a distinctly female profession? Why, after nearly two decades of relative inertia, did university men choose this moment to take up a scheme of social action? It will be argued below that after 1900 the new interest of university women in social service implicitly challenged the gendered assumptions emanating from the Department of Political Economy. Although their right to participate was never openly contested, by the end of the decade female students and alumnae found their activities devalued by a surge of popularity for the idealist message among members of the university's male community.

University Women and the American Settlement Movement

The British middle classes had become aware of the existence of an 'outcast' London in the early 1880s. In the years just before the First World War, many middle-class Torontonians experienced a similar social awakening, becoming convinced that a destitute population carried on a separate and isolated life in the city that they shared. Although middle-class perceptions cannot be isolated from considerations of class and ethnicity – horror of the slums, for example, can be seen as fear of the immigrant's 'otherness' – the general preoccupation with poverty and crime nevertheless reflected a critical situation for which the existing welfare structure was totally inadequate. As studies of Montreal and Toronto have shown, the economic expansion that Canada experienced after the turn of the century did not result in a higher standard of living for the working classes; instead, national prosperity was accompanied by extreme poverty among urban labourers.[3] Toronto's population had nearly doubled between 1861 and 1881, and its haphazard system of charity, run by volunteers and operated mainly through the city's workhouse, the House of Industry, was unable to alleviate widespread distress. During the winter of 1907–8, this destitution was forced onto the attention of the Toronto public as the city underwent a severe unemployment crisis, and the House of Industry became incapable of dealing with the extent of the poverty.[4]

At the University of Toronto, this sense of urgency was reflected in a steady growth of interest in social problems among both faculty and students. In 1906, James Mavor's survey of slum conditions among wage earners in Toronto had concluded that many of these families lived on the very edge of poverty. Following the unemployment crisis of 1907–8, other investigations confirmed and supplemented his results. In 1909 the Methodist church sent a group of Victoria College students to make a door-to-door survey of the downtown wards; the extreme conditions that they found were reported subsequently by an alarmed *Christian Guardian*. In 1911 a Civic Guild Committee on working-class housing was formed, chaired by another Toronto faculty member, E.J. Kylie, and in the same year a bleakly comprehensive study of the city's slums was released by the new Medical Health Officer, Charles J. Hastings.[5] While the creation of University Settlement in 1910 was the first official recognition of the university's new involvement in these issues, throughout the decade women's groups on campus had been forging close ties to the reform movement in the city.

By the end of the nineteenth century, women at Toronto were showing a concern for social issues that went beyond the evangelical focus of the mission work endorsed by the student Young Women's Christian Association (YWCA). The Toronto YWCA, which was first formed at University College in 1887, was as dedicated as the YMCA to 'developing Christian character among its members.'[6] Like other student YWCAs across Canada, the University of Toronto branch maintained an explicitly evangelical view of its purpose, in contrast to the growing reform interests characteristic of the American movement. Although by 1900 the national YWCA was reflecting the influence of the social gospel, shifting, like the Protestant churches, towards an acceptance of the need for social as well as individual redemption, the student associations on the whole were hesitant to expand their perception of evangelism.[7] But while the university YWCA resembled the men's association in continuing to assert that its 'extension work' was evangelical in aim, other women's groups at Toronto began seeking a more secular approach to social problems. In the period before the First World War, these groups became increasingly influenced by the goals of the American settlement movement, which elevated the social needs of a neighbourhood over the spiritual welfare of its individual inhabitants and, most important, valued the work of the committed professional over that of the casual volunteer.

The American movement then was undergoing a period of rapid growth, expanding from six settlements in 1891, to seventy-four in 1897, to over one hundred by the turn of the century.[8] In contrast to the primarily educational activities of Toynbee Hall, Hull House operated as the institutional headquarters of a large network of applied sociologists and social workers, some of whom were affiliated academically with the Department of Sociology at the University of Chicago. Under the leadership of Jane Addams, the Hull House workers believed that social problems could be alleviated only once quantitative evidence on those conditions was made available to reformers. In 1895, the residents of Hull House had published the innovative sociological study *Hull-House Maps and Papers*. Many workers at the settlement continued to devote much of their time to the collection of statistical information on urban conditions. Residential life in a settlement house proved to be appealing to female college graduates, who often sought an independent life away from home while wishing to preserve the sense of community they had experienced at university. The role of the settlement worker, as it was articulated by such pioneers of the American movement as Jane Addams and Lillian D. Wald, was to act as a mediator in the process of democracy, both by educating the inhabitants of a neighbourhood in democratic principles and by defending the rights of those inhabitants as citizens in the larger political process.[9] Jane Addams wrote in *Twenty Years at Hull-House* (1910): 'so far as a Settlement can discern and bring to local consciousness neighborhood needs which are common needs, and can give vigorous help to the municipal measures through which such needs shall be met, it fulfills its most valuable function.'[10] As a neighbourhood centre, a settlement was meant to facilitate contact between its educated middle-class residents and the predominantly 'foreign' population of its district and, by doing so, to break down the barriers thrown up by class and ethnicity. For Addams and Wald, the key aspect of a settlement's program was the organization of self-governing social clubs, in which a worker could gain an immediate knowledge of the concerns of the neighbourhood, while at the same time communicating to new Americans the ideals of democracy.[11]

The earliest references to the settlement movement in University of Toronto publications appeared in the late 1890s. In sharp contrast to those accounts written after 1907, they discussed American rather than British settlement houses, and emphasized the participation of women as well as that of men. In October 1897, for example, the Victoria College students' journal, *Acta Victoriana*, published a short unsigned article reporting on the involvement of 'many women undergraduates and alumnae' in college-affiliated settlements in the larger cities of the United States. University settlements, the article claimed, 'partake of the nature of club-rooms, and are equipped with reading-rooms and other facilities for the working-classes to improve the intellectual part of their being and to broaden their ideas of life.'[12] In December 1899, *Acta Victoriana* printed a longer article on the American movement by the Canadian social reformer and feminist Alice Chown. While Chown expressed her reservations about the suitability of settlement houses for Canadian conditions, she provided an approving description of American settlement work that was essentially faithful to the teachings of

Jane Addams. Chown explained that settlement workers took up residence in a congested district of a large city in order to create 'a social centre for the neighborhood.' She wrote: 'Their residence becomes the meeting-place, where neighbors learn to know each other, and are encouraged to co-operate in establishing clubs and classes for their own culture, or for the betterment of the community.'[13]

Under the leadership of the University College Alumnae Association, during the early 1900s Toronto women themselves explored the possibility of undertaking settlement work in the city, based on their knowledge of the American movement. At this time, university women were displaying the same tendency towards organization that since 1870 had resulted in the growth of national women's associations, a tendency exemplified by the formation of the National Council of Women of Canada in 1893. As at other Canadian colleges and universities, at Toronto the urge to create female clubs and societies accompanied the expansion of positions for women in such fields as nursing, teaching, and household science.[14] From the time of its inception in November 1898, one of the primary concerns of the University College Alumnae Association was to help female graduates find suitable jobs. The organization's initial interest in settlement work seems to have been sparked by this consideration. An occupations committee was immediately set up to inquire into careers that might be open to university-educated women. By 1900, the committee was collecting information on those jobs it considered to be better paid and 'more congenial' alternatives to teaching. Having recently affiliated with the Toronto branch of the National Council of Women, the executive of the Alumnae Association first decided to gather details on settlements in June 1900, when it appointed two members to join a subcommittee, organized by the Local Council of Women, to investigate settlement work among 'factory girls.' The following year, in April 1901, the subject was explored thoroughly at the Alumnae Association's annual meeting. The speaker gave an address that, like Alice Chown's article, portrayed American settlement houses as residential neighbourhood centres designed to promote social contact. 'The work is going on in many large cities,' the minutes recorded, 'and largely with the same leading principle through all, that of being neighborly and leading the poor and ignorant to better things not by trying to preach doctrines but by living a life that is higher than theirs but among them.' In an enthusiastic discussion after the address, members contemplated starting settlement work in Toronto, and suggested asking the Ontario Medical College for Women to join them.[15]

Although this plan did not materialize, women at the university soon were given a good opportunity for social service, when Toronto's first settlement,

Evangelia House, was opened in 1902 by an American settlement worker, Sara Libby Carson. Located in the eastern part of the city, Evangelia House originally functioned as a centre for the female factory workers of its neighbourhood, and in its early years was known informally as the 'Young Women's Settlement.' It gradually began to organize more activities for children, however, and later became the first agency in Toronto to provide a supervised playground and a nursery school.[16] Carson modelled Evangelia House on the more established American institutions, such as Hull House, or Lillian Wald's Henry Street Settlement in New York. Carson had attended Wellesley College in Massachusetts, and she subsequently exhibited the commitment to social activism that was characteristic of her fellow graduates.[17] In 1897, she had founded a settlement, Christadora House, in a section of New York that was largely populated by recent immigrants. This previous experience, combined with her college affiliation, connected her to a network of active social workers and reformers in the United States. Although Carson also had links to evangelical reform groups – she held positions in the National YWCA in both the United States and Canada, and after 1912 supervised the group of Presbyterian settlement houses – she approached her work from the perspective of the American social-settlement movement. Ethel Dodds Parker, who worked under her at St Christopher House in 1914, later wrote: 'While a warmly religious person, she made no church connection in Canada, but she was the only experienced person at hand and to her was given the task of developing the new chain of church Settlements across the country.'[18] Like Addams and Wald, Carson valued self-governing social clubs over classes as a way of conveying the value of democracy, and as the settlement worker's primary opportunity for contact and instruction. Under her influence, Evangelia's program was structured around the formation of clubs guided by residents and volunteers. By 1913 the settlement was conducting a variety of daytime and evening social clubs for both children and mothers.[19]

In 1902, Carson recruited support for her project by addressing women's organizations on campus, including the Victoria College YWCA and the University College Alumnae Association. The minutes of the Victoria College YWCA meeting in March, for example, recorded that Carson spoke 'impressively,' and concluded: 'After a meeting of unusual interest and helpfulness the hour was brought to a close with a prayer by Miss Carson.'[20] In December 1904, a wider bid for volunteers was made to undergraduate women through *The Varsity*, which devoted one of its 'College Girl' columns to a description of the activities at Evangelia House. 'Many outsiders have volunteered for the work, but there is work for many more, and for this reason those in charge are making a special appeal to university women students to aid in bringing to them something of the advantages of education which we enjoy.' The extent to which social service at this point had become defined as a women's field is indicated by the fact that *The Varsity*'s article assumed a settlement was by its very nature a female institution, operated by and for women.[21] That year the staff of Evangelia House proposed that closer contacts be made with university women by forming chapters of the settlement that would contribute financially, elect members to sit on its council, and send junior members into short-term residence. By 1910 chapters of Evangelia House had been set up by the Alumnae Association, the Women's Literary Society, the women of Victoria College, and the female undergraduates of Trinity housed at St Hilda's College. (Trinity College had affiliated with the University of Toronto in 1904.)[22] Carson by then had turned her attention to other projects, and the settlement had been placed under the direction of a graduate of Trinity College, Edith C. Elwood. In an interview years later, M.M. Kirkwood, who lived as a student at St Hilda's and would later become principal of the college, remembered Evangelia House as an integral part of campus life. It was a time when, through Elwood's influence, it became a 'college custom' for St Hilda's students to go to the settlement once a week to help with its clubs.[23] Although positions for women in settlement work remained limited until the expansion of the movement throughout Toronto after 1911, the Alumnae Association's original interest in its employment potential was to some extent justified. By 1904, two of the five permanent staff members at Evangelia House were graduates of the university; in 1906 the Alumnae Association included these statistics on settlement work – along with those on such other occupations as journalism, business, and the civil service – in its annual report on jobs taken by women graduates.[24]

When University Settlement was founded at the end of the decade, women's colleges and societies at the University of Toronto had established an accepted pattern of cooperation with Evangelia House. But unlike University Settlement, Evangelia was at no point officially connected to the university, and the settlement work of female students and graduates received little publicity or support from the wider academic community. After 1907, this segregation would become more and more pronounced as a new generation of young male academics began to disseminate idealist convictions beyond the classrooms of the Department of Political Economy. The settlement work undertaken by university women at Evangelia House was defined by the priorities of the American movement, and was associated with the emerging field of professional social work. By contrast, male students and faculty at Toronto increasingly came to regard social service as a voluntary and masculine responsibility.

University Men and the Transition to Social Action

By 1910, a like-minded group of academics had emerged at Toronto, represented by such men as S.J. McLean and S.A. Cudmore in the Department of Political Economy, E.J. Kylie in the Department of History, and the new president of the university, Robert A. Falconer. In their own careers, McLean, Cudmore, and Kylie demonstrated the commitment to civic duty characteristic of their generation: while Kylie combined an involvement in municipal affairs with his teaching at the university, both McLean and Cudmore ultimately left their academic positions to take up appointments in public service. Placing their hope in the power of research to solve contemporary problems, they all shared the belief that 'scientific' knowledge needed only to be united to the moral incentive of idealism to bring about social betterment. Through their writings and speeches, these faculty members conveyed an ethic of service that presented social reform as a man's responsibility, but not, however, a man's career. Like the young men of Toynbee Hall, Toronto's male graduates were to apply their expertise to the problems of poverty and to bring that knowledge to bear on their employment in other fields. Direct social action, such as settlement work, was seen as a way of gaining experience and accumulating information, which could then be applied to social issues from a man's more remote – but powerful – vantage point in the working world. The acceptance of the idealist and empirical approach was facilitated at Toronto by the widely held assumption that the participation of men, at any level, was innately more important than that of women. By prizing voluntary and temporary service over career-oriented social work, this approach questioned the very legitimacy of social service as a female endeavour.

Through his position as a lecturer in the Department of History, and particularly as the editor of the alumni magazine *University of Toronto Monthly*, from 1909 to 1911, E.J. Kylie became a strong advocate of T.H. Green's vision of active citizenship. In 1901, he had graduated in classics and history from Toronto. Having been awarded a Flavelle travelling fellowship, he had spent the next three years at Balliol College, Oxford. Although Green and Arnold Toynbee had been dead for almost two decades, the ethos they had fostered still animated the college. After Benjamin Jowett's death in 1893, James Mavor's former professor at Glasgow, Edward Caird, had been appointed master of Balliol. A committed follower of Green, Caird ensured that the college's ethic of service continued to be transmitted to yet another generation of students.[25] Kylie was deeply impressed by Balliol and, upon his return to Toronto in 1904, attempted to promote its ideal of citizenship among male undergraduates at the university. In *The Varsity* of December 1904, Kylie wrote admiringly of the advantages a student gained by living in Oxford's cultured surroundings and receiving a liberal education intended to be not just practical, but self-sufficient. 'With his better trained judgment and more cultivated taste,' he asserted, 'such a man will perform even his more purely professional tasks with greater facility and thoroughness, and in the discharge of the broad duties of citizenship will display deeper insight and greater grasp than one more narrowly educated.' For Kylie, the exercise of citizenship was an explicitly masculine responsibility, and therefore the acceptance of those duties was the supreme exhibition of manliness. The 'final expression of the Oxford ideal,' he concluded, was to be found in Jowett's response to an American writer who, upon entering the Balliol quadrangle, asked what was made there. Jowett had replied, according to Kylie, 'we make men.'[26] In October of the following year, Kylie carried this message to the Canadian Club at St Catharines, Ontario, suggesting in his lecture that the University of Toronto should try to emulate the thorough moral education imparted by Oxford. The *Toronto Star* summarized the address: 'Oxford aims first at making its students good citizens.'[27]

Kylie himself tried to live up to this ideal by actively supporting public housing in the city, and to this end he was chairman of Toronto's Civic Guild Committee on working-class housing in 1911, and was subsequently director of the Toronto Housing Company. Under his editorial guidance, *University of Toronto Monthly* began to raise the issue of slum reform. As will be seen below, a few key articles appeared that suggested the possibility that idealist solutions could also be applied to the Canadian situation. When the war began in 1914, Kylie immediately volunteered. His death only two years later of typhoid fever was extensively reported in the press, and his story became used as an example of patriotism and self-sacrifice.[28] In May 1916, the *Toronto Globe* printed a tribute to Kylie that was typical of the many obituaries written for him. 'In him were mixed those elements of personality and breeding and discipline which give an air of distinction without aloofness, of personal charm dignified with sincerity of purpose, the soberness of the "Balliol mind" touched with the unexhausted human emotion.'[29]

Kylie's frame of mind was represented in the Department of Political Economy by two of James Mavor's young recruits: S.J. McLean, who was appointed in 1906 and, after McLean's resignation in 1908, S.A. Cudmore. Characteristic of Toronto graduates in political economy, McLean and Cudmore combined an absolute faith in the importance of empirical research, on the value of statistics and the accumulation of facts, with an idealist conviction that these facts must contribute to social reform. One of Mavor's first honours students, McLean graduated from Toronto in 1894, and then left Canada for several years to pursue graduate work at Columbia and Chicago. In 1906, he resigned his position teaching economics at Leland Stanford University to accept an associate professorship at Toronto, hoping to pursue what he described to President Loudon as the 'practical side of Economic work – transportation, banking, commerce etc.' Perhaps finding his work at Toronto too limiting, or perhaps finding Mavor himself too uncongenial – Mavor thought McLean 'really a dull man' – two years later he accepted an appointment to the Board of Railway Commissioners for Canada.[30] McLean's abandonment of academia was permanent, and he spent the rest of his career in public service, ultimately becoming assistant chief commissioner of the railway board after 1919.[31]

While studying for his Ph.D. at Chicago in 1897, McLean had published an article in *The Canadian Magazine* entitled 'Social Amelioration and the University Settlement,' which provided an eager description of Toynbee Hall and its intellectual origins. Like Kylie, McLean believed social reform to be the domain of educated middle-class men, and he explained that the university settlement idea was a product both of the sense of duty instilled in young Oxford and Cambridge students and of a new confidence in the ability of 'trained men, cognizant of actual facts,' to precipitate social improvement. He assumed that, through teaching the lower classes the 'ideals of a nobler citizenship,' university men themselves would become better educated in the needs of modern society, and therefore better fitted for their permanent careers. For McLean, the bond between Toynbee Hall and the world of political power was obvious. 'Men of renown consider it an honour to be permitted to help on, in any way, the work which it has undertaken.' He concluded: 'To go among such classes, to investigate their life, to render them help and guidance, to point out to them higher ideals and render easier their struggles upwards towards respectability, is the peculiar phase of usefulness with which the Settlement is concerned.'[32]

McLean's successor, S.A. Cudmore, was appointed an instructor in the Department of Political Economy in 1908. Cudmore had graduated in political economy from Toronto in 1905, and, following Kylie, had been sent to Oxford on a Flavelle fellowship. Although he worked under Mavor much longer than McLean, in 1919 Cudmore also gave up his academic career for a life in public service, becoming chief general statistician for the Dominion Bureau of Statistics.[33] In December 1909, while still a junior lecturer, Cudmore wrote an article entitled 'The Condition of England' for *University of Toronto Monthly*, an essay that exemplified the alumni magazine's direction under Kylie's editorship. In May of that year, the British liberal politician and journalist C.F.G. Masterman had published his pessimistic criticism of contemporary society, *The Condition of England*.[34] By presenting a bevy of statistics, Cudmore strongly refuted the suggestion that the British masses were in a state of degeneration, arguing with feeling that 'the heart of the Empire' was still sound. (Cudmore's stay in Britain just after the 'New Imperialism' reached its peak seemed to give him – as it had earlier for Kylie – a heightened respect for the ambitions of Empire.) Instead of becoming degraded, he stressed, the British race had increased in vitality, and this social regeneration was the direct result of the idealist movement that had swept through the ancient universities. 'Hundreds of Oxford and Cambridge graduates and undergraduates are giving their lives to the work of raising the people,' Cudmore maintained, describing how the 'best men' from the universities were sacrificing their leisure to work in settlements and curacies in the slums. In common with both Kylie and McLean, he emphasized the fact that university men possessed the advantages of empirical training and a heightened awareness of their obligation to be useful citizens. Cudmore wrote: 'No nation has ever in the history of the world been blessed with so many trained unselfish workers for the good of the race, and not a few of these have laid down their lives at their self-sought post of duty.' He went further than Kylie and McLean, however, by concluding his article with an urgent plea for Toronto undergraduates to follow the example of Oxford and take immediate social action. Pointing out that local arm-chair critics of Britain should look to conditions in their own city, Cudmore appealed for a similar social regeneration in Toronto. 'Within a mile of our University we have a slum as vile as the worst in London stretching westward and engulfing new streets from year to year,' he warned. 'The smells of the slum and the sounds of the slum and the sights of the slum are at the very gates of our University, if we will only open our eyes to see.'[35]

By the time this article appeared in 1909, the city already had a thriving settlement, Evangelia House, and the problem of Toronto's slums had for years been debated at the meetings of female students and graduates. Yet Cudmore's essay presented the idea of a settlement house as something entirely new to the university community and, most significant, as an imperative civic duty that for too long had been neglected by those most qualified to act: the Empire's 'best men.' His article, therefore, indicates an important step in what was to be a rapid acceptance by male undergraduates of their central responsibility for social service. In the process of translating ideology into social action, the university's new president, Robert A. Falconer, played a crucial role. His public lectures preached a popularized form of idealist and empirical beliefs, presenting the settlement idea as the perfect outlet for both scientific training and humanitarian feeling – or 'science and sentiment' as he reportedly told students at Victoria College in 1910[36] – and it was his compelling exhortation to seek the 'highest good' through service that most clearly articulated what would become a distinctive Toronto ideal.

As the idealist ethic had gained 'scientific' authority by its association with empiricism, it also continued to appropriate the moral authority held by evangelism. Robert Falconer was appointed to the presidency of the university in 1907, following the resignation of James Loudon during the previous year. Through Falconer's public speeches, male students were urged to make a personal sacrifice that, in his conception, would not only ensure their salvation, but would express that potential for citizenship indicative of manhood. Falconer himself had been exposed to philosophical idealism while studying at Edinburgh University in the late 1880s, and his childhood grounding in evangelical morality made him particularly sensitive to the persuasiveness of the idealist ethic.[37] In his inaugural address in September 1907, Falconer asserted his view that the university's chief goal was to maintain the ideal or spiritual element in national life, a task only made possible through the cultivation, as he put it, of 'the nation's chief wealth – its manhood.' Denouncing intellectual aloofness as the 'besetting academical sin,' he argued that the real university ideal was one of cooperation and service, in which the student was obligated to address the problems of contemporary society. In agreement with both W.J. Ashley and James Mavor, Falconer believed that the natural and most significant consequence of empirical study was the development of individual character, and that the ultimate objective was to motivate the student towards social activism. 'It should,' he claimed, 'fit him to observe the social and political situation, awaken in him human sympathies and the desire to emancipate his fellows from the ignorance and prejudice which are breeding evil.' This moral awakening was, in Falconer's mind, the fundamental prerequisite to social reform. He was able to reconcile the collectivist aspects of his idealist beliefs with his Christian commitment – as a Presbyterian minister – to individual regeneration. It was a point he stressed in his inaugural lecture, assuring his audience that 'the highest type of citizenship cannot be permanently trained apart from a sense of obligation to and reverence for the moral order which is Divine.'[38]

In October 1910, Falconer preached an equally characteristic sermon before a large audience of students and faculty in Convocation Hall. As reported in The Varsity, he based his sermon on the story of the rich young man who would not renounce his possessions to follow Jesus and bear the burden of his message. Falconer warned that wealth, social position, and intellectual training were all dangerous, as all had the potential to isolate the individual from the rest of humanity. Urging his listeners to break down those barriers, he maintained that the advantages of education had to be carried to those who lacked them. 'Find the highest good by serving your fellows,' he entreated, 'through your intellect, your wealth, your position, or whatever talent you may possess.'[39] In Falconer's speeches, the evangelical impulse was assimilated into a much larger concern for humanity, as he attempted to convince students that individual and social regeneration were inseparable, and that true social service required direct contact with those in need.

During the early years of Falconer's presidency there was, in fact, a noticeable alteration in the general character of the male students. The explosive behaviour that had marked Mackenzie King's generation began to be replaced by a more sober attitude, springing from an increased consciousness of the responsibilities of social position. A greater respect for authority led to the regulation by student organizations of the ritualized forms of student rowdiness: initiations became more standardized and tended to involve athletic contests between seniors and freshmen rather than the surprise attacks typical of the late nineteenth century.[40] In January 1907, a Board of Student Control was established by the student-run University College Literary Society, with a mandate granted by the college council to prevent 'improper behaviour' among the male students. 'Ungentlemanly or flagrantly immoral conduct,' the constitution read, 'interference with the rights of others, and behaviour which tends to prejudice the interests of the university shall fall within the cognigance [sic] of this Board.'[41]

After 1908, this change among male undergraduates was precipitated by a growing awareness in the university of the city's poverty crisis, and Toronto men, like their female colleagues earlier in the decade, began to give prominence to social topics in their meetings, discussion groups, and publications. In April 1908, *Acta Victoriana* printed an essay entitled 'Religious Life in Oxford,' in which the writer, E. Brecken, described the social service undertaken by Oxford students. Like Kylie and McLean, Brecken drew attention to the importance of the settlement movement in preparing Britain's finest young men for their future positions of power. 'England is on the verge of a tremendous social revolution,' he wrote, 'and it is well that among her students there are being trained men who in years to come will from the floor of the Commons, from the editor's desk, or from the pulpit, meet the inevitable crisis with a sympathetic understanding and unselfish devotion to the highest good.'[42] In February 1910, two months after Cudmore's 'The Condition of England' was published, *University of Toronto Monthly* printed a second powerful evocation of the settlement idea. Written by a student of Balliol

College and a former resident of Toynbee Hall, S.G. Tallents, the article graphically described the work of the original university settlement, juxtaposed against the 'darkness and the filth and the misery of East London.'[43] By the end of the year, a third article – unsigned but possibly the work of the editor, E.J. Kylie – had been written in *University of Toronto Monthly* concerning the settlement movement. Referring to University Settlement, which recently had been opened on Adelaide Street West, the writer stressed that although the settlement incorporated the charitable impulse usually found in mission work, its main object was to allow the students themselves to come to a scientific understanding of poverty. University Settlement's ambition was far from narrow, the writer insisted: 'Its aim, the permanent elevation of the entire community to a better mode of life, involves the practical application of every science and branch of knowledge in existence.'[44]

While previous articles in university publications had seen settlement work as a distinctly female occupation, and had discussed it in terms of the American movement, after 1907 the settlement idea gained a new character on campus as an embodiment of a masculine ideal of service. As male students at the university became increasingly preoccupied with social questions during the winter of 1909–10, a growing number became united behind the plan of a university settlement, which, they hoped, would offer them a distinctive role in social regeneration. Cudmore's anxious appeal in 'The Condition of England' was published in December, and in February a new undergraduate magazine, *The Arbor*, included a response by a third-year student at University College, A.M. Goulding. 'The need of a University Settlement has long been vaguely felt among the undergraduates,' Goulding pointed out, urging that the time to take action had arrived. He acknowledged the existing involvement of university women in settlement work, but dismissed it as 'an experiment,' claiming that 'it can scarcely be considered as fittingly representing the University.' Although Goulding argued against excluding women from participating in a university settlement, he followed Cudmore in promoting it as an opportunity for service that was uniquely appropriate for university men. He asserted: 'It is about time that the four thousand undergraduates in Toronto should awake to a sense of responsibility in this matter and make their settlement work bear some fair relation to their numbers and ability.' Criticizing the limited scope of the student YMCA, Goulding stated that a settlement should not be confused with a mission, but was an institution with a permanent resident staff dedicated to education 'in its broadest sense.' He expressed his acute sense of frustration at Toronto's lack of progress, blaming the university YMCA, which, he asserted, seemed to have 'lapsed into a condition of almost senile decrepitude from a dearth of active outside work.' 'The average undergraduate may not be very keen on Bible study as an end in itself,' he concluded, 'but that is no reason for supposing him incapable of practical Christian work.'[45]

Goulding's article drew attention to the fact that while support for a university settlement existed among the male undergraduates, what was needed was a group or individual with the necessary resources to carry the idea through to completion. In 1902, Sara Libby Carson had provided women at the university with a forum for social service when she had opened Evangelia House. In the summer of 1910, a young Methodist minister, J.M. Shaver, gave university men a similar opportunity for action. Working through the YMCA, he was able to mobilize extensive backing for the creation of a new settlement house.

Although most YMCA leaders at both the national and the branch levels steadily resisted the influence of the social gospel, after the turn of the century the association continued to attract members who adopted a broader interpretation of its evangelical mandate.[46] Between 1908 and 1911, the University of Toronto YMCA bowed to pressure – both from members within its ranks like J.M. Shaver and from the wider university community – and allowed itself to become the agency through which University Settlement was launched. Yet even as it expanded its focus to accommodate the students' interest in social service, the university YMCA firmly maintained its perspective as an evangelical organization. During the 1907–8 academic year, Toronto students helped conduct Sunday schools and prayer meetings at the LaPlante Avenue Mission and the Fred Victor Mission. The association's annual report suggested the possibility of establishing its own 'settlement house'; the following year, the annual report observed that despite branching out into medical work 'the note of active evangelism has been maintained – a necessary condition for successful Settlement work under the University YMCA.'[47] While this condition would ultimately prove to be divisive, the initial participation of the university YMCA was crucial, as it provided the financial support and organizational framework necessary to get the project off the ground.

J.M. Shaver had decided to go into the Methodist ministry at the age of sixteen, after experiencing the intense religious conversion that characterized evangelical revival meetings. 'Those were days of hell fire preaching,' he later remembered, 'and it took firm hold of me until I decided that at the first public opportunity I would take my stand for Christ.'[48] Shaver was granted special ordination by a Methodist Conference held in 1901, but it was not until 1908 – when he was thirty-two years old – that he began studying theology at Victoria College. After he left Toronto, Shaver's subsequent career was dedicated to mission work for the Methodist church, helping immigrants become, as *The Christian Guardian* put it, 'Christian, Canadian, citizens.'[49] In 1912, he was appointed the first superintendent of the Wesley Institute, a Methodist mission established in the impoverished 'Coal Dock' area of Fort William, in north-western Ontario. In order to gain the cooperation of other local churches, Shaver originally agreed not to undertake any evangelical activities, and the mission instead concentrated on teaching English and the ideals of British civic life to the mainly immigrant population. He left the Wesley Institute in 1921, and for the next twenty years held the position of superintendent at the All Peoples' Mission in Winnipeg. Unlike one of his predecessors as superintendent, the politician and reformer J.S. Woodsworth, Shaver accepted the collectivist implications of the social gospel's message only to a limited degree, and his recognition of the necessity for social reform does not seem to have shaken his allegiance to a broadly defined evangelism. Throughout his years of mission work in the slums of Toronto, Fort William, and Winnipeg, Shaver maintained the convictions of his youth, continuing to equate the reform of society with the individual's redemption through Christ.[50] Two years after his appointment to All Peoples' Mission, he described his future task to be 'to try to win the New Canadians in as far as I can to the real new life in Christ that they may pass it on to others in our beloved Canada and ... I do pray that some may even join our little army of the Kingdom in China and Japan.'[51]

While a student at Victoria College, Shaver had been drawn towards mission work through his participation in a program of 'aggressive evangelism' organized by the Methodist church. Taking advantage of an expected visit to Toronto by a famous evangelist, Gipsy Smith, in April 1909 the Methodist church sent Shaver and eleven other 'Vic boys' to make a door-to-door survey of the downtown slum districts. Although the students were mostly to inquire into the religious outlook of the inhabitants and urge them to attend the Gipsy Smith meetings, they also were to report on the conditions that they found. In an article entitled 'In the Slums of "Toronto the Good,"' *The Christian Guardian* was horrified to relate that moral and religious destitution was extreme and that sanitary conditions were of the most appalling kind. 'So evil, indeed,' the magazine claimed, 'were the conditions brought to light that one of the students, who had worked for five years in the Whitechapel district in Old London, stated most emphatically that Toronto quite outclassed even that notorious old-world slum in the moral and physical conditions of some of its down-town districts.'[52] A committee for 'aggressive evangelism' was appointed under the direction of the City and Fred Victor Mission Board. With Shaver as chairman, the students followed up their original survey by conducting evangelistic services and canvassing non-churchgoers during the summer. 'We preached on street corners and in tents, on vacant lots, prayed together, and in the peoples' homes, [and] visited the saloons,' Shaver recalled.[53] Although the primary incentive of the campaign was missionary, the students again were authorized to gather facts on such aspects of slum life as overcrowding and poor sanitation. In October, *Acta Victoriana* was able to report that 'a great deal of valuable information regarding social conditions has been collected.'[54] Victoria's connection with the Fred Victor Mission was then more firmly established by the formation of the Students' Social and Evangelistic Department of the Mission Board, a department that continued to conduct street meetings and house-to-house visitations with the intention of reclaiming slum-dwellers for the Methodist Church.[55]

The students' campaign encouraged a new attention at Victoria College to urban conditions and mission work. At the beginning of the 1909–10 term, the Students' Christian Social Union was organized by a theology student, Arthur H. Burnett, to explore issues relating to the Methodist church's involvement in social questions. A member of the students' campaign during the summer, Burnett had been particularly attracted to the possibilities of applied sociological research, and had taken numerous photographs of the slums that were later used by Toronto's Medical Health Officer, Charles J. Hastings. (Burnett's experience in Toronto prompted him – in contrast to J.M. Shaver – to pursue a career in professional social work, and in 1912 he enrolled in the New York School of Philanthropy.) In January 1910, the Students' Christian Social Union initiated a series of lectures and student conferences on social questions designed by Burnett.[56] Once the program had been distributed over the Christmas holiday to all Victoria College students, *Acta Victoriana* reported that 'great interest has been aroused,' and commented: 'The world is becoming deeply interested in these questions, and the church must make her influence felt in no uncertain way. But how can she do so if her leaders are not well informed on these tremendous problems?'[57] In February 1910, the Theological Club of Victoria College invited the provincial superintendent of neglected and dependent children, J.J. Kelso, to deliver an address on 'The Effect of Heredity and Environment on Morality.' According to Kelso, after the address both Shaver and Burnett consulted him privately for suggestions on how they could initiate social action among the students.[58] In May, President Falconer delivered the final lecture of the union's program, appropriately entitled 'The University Student and the Social Problem.' As it was reported in the *Toronto Mail*, Falconer argued that the discrepancy between rich and poor created by modern society could be most effectively reformed by university students 'actuated by the great Christian dynamic.'[59]

While Arthur Burnett was exploring the sociological implications of the social gospel, J.M. Shaver was focusing his energies towards a redirection of the university's traditional mission activity. Through his position on the Victoria College YMCA executive for 1909–10 and, during the following year, as associate secretary and settlement convenor on the YMCA federal executive, Shaver managed to encourage support among the membership for the creation of a settlement sponsored by the association. Every Sunday afternoon throughout the academic year of 1909–10, for example, he promoted the discussion of social questions by conducting a class for the YMCA on 'City Problems.'[60] In the annual report for 1909–10, the general secretary, Paul R. Brecken, explained that the YMCA's student leaders had long held the conviction that the methods used in its mission work provided 'little opportunity for extension or permanence.' The establishment of a settlement had been undertaken, he continued, because of the growing realization of the responsibility that university students had towards the residents of the 'lower parts' of the city. Not all the officers, however, appeared to be committed to changing the YMCA's evangelical focus. In the same report, the city-missions convenor (who was replaced by Shaver in the following year) expressed his hope that the work carried on at the Hayter Street Mission and the YMCA Boys' Club would be increased during the following year, as it tended 'to uplift souls less fortunate than we.'[61]

In the fall of 1909, President Falconer had approached Shaver and asked him to help plan a university settlement, but the final decision by the YMCA executive to go ahead with the project had been sparked in March 1910 by the unexpected offer of the Massey family to build a substantial student centre on campus.[62] In February, the YMCA had raised $16,200 from student subscriptions in order to finance a new university YMCA building. Since the Masseys' proposed centre, Hart House, would accommodate the association in some style, the executive was therefore left with a large amount that it might contribute towards a university settlement. On 15 March, Paul Brecken announced the YMCA's intentions in the student newspaper, and urged all male undergraduates to back the undertaking. In its editorial, The Varsity expressed its wholehearted approval of the settlement, which, it hoped, would inspire university men to use their superior education to elevate the lives of the poor. 'A well-organized social settlement with facilities for promoting the physical, mental and spiritual welfare of the vast neglected and degraded portion of Toronto's population, would give the undergraduates of this University an opportunity for social service which would be of incalculable benefit.'[63] From the beginning, *The Varsity* supported the view that settlement work was an explicitly masculine activity. One typical editorial in November 1911 urged university men to give both their money and themselves to the cause of the settlement. 'Actual inculcation of decent, manly ideas into the minds of those people, who have found the State less kindly than you have and whose experiences have led to a sordid view of life,' *The Varsity* enthused, 'is the kind of constructive work that a University man should favor, with a share of his time at least.'[64]

Despite the participation of the YMCA, the original constitution of University Settlement was a clear statement of the moral and scientific underpinnings of the emerging Toronto ideal. The board of directors – formally established in October 1910 – was dominated by Robert Falconer, who, as president of University Settlement and chairman of the board, was largely responsible for determining its policy.[65] Falconer received strong support on the board from the university's new associate professor of political economy, G.I.H. Lloyd, who had been appointed to replace S.J. McLean in September 1909. After graduating from Cambridge University in 1896, Lloyd taught for twelve years at the University of Sheffield, where he established contacts in the British settlement movement; since 1897, for example, he had given special courses in 'Social Economics' to Sheffield's social workers, and in 1899 he had spent several months visiting Toynbee Hall.[66] The board's first publicity pamphlet declared that the aim of the settlement was 'to bring the University Students into direct contact with those living amidst the unfortunate social conditions of our modern cities and thus broaden the one and elevate the other.' This idealist faith in the value of personal communication between the classes, and in the importance of community reintegration, was then united to the goal of empirical social research that had been cultivated at Toronto since the appointment of W.J. Ashley. University Settlement, the pamphlet announced, was to be 'an institution where all kinds of social work and investigation could be carried on.'[67]

After 1900, social service became a disputed field at the University of Toronto, as men and women competed to define an approach to reform. By 1910, the prevalence of idealist and empirical assumptions ensured that the university's first official response to the poverty crisis would be to offer the assistance of its young men and, at the same time, to overlook the long-standing commitment of university women to neighbourhood work at Evangelia House. The new authority of this social ideal determined that once the university decided to take action it would seek to emulate, as much as possible, the then famous efforts of Oxford University. Like Toynbee Hall, University Settlement was opened to provide university men with first-hand experience of urban slum conditions, and initially only men were accepted as resident workers or volunteers. Yet unlike the founders of Toynbee Hall, the directors of University Settlement did not institute a policy that deliberately excluded women; rather, the social-work activities of female students were ignored, undermined by the belief that service was primarily a masculine responsibility. While university women developed professional interests, Toronto men were taught to regard active social service as a temporary means of expressing their awakened sense of civic responsibility and as an opportunity to accumulate valuable knowledge that they could later apply to their decisions in the workforce. The establishment of University Settlement was therefore a belated attempt to imitate Toynbee Hall, and, in its implications, was an effort to resist the growth of professional social work. This attempt would ultimately prove to be impossible. Throughout the early years of the settlement's existence, the board would struggle to fulfil its idealist mandate in a series of unsatisfactory models, trying at first to accommodate the evangelical requirements of the YMCA, and then, more important, grappling with the feminizing implications of American applied sociology.

4

The Search for a Model:
University Settlement, 1910–1918

In their first publicity brochure, the directors of University Settlement had sounded confident that their combined goals could be instilled into the daily operations of the new agency. The settlement's initial years, however, were marked by the board's repeated failure to find a model that could attain these goals. During its first year, the management of the settlement was impaired by conflict between idealist and evangelical interpretations of social service, which, at the most simplistic level, pitted collectivist views of poverty against the individualist emphasis on sin and redemption exemplified by the university YMCA. Although the idealist ethic stressed the need for personal contact between individuals from different classes, the implications of its philosophy were fundamentally collectivist: by aspiring to bring classes together in a shared citizenship, the idealists were envisioning poverty as a problem for which the entire community was responsible. Moreover, the empirical elements of the directors' thought required that social problems be viewed not as originating in the moral defects of individuals, but rather as environmentally determined obstacles that could be investigated and ultimately removed. After 1911, the evangelical influence of the YMCA withdrew from the board of University Settlement, and the directors once again attempted to find a model that would leave them free to pursue the logic of their ideology to its full extent. Choosing to cultivate the empirical side of their mandate, and influenced by the university's preference for applied social research, the members of the settlement board then looked for a more appropriate model in the sociology of the early Chicago school.

The Rejection of Evangelism

From the start there was considerable confusion between the members of the board and the resident workers over what their aims should be; as a result, the early history of University Settlement suffered from a noticeable lack of direction. While the board of directors, dominated by Robert Falconer and G.I.H. Lloyd, regarded University Settlement as a vehicle for community reintegration and social research, J.M. Shaver, and through him the YMCA, conceived of it as an opportunity to use the techniques of mission work to bring about both social and spiritual renewal. In the summer of 1910, advocates of the two positions were forced, in effect, to face each other across a table, as both sides attempted to assimilate their often incompatible expectations into the program of the institution. Consequently, the federal executive of the university YMCA soon was anxious to officially disengage itself from the settlement. In June 1910, President Falconer explained the association's position to M.W. Wallace, a faculty member who would later join the settlement board. 'It is the desire of the YMCA,' Falconer wrote, 'to put this under the direction of an independent committee, and while the YMCA will stand behind it financially for some time and use all their endeavours to get it underway, they do not wish it to be a YMCA Settlement, but rather a University Settlement.'[1] Yet despite this detachment, the participation of J.M. Shaver assured that for the first year the association would continue to assert considerable influence over the activities of University Settlement.

J.M. Shaver had prepared a report on the proposed settlement in May 1910, and had been appointed to confer with the university YMCA's board of directors to plan details, but by the summer the project still was not clearly defined. At a meeting in Falconer's office in June, an organizing committee was chosen to secure a house and to get the work in progress before fall.[2] Reporting to the president, however, the committee confessed that it was unsure as to the general purpose of a settlement, and that it was waiting to receive pamphlets from American settlements describing their work. 'It is unnecessary to state that we feel the organization here drafted is very vague and indefinite but we hope it will be sufficient,' the committee concluded.[3] That summer Shaver was appointed resident secretary, and he and his wife moved into a house on Adelaide Street West that had been renovated to provide both living quarters and public rooms. Writing over twenty years later to J.J. Kelso, Shaver remembered coming to him with the many problems he had encountered, as he put it, 'in those early days when my young wife and I were making ventures out into an experience which was entirely new to both of us.' 'The fact that I could go to one of the directors whose ... ideals were so tempered with sane, common sense,' Shaver wrote, 'and who, with it all, had a real sympathy for the man who had his hands actually on the task, was a source of great comfort to me, a comfort more than I am able to describe to you.'[4] The lack of practical guidance which Shaver received from the board of directors can be at least partially explained by the fact that the directors themselves had no clear conception of how to translate their ideals into action. In the absence of a more satisfactory model, the settlement's initial program, although officially nonreligious, was comparable in structure to the more familiar efforts of such church institutions as the Methodist Fred Victor Mission.

Like the city mission work that had been carried out by the University YMCA for the last twenty years, the activities of the settlement staff during its first winter were intended to distract the boys of the neighbourhood from pursuing less wholesome entertainment in the streets. The settlement was housed south of the university in a modest three-story house in the centre of one of Toronto's congested manufacturing districts. The area was described in the publicity pamphlet as consisting of 'large families of laboring people,' most of whom were recent immigrants paying high rent. While the text of the pamphlet indicated the idealist ambitions of the board, the illustrations that accompanied it betrayed the more immediate concerns of the residents on the spot. One photograph, for example, showed a group of barefoot and untidy boys sitting on a mound of dirt. The caption beneath read: 'Some who spend their evenings in the street.' A second photograph displaying a small child (again barefoot) lying on a doorstep, revealed a more sinister aspect of slum life, and was included without comment.[5] The main focus of the work among boys was the athletic program operated by E. Murray Thomson, a student at University College, who, along with W.A. Scott of Medicine, lived with Shaver and his wife in the settlement building. Thomson organized an athletic club, established a team for the city's junior rugby football league, and created gymnasium classes for the younger boys. Other students from the university volunteered to help conduct the classes and to supervise hockey games in a public rink located across the street from the settlement. The program was planned to keep the boys busy and to encourage them to emulate the manly accomplishments of Thomson and other popular university athletes. According to Shaver, as he reported to a university YMCA meeting in November, the boys tended to be suspicious of the volunteers at first, but gradually became enthusiastic once their confidence had been gained.[6]

In his annual report, made public in June 1911, Shaver was able to present some impressive statistics. The report stated that ninety boys were registered at the settlement, with an average evening attendance at the rooms of thirty-two. While Shaver's report emphasized the work among boys, it also revealed that the residents had responded to other, perhaps more urgent, requirements of the neighbourhood. Two additional aspects of the settlement's activities, the medical dispensary and English-language classes, were shown to have been in equally high demand over the winter. By June a large number of male student volunteers were engaged in what was categorized as 'Foreign Work'; eighty-two people were reported attending the evening English classes. The free medical dispensary had also been extensively used: since the previous summer when the settlement's resident medical student, W.A. Scott, had opened it, the dispensary reported giving medical and dental care to one hundred different patients.[7] The positive nature of the resident secretary's report, however, masked the dissatisfaction with the program that had been growing throughout the university.

By January 1911, it was becoming increasingly clear that the uneasy alliance between representatives of the evangelical and idealist approaches was untenable. Although it was acknowledged, as Falconer expressed it, that the movement had 'life about it,'[8] the settlement's program fell far short of the aims outlined in its original publicity pamphlet. While these aims had echoed the idealist goals that had been incorporated into Britain's original settlement movement, the actual activities of University Settlement during its first year had little in common with the educative program established by its prototype, Toynbee Hall. The efforts of Toynbee's male residents had focused traditionally on the transference of university culture, in the form of art, literature, and science, to the working classes of London's East End. The ambition of the Toronto directors to achieve social and cultural reintegration, however, was difficult to locate in either the athletically oriented program for boys or the more practical labours of those at the dispensary. Moreover, if the idealist goal of 'broadening and elevating' was being neglected, then so was the accompanying aim of empirical research, since the program did little to facilitate the board's stated intention of using the settlement as a centre for original social investigation.

As male undergraduates responded to President Falconer's stirring appeal to find the 'highest good' through social action, they became more and more impatient with the evangelical focus of the university YMCA. During its first year, in fact, the settlement's popularity among the student body seemed to depend on an assurance that the project signified a definite break from the traditional mission work of the YMCA. In October 1910, for example, an editorial in The Varsity urged support for University Settlement, but took care to point out that 'the work is not directly religious at all.' Similarly that following January, at the beginning of the student YMCA's campaign to raise funds for the settlement, The Varsity praised its work, and stated that the house was 'in no sense a "mission."' 'It encourages those with whom it comes in contact to attend some church,' the editorial conceded, 'but there are no religious meetings.' Another article a week later again stressed that University Settlement was not 'directly religious,' and that its nature should appeal even to those students who were not interested in the regular work of the YMCA. *The Varsity* editorial went on to describe the settlement's purpose in the idealist language that was by then commonplace in university publications. 'It aims to raise the standard of citizenship within its sphere of influence, and to extend some of the advantages which we as students enjoy, perhaps without a thought to those less fortunate ones who labor all around us.' This appeal was successful, and by the end of January the campaign organizers were able to announce that their goal of raising $2500 had been satisfactorily met.[9] Yet, as the editorials in *The Varsity* revealed, many undergraduates were hesitant to support an agency that was sponsored by the YMCA.

The rejection of mission work by both board members and students led to the creation in September 1911 of another settlement, Central Neighbourhood House, which from then on would function as a rival to University Settlement in recruiting volunteers and financial support from the university community.[10] Although Central Neighbourhood House was a private venture, the three men responsible for its establishment all had ties to the university: Arthur H. Burnett and George P. Bryce, both theology students at Victoria College, and J.J. Kelso, who would remain a member of University Settlement's board until after 1914. Bryce had spent the summer of 1909 with Shaver and Burnett conducting the aggressive evangelism campaign for the Methodist church. Like Burnett, he had subsequently pursued an education in social work at the New York School of Philanthropy.[11] Kelso had been advocating the importance of settlement work since visiting Hull House in Chicago in the 1890s, and, in March 1909, had made a suggestion to Falconer, which was tactfully declined, that Toronto's House of Industry might be moved to the country and the building renovated to accommodate a 'communal social centre' supervised by the university. According to his own account, Kelso also had played an active role 'as instigator and consultant' in the establishment of University Settlement.[12] While there is little evidence to support the view that Kelso's influence was essential to that project, he did act on both the organizing committee and the first board of directors. By contrast, Kelso's involvement in the formation of Central Neighbourhood House was much more direct. Having previously conferred with Burnett and Bryce, in May 1911 Kelso chaired a meeting held at City Hall at which it was proposed to establish a new settlement in 'The Ward,' an area east of University Settlement that was then notorious as Toronto's worst slum district. At the meeting Kelso explained that the aims of the project were unlike those of the missions that already existed in the area. Workers at Central Neighbourhood House, he insisted, would 'emphasize matters of common agreement instead of making prominent the points of greatest difference' – an assertion that gains significance in light of Kelso's own experience on the board of University Settlement. Kelso was elected chairman of the board of Central Neighbourhood House, and, in the fall of 1911, the new settlement opened with Bryce and Burnett as its first resident workers.[13]

Under the headship of Elizabeth B. Neufeld, who was a graduate of the New York School of Philanthropy, Central Neighbourhood House became dedicated to training immigrants in the duties of citizenship; its workers adopted the mediating role pioneered by Hull House in Chicago. Compared to University Settlement, the new agency from the beginning offered female members of the university an active role, and women on campus responded positively to its establishment. Like the residents of Hull House, staff members at Central Neighbourhood House devoted much of their time to efforts at municipal improvement, lobbying for such causes as improved working-class housing, a minimum wage, and local playground facilities.[14] During the years of Neufeld's leadership, the settlement became well known for its activist position. Ethel Dodds Parker, who was then working at St Christopher House, remembered, as she put it, that Central Neighbourhood House 'really hammered at civic reforms.'[15]

In November 1911, Arthur Burnett published an article entitled 'The Conservation of Citizenship' in *Acta Victoriana* that drew attention to the differences between Central Neighbourhood House and University Settlement. Burnett argued that the goals of 'true settlement work' (an unacknowledged dig at University Settlement) were to educate immigrants in the value of democracy, while pursuing the interests of the neighbourhood within the larger community. Concluding the article with an invitation for students to visit Central Neighbourhood House, he scornfully attacked mission work of any variety. 'It will be seen that settlements fundamentally differ from "missions,"' Burnett maintained, 'whose inadequate and frequently vicious charities and whose preaching services are rapidly becoming obsolete: as though the poor were especially anxious to be sermonized!'[16] While the founders of Central Neighbourhood House conceived of their project as a definite rejection of evangelism, they also were self-consciously applying the model of an American social settlement, like Hull House, to conditions in Toronto. By doing so, they necessarily brought a third influence, that of applied sociology, into the debate over the mandate of University Settlement.

The appearance of Central Neighbourhood House as a competitor drew attention to the failure of J.M. Shaver's program to maintain fully either the idealist mandate of the board or that 'note of active evangelism' that the YMCA had considered a necessary condition for its settlement work. Although its program was structured like that of a mission, and Shaver himself (as *The Varsity* suggested) almost certainly attempted to inject a religious element into his work, the settlement's official policy prevented any explicitly evangelical activity. The YMCA's discontent with this situation was evident in its decision, announced in October 1911, that from that point onward it would be considered completely distinct from University Settlement. Not only did this decision signify a clear victory for advocates of the Toronto ideal, but it irrevocably challenged the authority of evangelism to continue to limit social action among students. The new agreement left the settlement in the control of the board of directors, which was to be composed mainly of graduates and faculty members, in consultation with a student committee, chosen, as *The Varsity* reported, 'from all faculties and years without regard to denomination or religious activity.' 'It has been felt for some time,' *The Varsity* claimed, 'that many men have the idea that the Settlement is an evangelical work. Such, however, is far from the case. The Settlement affords to men of the University an outlet for the broad humanitarian spirit which the college course helps to promote.'[17] The rejection of evangelism was reinforced that fall by significant changes on the settlement's board of directors and among its resident staff. An updated publicity pamphlet for University Settlement revealed the board's new composition: the YMCA's principal representative, G.A. Warburton, was conspicuously absent, while the idealist ranks had been fortified by the addition of E.J. Kylie. The most important change, however, was in the board's choice of a new head worker for the settlement. J.M. Shaver had decided to leave Toronto to pursue his career in the Methodist church, and, in June 1911, Milton B. Hunt of Chicago had accepted the position of resident director of University Settlement.[18]

Throughout its remaining years on campus, the YMCA would steadily lose ground among students at the University of Toronto. Yet while it was no longer able to exert its old influence, the association did establish a polite, if rather distant, relationship with those students who were interested in social service. The university YMCA promoted University Settlement in its students' handbook, which was distributed to first-year undergraduates each fall, and continued to raise funds for the agency during its annual campaigns. Beginning in 1913, the federal executive began appointing a social-service secretary to coordinate the placing of male student volunteers at the various settlements and missions in Toronto.[19] With the outbreak of the First World

War in 1914, however, many of the regular activities of the university YMCA were curtailed. Its membership began to dwindle as more and more students enlisted to fight overseas.

In contrast to the men's association, after 1910 the student YWCA began to demonstrate a new awareness of the potential of social work as a female occupation. The YWCA also maintained a social-service coordinator, but, unlike the YMCA, it organized a growing number of classes in social study as well as providing female volunteers for its extension work in the city. The University College YWCA, for example, received advice on openings for women in social service from St Christopher House workers in 1916, and from J.J. Kelso in 1918.[20] As interest in the professional aspects of social work grew, there was a corresponding decline in concern for the more traditional areas of the YWCA's commitment to service. Foreign mission work was most affected; in 1916 the YWCA reported in the undergraduate yearbook, *Torontonensis*: 'For reasons difficult to discover, Mission Study does not arouse much interest among the women and it has been no easy task for the convener to organize classes.'[21]

After the First World War, both the YMCA and the YWCA rapidly lost what was left of their once authoritative status on campus. At Toronto, as at other Canadian universities, students bruised by the war were recoiling from organized religion and embracing the more direct and personal approach to spirituality preached by Henry Burton Sharman, the leading proponent of the Student Christian Movement in Canada.[22] The university's postwar mood was expressed forcefully in a report to the Toronto district committee of the YWCA, submitted by Ruth E. Spence, the district student secretary, in November 1919. 'Renewed, abounding life in all the college is very striking in this first year after the war,' Spence commented. 'One indication of this ... is a certain spirit of *storm and stress*, more or less articulate among the wide-awake students – a restlessness and impatience with conventionalism, an intolerance of anything that smacks of complacency or insincerity, and a desire to subject the YWCA to a searching test as regards both its purpose and its achievements.'[23] The student leaders of the YMCA also realized what they were up against. In 1918 the general secretary, R.B. Ferris, wrote anxiously: 'Just six more weeks until College opens, and then – what! Are we going to square-up to the problems that face us in Toronto University?'[24]

The most serious criticism levelled at both associations on campus was that by becoming concerned with such secular details as boarding houses and fund-raising, they had been neglecting their original spiritual mandate. Considering their initial reluctance to expand their evangelical activities into the area of social service, it is ironic that, as the student leaders began to reexamine their work after 1918, this particular aspect of the organizations' secular work started to be questioned. At the YMCA's student secretaries' conference at Lake Couchiching, the association's role in coordinating volunteers for social agencies was challenged. 'What is the relation and message of the Social Service movement to the Association and the secretaries?' the seminar program asked. 'Shall we follow a large program of community social service even though our student leaders are inefficient and uninterested?'[25] In a similar fashion, the executive of the university YWCA was also reconsidering the importance of its social-service activity. In June 1920, the findings committee of the central women's student conference decided that social study should be regarded as a phase of mission study, because, its report stated, 'the primary responsibility of students is rather along the line of study and thought than of actual Social Service.'[26] In December 1920, the board of directors of the university YMCA was informed by a committee of the federal executive that a majority of the students taking an active interest in Christian work were in favour of substituting the Student Christian Movement for the YMCA. Thus, in 1923, male and female students were brought together in the formation of the University of Toronto Student Christian Association.[27] The committee of 1920 made it clear that many students believed that the YMCA had lost sight of its true spiritual purpose by focusing its attention on the secular branches of its campus work. The report stated: '[The Student Christian Movement] lays stress on the study of the life and teaching of Jesus, rather than on the performance of various social and organising functions which have hitherto taxed the energy of those most interested in the work, and which have obscured the religious purpose about which a Christian Movement ought to centre.'[28]

The Chicago Experiment

By October 1911, the withdrawal of the YMCA from the management of University Settlement had left the social-service field open to the influence of Robert Falconer and his supporters on the board of directors. As the results of the first year had shown, however, there was an obvious gap between the ideal of the settlement as it was interpreted by the board and the actual possibilities of the program as it was carried out by the residents and volunteers. The publicity pamphlets distributed at the beginning of each fall session continued to indicate what it was that the board hoped to accomplish, yet there was a growing discrepancy between the ongoing activities that they described and the goals that they projected for the future.

In their pursuit of a more suitable model – and perhaps determined to dis-

tance themselves from any hint of mission work – the members of the settlement board looked south to the group of applied sociologists centred at the
sociology department in the University of Chicago, known collectively by
historians as the 'early Chicago school.' Since the appointment of Albion
Woodbury Small to the first American chair of sociology at Chicago in 1892,
social research at that university had been linked to the inductive method
and, like applied political economy, had been directed towards the gradual
reform of society. Although in the 1920s a second generation of sociologists
would shift the emphasis of the Chicago school away from social reform and
towards theoretical sociology, initially the department's applied orientation
led many Chicago academics to develop a close working relationship with the
sociologists and social workers based at the Hull House settlement. It was
part of the Hull House philosophy, as Jane Addams expressed it, that the ine-
qualities of modern life could be challenged and alleviated by educated lobbyists able to back their policy with indisputable quantitative evidence. As the
Hull House residents themselves often were former students, or were affiliated professionally with the Department of Sociology, a network of cooperation between settlement workers and academic sociologists was established
during the years before the First World War. In 1908, the Chicago School of
Civics and Philanthropy was formed as a training institute for social workers,
and under the guidance of two faculty members, the social scientists Sophonisba Breckinridge and Edith Abbott, it began to accommodate the practical
research interests of this network. Until the war, the Chicago School of
Civics and Philanthropy primarily functioned as a centre for the investigation of urban conditions, offering students a broad education in public-
welfare administration and the social sciences. The school existed as an
independent institution until 1920, when it became the graduate department
of social work at the University of Chicago.[29]

   The board of University Settlement at Toronto recruited first Milton B.
Hunt, and then his successor, Norman J. Ware, from the community of sociologists affiliated with Hull House and the early Chicago school. From 1911
to 1915, Hunt and Ware attempted to transform University Settlement into
a neighbourhood centre for social research and civic betterment; a centre
that, like Hull House, would reveal the moral and empirical priorities of
applied sociology. To a great extent, the Chicago influences were perfectly
suited to the intellectual environment of the University of Toronto. Since the
late 1880s, students of political economy had been taught by Ashley and
Mavor that the empirical study of society was justified by its moral utility, as
'scientific' methodology would provide the information necessary to alleviate
social problems. But by turning University Settlement over to the influence

of Chicago sociology, the board members were unknowingly striking at the foundations of masculine exclusivity that had for years defined this tradition. In the United States, the close ties between Hull House and the Chicago school had ensured that, as an academic discipline, applied sociology would become increasingly identified with the development of female-dominated social work.

As early as the summer of 1910, the settlement board had been anxious to gain information on the activities of the more established settlements in the United States, and, in March 1911, J.M. Shaver had visited the two leading settlements in Chicago, Hull House and Chicago Commons.[30] In a letter of introduction to Graham Taylor, the warden of Chicago Commons and president of the Chicago School of Civics and Philanthropy, Falconer had stated the situation at Toronto quite frankly. 'The Settlement was started a year ago in a tentative way,' he had explained, 'and Mr. Shaver is now intending to visit Chicago in order to gather some suggestions as to the way in which the work might be conducted.'[31] By June, the board's decision to align itself with the Chicago movement had been confirmed by the appointment of a former resident of Hull House, Milton B. Hunt, to the position of director. Falconer had written to him optimistically: 'This we hope may prove to be the beginning of better things.'[32] Unlike that of J.M. Shaver, Hunt's background was academic. After graduating in political and social science from Brown University in 1909, he had spent a year at the Chicago School of Civics and Philanthropy, where he had participated in one of the housing surveys characteristic of the school. Hunt had made a special study of the single male immigrants who lived in the boarding houses surrounding Chicago's steel mills and stockyards, and his results had been published along with others of the survey in the *American Journal of Sociology*.[33]

During the two years of Milton Hunt's appointment at Toronto, the authority of the early Chicago school affected, but did not completely alter, the mandate of University Settlement. From the time of his first contact with the directors of the board, Hunt had made it clear that he would attempt to incorporate Hull House's emphasis on mediation and research into the program of the Toronto settlement. In June 1911 he had written to M.W. Wallace: 'The possibilities look very great to me both for a successful neighborhood centre interpreting the needs of the neighborhood to the city at large and as a school for opening the possibilities of social work to the students in the University.'[34] In the new publicity pamphlet for the settlement distributed that fall, Hunt's perspective appeared most strongly in the prominent placement of a quotation by Jane Addams, which expressed her view of the settlement as an interpreter of democracy. 'To know when democracy fails, how the people live, what their problems are and how they may be helped can be accomplished only by constant daily association and study,' the quotation read. The pamphlet's description of University Settlement's own aims, however, demonstrated the persistence of the board's idealist beliefs. Of the three goals stated in the pamphlet, only the third – 'to establish in the community a permanent socializing agency for bringing about civic better- ment' – expressed Hunt's accent on the settlement's role of mediation. In contrast, the other two aims displayed remnants of the board's original intentions. The statements that the settlement was 'to bring University life to bear on the problems of the city' and 'to afford students the opportunity and privilege of enjoying and having a part in social welfare work' evoked the board's continued faith in the importance of personal contact between the advantaged and disadvantaged members of society.[35]

Although the board members clung to the tenets of their original ideal, they were required to give up the settlement's identity as an exclusively male enterprise. Milton Hunt's appointment had directly exposed University Set- tlement to the influence of American social work, and this influence could only strengthen the collaboration that already existed between university women and Toronto's social-work community. In October 1911, *The Varsity* had announced the YMCA's decision to withdraw from the settlement work, and had added the news that from then on women were to be involved in the program of University Settlement. 'New Plan Adopted – Ladies To Be Asked.'[36] Female undergraduates responded energetically to this invitation, and during the 1911 campaign for funds, women from Victoria, Trinity, and University colleges, and from the Faculty of Education, all contributed money to support the settlement. That fall, two classes of girls started doing matriculation work in English literature under the direction of female stu- dent volunteers, and a 'Ladies' Committee,' headed by G.I.H. Lloyd's wife, was formed to assist the board of directors. By 1912, an evening social club consisting of twenty-five members had been organized for the women of the neighbourhood. In addition to the English classes, sewing classes had been initiated by students from the School of Household Science. The participa- tion of university women was made official in 1912 when the board appointed Mabel F. Newton, formerly a municipal sanitary inspector and health visitor in England, to be in charge of the settlement's growing pro- gram for girls and women.[37]

Yet despite his ambition to transform the settlement into a neighbourhood centre, Hunt, like Shaver, seems to have found it difficult to translate either his own ideals or those of the board into practice. Apart from the addition of clubs and classes for girls and women, under Hunt's direction the program changed little from that initiated by Shaver in 1910. A brochure of 1912 shows that the work among boys, the free dispensary, and the English classes remained the primary focus of the settlement's activities. Although this pamphlet, like the previous one, indicated that the directors planned 'to make the Settlement a centre to which we may bring trained workers to study the needs of the locality,' there is no evidence that Hunt was able to organize any extensive investigation of social conditions.[38]

By March 1913, Milton Hunt had resigned, leaving University Settlement down in its attendance figures and, to use President Falconer's words, 'in a somewhat critical condition.'[39] Arthur Burnett wrote from the New York School of Philanthropy to apply for the position, but the board again appointed a Chicago man, Norman J. Ware. Ware was a Canadian, and a graduate of McMaster University. He had recently completed his doctoral degree in sociology at the University of Chicago under the direction of Charles R. Henderson.[40] Henderson believed that the sociologist had a moral responsibility to guide public opinion; like other applied sociologists of the early Chicago school, he maintained that statistical research could be utilized to bring about social reform. In addition to his work at the university, Henderson was also an instructor at the Chicago School of Civics and Philanthropy, and he was committed to the importance of investigation into such urban conditions as unemployment, crime, and juvenile delinquency. He was particularly supportive of settlement work, and collaborated with both Jane Addams of Hull House and Graham Taylor of Chicago Commons.[41] While in Chicago, Norman Ware had gained considerable experience in applying empirical research to questions of public policy; as Henderson's assistant he had been connected with commissions on industrial accidents and diseases, vice, and unemployment. Like Hunt, Ware had also become familiar with settlement work, spending one winter at Hull House as director of the boys' department.[42]

Even though Norman Ware had a background in applied sociology through his work under Henderson and Addams, the board of University Settlement became apprehensive that his interests were overly theoretical. In May 1913, Ware wrote to J.J. Kelso to express his desire to be allowed to teach a course at the university in addition to his duties at the settlement. 'I am rather anxious about this,' Ware confessed, 'as I do not wish to get out of academic work altogether and I believe the combination can be carried on with great profit.'[43] The board disagreed, and after interviewing Ware, Falconer was provoked to express the directors' fears that Ware did not share their approach to settlement work. Writing to him in June 1913, Falconer bluntly stated that the board did not wish to appoint anyone as head whose interests were mainly 'academic and theoretical.' He then summarized the directors' perspective: 'Interest in people is what we want: we are looking for a man who can throw himself into the life of others and thereby lead his fellows to a higher understanding of what they can and ought to do in helping them both in the way of preventing and of solving social problems.' Falconer concluded that the members of the board were doubtful whether Ware's main concerns lay in that direction, but, if after knowing their views he still wanted to take the position, they were willing to offer it to him on trial for one year.[44] The reaction of the directors to what they suspected were Ware's theoretical tendencies reveals a glimpse of the university's deeply rooted hostility to forms of empiricism that could not be justified morally. As will be seen below, this preference for applied research over academic theorizing would continue to shape the academic development of both social work and sociology at the University of Toronto.

While the board expressed its doubts privately, in public Norman Ware's period at the settlement was inaugurated with considerable enthusiasm. A brochure of 1913, which seems to have been written by Ware himself, announced that University Settlement was entering upon a new epoch in its history, and eagerly prophesied that this would be 'the golden age of achievement.' The new stage was to be marked by both a physical and a 'psychical' change. In addition to a move eastward to a more spacious building on the corner of Peter and Adelaide Streets, the settlement was to undergo a redirection of its goals and objectives. The pamphlet explained that the new 'plan of action' was three-fold: 'to organize the social workers of the city around the University Settlement as a centre; to carry on the more scientific work of investigation and study of social problems, and to experiment and initiate in new lines of social or Settlement activity.' Despite the brochure's emphasis on innovation, however, the 'psychical' change was in reality a more strident restatement of the empirical aims that had been incorporated into University Settlement's official policy since 1910. More specifically, Ware's view of settlement work, like that of Milton Hunt, was based on the teachings of Jane Addams. Ware's claim that the settlement should act as a centre for Toronto's social workers obviously relied upon the example provided by Hull House. For Ware, it was essential that social workers lived in residence at the settlement if they were to function effectively as interpreters of democracy to the community. 'A long-distance attempt to carry on certain classes and clubs is not a Settlement,' the pamphlet stated. 'One must first live and understand the life of the neighbourhood, and then express and organize it for neighbourhood ends.' Like Addams, Ware also believed in the value of civic education, and the brochure announced that the settlement's classes would be replaced by 'clubs,' because, it explained, 'the latter is a training in democracy and the former is not.'[45]

Unlike both Shaver and Hunt, Norman Ware seems to have been able, to some degree at least, to instil his ambitions for the settlement into its daily program. In a pamphlet dated December 1913, several notable changes are evident in the activities of University Settlement. In addition to the medical dispensary, the English classes, and the boys' athletics, the settlement held weekly seminars for the study of social problems, and hosted the meetings of the Social Democratic Society and the Junior Suffrage Society. As Ware had promised, there was a marked increase in clubs, both social and educational, for men, women, and children. The women's department in particular had expanded under the direction of Mabel Newton, and now included a kindergarten and classes for girls in cooking and dancing. After falling dramatically during Milton Hunt's tenure, attendance at the settlement was rising steadily; by November 1914, *The Varsity* could announce that instead of the workers going out to the people, the people were coming in to the settlement.[46] During his two years at Toronto, Ware was also able to pursue his intention of making the settlement a centre for research and social-work initiatives. At that time the city was in the midst of a severe depression, and throughout the winter of 1913–14 Ware investigated the high levels of unemployment and conditions of relief among Toronto workers. By the beginning of the First World War, University Settlement was providing a local base for the activities of other social-work organizations, housing, for example, the District Social Conference (which in 1914 united with other district councils to form the Neighbourhood Workers' Association), the Social Workers' Club, and the public-health nurses, who used the settlement as the local headquarters of Toronto's Department of Health.[47]

Although Norman Ware was more successful than Milton Hunt in applying Chicago principles to the work of the settlement, it was equally impossible for him to satisfy both the idealist and the empirical aspects of the board's requirements. Falconer's injunction that Ware 'lead his fellows to a higher understanding of what they can and ought to do' relied on a projection of the settlement worker's role that was delineated by the code of moral certitude integral to the idealist ethic. This projection did not necessarily conflict with the settlement's research mandate, but rather was ultimately irrelevant to it. If Ware was preoccupied investigating the causes of unemployment, it could reasonably be argued that he was neglecting his moral responsibility to elevate those around him. The model adapted from Hull House proved to be as unsuitable as that derived from the religious missions; while the directors did not wish their settlement to reflect the evangelical interests of a church mission, neither did they want to see its program become completely devoid of spiritual purpose. By introducing the influences of applied sociology into the program of University Settlement, however, Hunt and Ware had shifted the grounds of the debate. Even though the board members no longer had to contend with evangelism, their adherence to the Toronto ideal was to be increasingly challenged by the priorities of professional social work.

By 1915 the settlement's directors were forced to further alter their policy to accommodate the expansion of social work in the city of Toronto and, more pragmatically, to compensate for the enlistment of young men to fight overseas. When Ware resigned in March, the reality of the war made any attempt to fully reorganize the settlement impossible. The board requested Sara Libby Carson, who was by then supervising the Presbyterian church's chain of settlements, to spend part of her time directing University Settlement.[48] Although Carson only remained in charge until 1917, her appointment established a pattern of female leadership that would remain unbroken for the next forty years.[49] She restructured the program to resemble that of Evangelia House, giving preference to self-governing social clubs and hiring female university graduates to assist her. Although the settlement was open to both men and women, after Carson's tenure it primarily directed its attention towards meeting the needs of mothers and children from the neighbourhood. In addition to various clubs for children and adults, during the interwar years University Settlement offered a mixture of recreational and educational activities, including a circulating library, a music school, a nursery school, and a summer camp. The settlement also continued to provide a well-baby clinic under the supervision of the Department of Health.[50]

In 1914, the University of Toronto responded to the requirements of the emerging profession by forming the Department of Social Service, and from that point onward the program of University Settlement was affiliated with the social-work course. Each year, two social-work students lived in residence at the settlement, while others participated in its activities through the department's fieldwork program. During the war years, the settlement was operated by a growing number of trained social workers: between 1915 and 1918 three of the resident staff were graduates of the new department, while many of its volunteers were enrolled in the course part-time.[51] After their invitation to help in 1911, undergraduate women had started to divide their loyalties between Evangelia House and University Settlement. In November 1915, the Alumnae Association decided to offer financial support to both institutions. Within a few years other female organizations, such as the Women's Undergraduate Association, were routinely supplying contributions to University Settlement.[52] By the end of the First World War, social service at the university could no longer be defined as a uniquely masculine responsibility, and administrators were forced to acknowledge that both University Settlement and the new Department of Social Service had become centres of activity for female social workers.

5

Skill or Knowledge?
Training for Social Work, 1914–1918

The establishment of the Department of Social Service in the fall of 1914 was the university's attempt to exert academic authority over the development of the new profession of social work. At this time, social workers in Canada, as in the United States, were trying to shape their professional identity around the acquisition of a specialized skill. By 1918, differential casework was seen by many as the principal technique that distinguished the professional from the volunteer. In devising the curriculum for the department, however, the members of the social-service committee minimized the importance of technical or vocational training, and chose instead to create a program that offered a broadly based academic education in the social sciences. By doing so, the committee members brought the Toronto course into a much wider debate that was then characterizing the evolution of social-work education in both Britain and the United States. Was the aim of this education to train skilled workers for the growing number of agencies, or was it to produce a class of welfare policy-makers who would be equipped to explore the deeper issues affecting economic and social change? At Toronto, the decision to reject the vocational approach to social-work education was influenced by the same intellectual assumptions that had formulated the policy of University Settlement, and the department, like the settlement, was constructed to express the university's continued faith in social progress and the moral rationality of human endeavour.

On a more general level, the university's attitude to social-work training had its foundations in a tradition of professional education that reached back into the nineteenth century. As R.D. Gidney and W.P.J. Millar have argued, in Ontario the authority of the three principal learned professions – medicine, law, and the ministry – relied on the ideal that a 'professional gentleman' possessed social and cultural advantages that could only be acquired by a classical or 'liberal' education. The more specialized aspects of training required by each profession were incorporated into a general program that included classics, mathematics, and philosophy. The earliest history of the University of Toronto was closely tied to this ideal, as it was considered essential that a provincial university be established to provide the education necessary for the creation of a leading professional class. Even as the concept of a liberal education was expanded to accommodate such modern subjects as science, history, and English, at the end of the century the belief persisted that the university ought to provide its graduates with instruction in moral character, and with cultural advantages that went far beyond specific technical skills.[1] The committee's rejection of a technical view of social-work education, therefore, was in part an affirmation of the university's traditional involvement in professional training, and, as such, was an assertion of the importance of academic knowledge in professional work.

The debate over social-work training, however, focused more specifically on considerations of gender. The ideal of a professional gentleman was an explicitly gendered construction, Gidney and Millar claim, and the abstract knowledge upon which each profession was based allowed professional men to differentiate themselves not only from other male workers but from women. The assumption that a profession was, by definition, a masculine calling threatened to devalue any occupation in which large numbers of women participated.[2] Social work was a field that predominantly attracted women, and its claim to professional status thus fundamentally challenged the nineteenth-century interpretation of a profession. After the turn of the century, many social workers, like nurses, chose to support this claim by asserting the importance of their own specialized technique.[3] By contrast, the university's creation of an academic curriculum was an attempt to lend the new female occupation an older form of authority, one traditionally conferred on the masculine professions by a liberal education.

At Toronto and beyond, the assumption that academic knowledge was innately masculine would shape the development of both social work and sociology within the university system. In Britain and the United States, the identification of theoretical or academic social study as a masculine activity increasingly would limit women to the field of practical social work. By the 1920s, female sociologists in the United States would find themselves largely excluded from the academic establishment, and confined instead to participation in a separate network of applied sociologists, settlement-house residents, and social workers.[4] While technique in social work would be seen by many to be a feminine skill, suitable to the nurturing and communicative qualities attributed to women, sociological theory would be pushed further into the domain of the male social scientist.[5] By designing a curriculum that offered an academic grounding in the social sciences, the founders of the department at Toronto were also contributing to a gendered view of social work, and were hoping to elevate the profession by attracting young men to a career in social service. Settlement work had been promoted as a temporary way for men to gain knowledge of social problems that they could then apply to other fields, but it was anticipated that the Department of Social Service would be able to draw men permanently into social work's policy-making and administrative positions.

Social Work as a Profession

The creation of University Settlement in 1910 had been most directly a reaction to acute poverty in the city – a realization that had spread quickly after the period of high unemployment during the winter of 1907–8. Although not founded until 1914, the Department of Social Service was also a response, by administrators and faculty, to this shared sense of crisis. The actions of those in the university are thus best understood in light of the developments taking place among the city's nascent social workers. While University Settlement was experiencing the difficulties of its first few years, important areas of social-service activity in Toronto were gradually moving out of the voluntary sphere and into the realm of paid social work. Like nurses during the interwar period, social workers contested traditional views of male professionalism by primarily basing their claim to professional status on the possession of skills unique to their occupational training.[6] Since the turn of the century, casework had become the most important technique in American social work; as a special skill that could be acquired, it consequently helped to legitimize the work of the new professional. By 1914, a theory of differential casework had been developed that standardized social-work methodology.[7] As it was promoted by the social-work educator Mary E. Richmond, in *Social Diagnosis* (1917), differential casework allowed the social worker to suggest treatment for an individual or family based on an investigation of the existing external conditions, which she referred to as 'social evidence.' Richmond wrote: 'Social diagnosis is the attempt to arrive at as exact a definition as possible of the social situation and personality of a given client. The gathering of evidence, or investigation, begins the process, the critical examination and comparison of evidence follows, and last come its interpretation and the definition of the social difficulty.'[8] The historian Roy Lubove has pointed out that Richmond's reliance on social evidence was rooted in the assumption, soon to be challenged, that an objective environment in fact existed that could be both analysed and controlled. In the 1920s, her environmentalism would become unfashionable as many social workers, inspired by psychiatry, began to shift from an emphasis on external social conditions to a consideration of the inner mental process.[9]

In the decade after 1910, however, Richmond's conception of differential casework was at the height of its influence, and many social workers in Toronto began to use casework methodology. Following the appointment of Charles J. Hastings as Toronto's Medical Health Officer in 1910, public-health nurses were organized into a circuit of home and school visitors, and they increasingly adopted casework to help organize relief and investigate slum conditions.[10] In 1912, four district councils were established, allowing settlement and public-health workers from the poorer parts of the city to meet monthly to discuss the distribution of private relief. At that time, the city's public funds for non-institutional, or 'outdoor' relief, were still administered by the privately run House of Industry. In an attempt to improve the coordination of this outdoor relief, the municipality of Toronto requested that the four councils join together to form one central council. As a result, in January 1914 the Neighbourhood Workers Association (NWA) was created, under the secretaryship of Arthur H. Burnett, who was then working for the Department of Health. During the war years, the district secretaries employed by the NWA (whose salaries nevertheless were paid by the municipally appointed Social Service Commission) concentrated on developing uniform case records that, they believed, would facilitate a more rational allocation of both public and private charitable funds. By 1918, in addition to its mandate from the city to coordinate outdoor relief, the NWA represented over six hundred workers from such privately supported enterprises as missions, settlements, crèches, and relief societies.[11]

Toronto's settlement houses functioned at the heart of this community of paid and volunteer social workers, providing institutional neighbourhood bases for both public and private endeavours. By 1914, the settlement movement had grown rapidly: in addition to Evangelia House, University Settlement, and Central Neighbourhood House, it included St Christopher House, established by the Presbyterian church in 1912, and Memorial Institute, which was opened by the Baptist church in 1913. The spread of settlement houses allowed the public-health nurses to extend their activities throughout a large section of the city, operating out of University Settlement and St Christopher House in the area west of University Avenue, while to the east using the facilities at Central Neighbourhood and Evangelia houses.[12] Workers from the settlements were also original members of the district councils – University Settlement, for example, housed the conference for its area – and, after 1914, they formed the backbone of the NWA. Although the settlement houses to a great extent relied on the participation of volunteers, there was a new tendency to differentiate between unpaid and paid workers. In December 1918, Toronto settlement workers formed the Federation of Settlements, which, in keeping with the emerging professional orientation of the city's social workers, excluded volunteers by specifying that only the paid staff of the participating settlements were eligible for membership.[13]

Although they cooperated with each other professionally, the Toronto settlement houses reflected the extremely diverse ideological perspectives of their directors, and often embodied widely divergent mandates. This lack of unity was revealed openly by University Settlement's 1913 publicity pamphlet, in which Norman J. Ware found it necessary to state: 'It has been felt all along that a University Settlement should be somewhat different from other Settlements.'[14] Under the supervision of Ware and of Milton B. Hunt, University Settlement came closest in its policy to Central Neighbourhood House, as both at that point were non-sectarian institutions modelled on the American social settlement. By contrast, St Christopher House had been established by the Presbyterian church to fulfil a definite evangelical purpose, and was dedicated to the goals of 'Canadianizing and Christianizing.' Although the directors of St Christopher House were divided on whether they should give preference to the aspirations of the church's traditional or social-gospel factions, the settlement always maintained its character as a church institution whose primary role was to provide workers for the Presbyterian chain of settlements. Moreover, since the staff members at St Christopher House tended to be recruited through their local churches, the settlement's activities, such as the Sunday evening story hour, were often religious in nature.[15]

As Canadian social workers became more conscious of their status in the years leading up to the First World War, the University of Toronto was pressured to legitimize their occupation academically by instituting a course in social service. There was a concern among many in the field that Canadian students should be made aware of conditions specific to their own country, rather than be forced to seek social-work training in New York or Chicago. For several years, J.J. Kelso had been actively campaigning along these lines, and had recommended to the Ontario Legislature that a 'school of philanthropy' be organized in affiliation with the University of Toronto. John G. Shearer, the secretary of the Presbyterian church's Board of Social Service and Evangelism, was also anxious that the university provide courses to supplement the training that students received at St Christopher House.[16] In 1913, the Canadian Welfare League was formed in Winnipeg to facilitate research into social problems and to encourage reform at the community level. The idea of a nation-wide social-work organization that functioned independently from the churches had been fostered by J.S. Woodsworth, who had left his position as superintendent of Winnipeg's All Peoples' Mission to become the League's first secretary. The executive committee of the Canadian Welfare League included Kelso among its influential members, and the new association soon added its support to the scheme of a course in social work at Toronto.[17] In March 1914, *Acta Victoriana* published an urgently worded article by Woodsworth, writing in his capacity as secretary of the League, entitled 'Social Work as a Profession.' Arguing that complex and potentially chaotic changes were taking place in Canadian society, Woodsworth contended that properly trained social workers, along with those in the traditional male professions, were required to take the lead in reconstructing social life. 'To-day social work is coming to be recognized as a profession. The social worker stands side by side with the doctor, the lawyer, the minister, the journalist or the educator.' While insisting on the need for professional standards and technical instruction, however, Woodsworth also stressed the fundamentally moral dimension of social work. For Woodsworth, social work required theoretical as well as practical training, so that students could apply their knowledge to social problems, and ultimately perform their future responsibilities 'in accordance with the principles of social justice and welfare.'[18] Three months later, Woodsworth sent President Falconer a report containing the recommendations of the Canadian Welfare League's committee on social training in universities and colleges. Falconer promised to consider the suggestions carefully, but by that time the university's senate had already approved a curriculum for new courses in social service to be introduced in the fall.[19]

After 1910, there had been a corresponding growth of interest in social-work training among faculty at the university. By 1912, several Toronto academics had been giving informal instruction on social problems through a weekly lecture series sponsored by the Methodist Department of City Missions and Social Service, and held at the Fred Victor Mission in Toronto. During the winter of 1913–14, for example, two professors from Toronto's Department of Political Economy, G.E. Jackson and G.I.H. Lloyd, had participated in the program at Fred Victor, offering lectures on 'The Drift to the Cities' and 'Minimum Wage Laws,' respectively. The series had been advertised as being open to all those 'interested in social betterment,' and also had encompassed addresses by many Toronto social workers, including Elizabeth B. Neufeld, Sara Libby Carson, and Arthur Burnett.[20] In March 1913, T.R. Robinson, a professor in the Department of Philosophy, had consulted

J.J. Kelso for advice on developing social-service lectures in connection with his own courses in social ethics.[21] Although there is evidence that Falconer himself had been considering the creation of a university course on social questions as early as January 1908, the decision to go ahead with the program in 1914 seems to have been sparked by fear that a private group might establish a school on an independent basis, a strategy that had been successfully accomplished in 1898 by the New York Charity Organization Society when it inaugurated its Summer School of Philanthropy (later known as the New York School of Philanthropy).[22] In a handwritten memorandum in which he indicated his intention to ask the approval of the university senate for a scheme of special courses in social work, Falconer commented: 'This is in answer to requests from many different sources. If the university does not do something, less competent private undertakings may be formed for this purpose.'[23]

While it is not clear exactly which 'private undertakings' Falconer was most concerned to forestall, his subsequent actions indicate that he preferred to cooperate rather than compete with the more powerful lobbyists in the social-work community. By 1914, two voluntary, predominantly female organizations had been formed to promote the interests of social workers. In 1911, the Social Science Study Club was established to discuss social problems, with a mandate to encourage 'the enlightenment and formation of public opinion, first within the club and then in an ever widening circle outside.' The Social Workers' Club, which was organized the following year and housed at University Settlement, perceived its goals to be more professionally directed. At a meeting in May 1913, the Social Workers' Club announced its aims as follows: 'The cultivation of personal acquaintanceship among the members, their education in respect to all branches of social work, the increasing of efficiency and the raising of standards, the encouragement of co-operation amongst all agencies doing social work, and the fostering of social reform.'[24] Like J.S. Woodsworth, the members of the Social Workers' Club believed that social research should be applied, and regarded the improvement of society as a responsibility that should naturally be entrusted to those in the new profession. In 1913, the two clubs together arranged a meeting with President Falconer to discuss the possibilities of a course for social workers. A resolution was passed stating the need for such training, and was presented by Falconer to the board of governors. In March 1914, a special senate committee was appointed, which, in addition to Falconer, included James Mavor and Charles Hastings. The committee's report was adopted the following month, and the senate recommended that courses of instruction be established 'for persons who propose to become trained workers in Social Service.' In May, Falconer was authorized by the board of governors to establish for the winter 'vocational courses for social workers.'[25] The close cooperation between Falconer and the social-work community at this point was accentuated by the offer of a member of the Social Science Study Club, Sarah T. Warren, to pay the salary of the new department's director during the first year.[26]

Designing the Curriculum

Like the University Settlement board, in 1914 the social service committee was dominated by Robert Falconer and G.I.H. Lloyd, and the curriculum of the Department of Social Service was strongly influenced by the same convictions that had shaped the policy of the settlement.[27] The inductive approach to social study introduced by W.J. Ashley rested on the premise that society was subject to evolutionary forces, and would, by nature, change over time. The rejection of the deductive method and its fixed laws was therefore grounded in the teleological faith – much strengthened at Toronto by idealism – that society had the potential to change for the better. Empiricism was welcomed less for its intrinsic value, than for its utility in gathering facts and statistics that could then be applied to social problems; knowledge that could, ultimately, hasten social progress. The desire of groups such as the Social Workers' Club to facilitate social reform while raising professional standards harmonized well with this emphasis on the importance of applied over purely theoretical social study. The proposal drawn up in the spring of 1914 accentuated the need for a course that would act as an agent of social betterment, by producing graduates qualified to combat the problems of modern industrial society. 'There is,' the proposal stated, 'a growing demand for persons who are, by reason of personality, experience, and training, able to help in the difficult work of alleviating social misfortune and remedying social maladjustment.'[28] The university's long-standing trust in the potential of 'scientific' education when it was united to the moral impulse was revealed in the public statements of the department's purpose. As the *Calendar* for 1915–16 explained, the Department of Social Service was to afford 'an opportunity to the ablest and best young men and women to qualify themselves for service which is increasingly demanded on behalf of the social life and progress of the nation.'[29]

In planning the department's curriculum, Falconer and Lloyd showed their awareness of the issues that were then being debated by social-work educators in Britain and the United States. The first British program in social work, the London School of Sociology and Social Economics, had been set up in 1903 by the Charity Organisation Society. The course had its origins in the activity of the London Ethical Society, which had been formed in 1886 by followers of T.H. Green living at Toynbee Hall.[30] From their earliest efforts to establish a training course in the late 1890s, the founders of the London School of Sociology had attempted to solve a conflict that was central to social-work education: was the course to be primarily vocational and oriented towards training in technical skills and methodology, or was it to be broadly based, theoretical, and academic in focus? In October 1902, a conference had been held by the Charity Organisation Society to discuss the extent to which universities should participate in social-work education. The ensuing report had recommended that social workers be given both practical training and a theoretical background, but had not favoured seeking academic affiliation, suggesting that the teaching should be done by an organization independent of the universities. The new School of Sociology, therefore, had been conceived as a separate institution that could nevertheless offer academic education in addition to technical training. Under the directorship of a Toynbee Hall resident, E.J. Urwick, however, the curriculum emphasized courses in the social sciences, such as social psychology and economics, and provided little instruction on the development of vocational skills.[31] In his introductory lecture in October 1903, Urwick argued that while social workers needed to be trained in 'scientific' methods like physicians or surgeons, they should never consider themselves 'mere practitioners,' but instead should gain a full understanding of the social theory upon which their work was based. He stated: '[The social worker] must learn to realize the slow growth that lies behind each present condition and fact; to see in the social structure, whole or part, of state or of institution, the expression of a vital meaning; to feel beneath the seemingly plastic relationships of social life the framework of economic necessities; and to find in each casual tendency and habit the effect of slowly changing mental processes.'[32] Urwick wholeheartedly endorsed the idealist ethos that had been incorporated into the School of Sociology through its early links with the London Ethical Society and Toynbee Hall. Like Falconer and Lloyd, he was guided by the belief that society was morally defined. For him, as for many other idealists, social work was perceived as an endeavour that could give men and women access to that 'vital meaning' shaping their evolution towards a better society.

In 1912, the London School of Sociology strengthened its academic orientation when it became the Department of Social Science and Administration, housed at the London School of Economics and Political Science (LSE) and under the control of the University of London.[33] After the amalgamation, the department continued under Urwick's leadership until 1921, and during this period it retained its original emphasis on applied sociology, directed towards the amelioration of social problems. The *Calendar* of the LSE for 1913–14, for example, lists a typical lecture course offered by Urwick, entitled 'Moral Basis of Social Progress.' As it had before the amalgamation, the curriculum primarily consisted of courses in the social sciences, such as social economics, statistics, and sociology. These courses, the 1914–15 *Calendar* explained, were designed to provide theoretical background for the students' practical fieldwork under 'experienced administrators' in the various London agencies that cooperated with the program. 'In their theoretical work the students obtain, through lectures, classes, reading, and individual tuition, a knowledge of the relation of present conditions and efforts to the past history of industrial and social life, and to the generalisations of Economic Science and Sociology. The special aim of this side of their training is not to teach them to theorise, but to deepen their intelligent interest in everything connected with their subsequent practical work.'[34] The teaching of technical skills and methodology, however, was virtually absent from the curriculum, and it seems clear that the department assumed that most of whatever vocational training was necessary would be conveyed by the agencies supervising fieldwork. During Urwick's tenure, just one course on technique, 'Class in Methods and Details of Charitable Administration,' was included in the curriculum, and it was listed only from 1914 to 1919.[35] Although the department was oriented towards the solution of practical rather than theoretical problems, its courses in sociology overlapped with those taught by L.T. Hobhouse in the LSE's Department of Sociology; until 1915, in fact, social-work students were required to take Hobhouse's course 'Social Evolution,' among others. Hobhouse shared Urwick's faith in evolutionary social progress, a faith that, Reba N. Soffer has argued, limited the development of British sociology as an independent theoretical discipline before the Second World War.[36]

The LSE's Department of Social Science and Administration therefore expected to teach its students the academic principles underlying social work, rather than vocational procedures. As its name suggests, it was more concerned to produce welfare administrators than social-work practitioners. As a result, the amalgamation of the London School of Sociology with the LSE left a vacuum in social-work education, and by 1915 the Charity Organisation Society had joined with other agencies to create short-term certificate courses that aimed at providing strictly technical training for practitioners.[37] This division between teaching skills and imparting knowledge characterized early social-work education in other British cities. At the University of Birmingham, courses had been instituted for social workers after 1903 as a cooperative venture between the university and the city's settlement houses.

W.J. Ashley, who had left Harvard in 1901 to accept the chair of commerce at Birmingham, was the chairman of the social-study committee; like Urwick, he thought that the course's primary function was to provide students with an empirical and moral foundation upon which to build their future work. In a report of 1918, Ashley claimed that the aim of social study was 'to educate the citizen's understanding of the social life of which he is a part; to train and test his judgment in dealing with its complexities – for the good of his neighbours as of himself; to furnish him with a background of fact and ideal which shall throw light on all his practice as an administrator; to increase his power of dealing with people and their present difficulties; and to inspire him with faith in the value of his efforts.'[38] In formulating the social-work program at Birmingham, Ashley continued to place his confidence for social progress in the bond between 'fact and ideal,' which thirty years before had inaugurated the idealist and empirical tradition at the University of Toronto.

Social-work educators in the United States also were divided over the question of the profession's academic status. The debate between advocates of vocational training and academic education resulted in the adoption of very different curricula by the two founding American schools of social work, the New York School of Philanthropy and the Chicago School of Civics and Philanthropy. Originating in 1898 as a series of summer lectures sponsored by the New York Charity Organization Society, the New York School of Philanthropy took the vocational approach, and placed a growing emphasis on the importance of casework as the profession's primary technique. An independent organization, the New York school worked closely with the city's social-work agencies to train the large numbers of skilled workers that they required. By contrast, the Chicago School of Civics and Philanthropy after 1908 increasingly strove to gain academic legitimacy for social work. While most other early American schools were tending to follow the New York School of Philanthropy and focus on casework methodology, the Chicago School of Civics and Philanthropy resisted technical specialization and approached social work from the vantage point of early Chicago sociology. Under the leadership of Edith Abbott and Sophonisba Breckinridge, the Chicago program required its students to gain a firm understanding of scientific analysis and research in the social sciences, and to apply that knowledge to the solution of practical social problems. Like E.J. Urwick's program in London, the Chicago course attempted to produce broadly educated public-welfare administrators instead of the specialized practitioners requested by social-service agencies. In 1920, Abbott and Breckinridge succeeded in gaining full academic recognition for their institution by affiliating it with the University of Chicago as a graduate professional school, the School of Social Service Administration.[39]

At the University of Toronto in 1914, the curriculum of the new Department of Social Service was intended, at first, to serve as a compromise between the two conflicting approaches to social-work education. In the university's *Calendar* for 1915–16, it was announced that the Department of Social Service was to be a 'Canadian school of civic and social training,' and that it would combine vocational and academic instruction: 'The necessity has long been recognized for trained and qualified workers with a knowledge of the social problems and needs of the country, together with the technical training enabling them to take effective part in the social development of the Dominion.'[40] In designing the curriculum, however, Falconer and Lloyd gave little attention to vocational training, and clearly favoured the kind of broadly based academic education being pursued by Urwick and Ashley in Britain, and by Abbott and Breckinridge in Chicago.

By 1914, the university's preference for applied research had already prompted Falconer and Lloyd to import the sociological approach of the early Chicago school to restructure University Settlement. The influence of idealism, moreover, harmonized well with Toronto's traditional approach to professional education, as both schools of thought emphasized the value that academic knowledge would have for the male leaders of society. In addition to stressing the moral principles that lay beneath social work, Falconer and Lloyd directed their program towards training the administrators and civil servants who would eventually shape social-work policy. The perspective of those on the social-service committee also corresponded with the continued belief at Toronto that the university ought to produce professional graduates of good character and broad academic interests. In an editorial in March 1914, *University of Toronto Monthly* welcomed the announcement that a Department of Social Service was to be set up in the fall, but warned against the university adopting the 'narrow' aim of merely equipping specialists for their definite callings. Instead, the editorial maintained, the university should attempt to merge the modern practical focus of vocational training with the traditional 'ethical spirit' of academic education. 'To attain to a finer sense of the *value* of life and at the same time to lose nothing of the wider, clearer perception of the *facts* of life which science has taught us, is the goal to which the university of to-day must try to find its way.'[41]

The University of Toronto's intellectual affinity with the idealist perceptions of academics like Urwick and Ashley was strengthened by Lloyd's personal familiarity with social-work education in London and Birmingham, which he had gained in his previous position at the University of Sheffield.[42] The original curriculum of Toronto's Department of Social Service closely resembled that of Urwick's Department of Social Science and Administration at the LSE. The proposal of 1914 placed an emphasis on the need for principles over techniques, and academic education over vocational instruction: 'Though vocational training must always be subordinate in importance to personal aptitude and general education, yet the nature of the task which confronts the social worker makes some special preparation increasingly necessary. The efficiency of the social worker will be largely increased if he has learned to utilize the experience of others and rely on precepts and principles already tested and established.'[43]

The department's curriculum from 1914 to 1918, during the tenure of its first director, Franklin Johnson, Jr, remained much the same as when it first was planned by Falconer and Lloyd. Within the framework of applied social study, the course combined a theoretical grounding in the social sciences with practical information on such topics as criminality and contagious diseases.[44] The program was divided into two sections: lecture courses to provide theory, taught by members of the university, and discussion classes led by active social workers that were meant to bear 'directly on the everyday experience of the student.'[45] In the first year, for example, the lecture courses included 'Social Economics' by G.I.H. Lloyd, 'Social Psychology' by the philosopher George Sidney Brett, and 'The Urban Community' by the sociologist Norman J. Ware. The discussion classes explored such topics as 'Settlement Methods' and 'Recreation'; in accordance with Falconer's previous recommendation, they were conducted by prominent Toronto social workers, including Sara Libby Carson, who was then supervising the Presbyterian settlements, and Elizabeth B. Neufeld of Central Neighbourhood House.[46] As in the Department of Political Economy, students in social service were expected to use their theoretical understanding of social conditions to realize moral purposes. The program incorporated a course on 'Social Ethics,' in which students wrestled with such questions as 'whether the subject of moral judgments is the *action* or the *motive*.' The essays written by one student in the class of 1916, Dorothy W. Eddis, ranged from a discussion on 'How do I distinguish right from wrong?' to an analysis of 'The Social and Economic Differences between Labor and other Commodities.'[47] In 1917, an optional second year was added to the program to provide more advanced instruction; a course on 'Social and Industrial Investigation,' which aimed to train students for government service, was included as an elective second-year course. With an emphasis similar to that of courses taught at the LSE and the Chicago School of Civics and Philanthropy, this class was specifically designed to prepare students for positions in public-welfare administration.[48]

Although they recognized the importance of practical education, Falconer and Lloyd gave only minor attention to the need for actual training in social-work methodology. In contrast to most American schools of social work at this time, the curriculum of the Department of Social Service at Toronto included, out of eight compulsory and eight optional courses, only two specifically dealing with technique: 'The Family and the Community,' which all full-time students were required to attend, and 'Charities,' which was an elective discussion course.[49] Between 1914 and 1918, both courses were taught by Arthur Burnett, who had received his own training, after leaving the University of Toronto in 1912, at the New York School of Philanthropy. By the time of Burnett's attendance, the New York School of Philanthropy had become almost exclusively oriented towards vocationalism and casework.[50] In accordance with his education in New York, Burnett's courses at Toronto were concerned with transmitting skills, particularly methods of differential casework. The *Calendar* for 1915–16, for example, gave the following description of Burnett's required course: 'The technique of charitable work; investigation, plan, application. Methods of administration; confidential exchange, records, conferences. Study of selected case records.' Similarly, his discussion course, 'Charities,' was intended to offer more advanced instruction in casework, and was organized to help students deal with the cases that they encountered during their fieldwork. In the original proposal for the department, fieldwork had been recommended as a third kind of instruction, which would be 'for the collection of information and critical first hand study of social questions.'[51] Fieldwork was initiated in 1914, and full-time students were required to devote ten hours a week to gaining experience in Toronto's agencies, which included University Settlement, Central Neighbourhood House, and the Social Service Department of the Toronto General Hospital. As with Urwick's course in London, it seems to have been assumed at Toronto that the students would receive most of their technical training through their fieldwork. During the department's first four years, however, the fieldwork program remained tentative and unorganized, with 'the problem of suitable field work' consistently striking the single negative chord in the director's otherwise self-congratulatory annual reports.[52]

Despite its limited attention to technique, the Department of Social Service immediately attracted the participation of those groups of social workers who were pioneering casework methodology in Toronto: the visiting nurses employed by the Department of Health and by the Board of Education. As in many large American cities, in Toronto some of the earliest people to use casework were the nurses and teachers who specialized in medical or school social work.[53] The department's enrolment for the first year reflected the particular interest of caseworkers, as the over two hundred and eighty part-time students included a large number of public-health and school nurses, as well as probation officers of the Juvenile Court and nurses-in-training from the Social Service Department of the Toronto General Hospital.[54] In addition to those who specialized in casework, the program also drew part-time students from Toronto's settlement houses, and during the first year paid workers from St Christopher House, Evangelia House, and University Settlement took courses. Of the eleven full-time students who graduated in 1915, eight would later hold permanent positions in settlement houses, or in such agencies as the NWA. One graduate from the first class, Ethel Dodds Parker, became a leading member of Toronto's social-work community, holding several prominent appointments, including the directorship of the city's Social Welfare Division from 1927 to 1932.[55] In 1915, the ties between the department and Toronto's professional social workers were strengthened by two developments: first, the decision by the city that all playground supervisors and assistants in its employment were from then on required to take the department's course on playgrounds and, second, the establishment by the Toronto General Hospital of a scholarship to enable its best part-time student enrolled in the medical social-service course to study full-time in the department for a year. In 1916, both the municipal Department of Health and the Board of Education followed the example of the city's Playground Department and required that their visiting staffs take specific courses given by the Department of Social Service. During the 1916–17 academic year, the department also conducted a study of the distribution of charitable relief from public funds for the city's Social Service Commission.[56]

'A Young "Ladies" Finishing School'

In designing the new program, the members of the social-service committee had sought continuity with the past, drawing their inspiration from the university's traditional reliance on the potential of its young men. The Department of Social Service, however, had been planned in the spring of 1914 for a world that would soon no longer exist. With the outbreak of the First World War that summer, male undergraduates were given a much more imperative call to service. In his opening address in Convocation Hall on 29 September, President Falconer urged the students to think about the struggle ahead and to be ready to defend their freedom with whatever sacrifice was necessary. 'The world is in agony,' he concluded, 'let this agony reach the depths of our nature also, so that it may purge our selfishness.'[57] In October, Falconer announced that the university would be forming its own officer training corps. His public appeal for volunteers was direct and stirring: 'We expect the men to come forward now.'[58] Within two months, more than 1800 had signed up with the officer training corps, and by the spring of 1916, over 1200 undergraduates had enlisted for active service, while the university's enrolment steadily dwindled.[59] By the end of the war, 5651 members of the university had enlisted, including 1881 undergraduates, of whom 613 had been killed in action or died on service.[60]

While the *University of Toronto Calendar* specified that the department received both men and women as students, wartime conditions accentuated the gender imbalance that already existed in social work, and by 1918 social service had become almost exclusively a women's program. During the first year there were just five part-time and no full-time male students, and the entire graduating class – and by extension the founding membership of the Social Service Alumni association – was female.[61] This discrepancy continued: between 1915 and 1918, only sixteen men were registered, compared to seven hundred and sixty-five women, and of these only five men studied in the department full-time.[62] In 1938, a survey indicated that since 1914 the department had graduated only fifty-three men, compared to four hundred and seventy-eight women.[63]

The identification of social work as a women's program was made official in the fall of 1920, when the university inaugurated a two-year 'Special Course for Workers with Boys.' The course was open to students in other departments, and was specifically designed to attract the young men who did not wish to take the entire diploma course in social work, but who intended, either as volunteers or paid workers, to lead the boys' programs operated by the city's social agencies. The *Calendar* for 1921–22 was careful to explain that boys' work not only provided men with a means of personal fulfilment but should be seen as a respectable male career. 'There is an increasing demand for Boys' Work Secretaries; the Young Men's Christian Association, local churches, settlements and Boys' Work Boards are in constant need of more and better trained men than are available. As an effective and satisfying form of social service, as well as a promising field for a vocation, specialized work with boys makes one of the strongest claims.'[64] While the creation of the special course in boys' work revealed the university's renewed desire after the war to attract men into the field of social work, it also indicated the degree to which enrolment in the regular course of the Department of Social Service had become regarded as unsuitable for young male students.

The curriculum had been intended to give social workers a sound academic background, but by 1918 the department had virtually no credibility in the university community. Agnes C. McGregor, a graduate of 1916 who for years served both as an administrator and a faculty member, later described the department in its early years as Toronto's 'step-child.' It was, she wrote, 'a small experimental department with no real status in the University, it had little prestige.'[65] At the most obvious level, this lack of status was due to the inadequacy of the first director, Franklin Johnson, Jr, and the scandal that subsequently arose concerning his academic qualifications. A more significant reason, however, was the program's close association with a female-dominated occupation, which, in the eyes of many, had no legitimate claim to professional status. In 1932, J.J. Kelso looked back with frustration on the development of the social-service program at Toronto. 'It was a great disappointment to me,' he remembered, 'to find when the course was actually opened that it was swamped with young women and the young men felt they were quite out of it. It seemed to be taken for granted that it was a woman's job and this is a big mistake for the key positions should be held by men.'[66]

As in their earlier search for the settlement's director, Falconer and Lloyd – who sat on both hiring committees – tried to find a male academic to head the department who would embody those intangible spiritual qualities they considered necessary for social service. In consultation with Sarah T. Warren, the member of the Social Science Study Club who had agreed to finance the appointment, Falconer started seeking advice from prominent American social-work educators in May 1914. In a letter that he sent to Charles R. Henderson of the University of Chicago, Graham Taylor of the Chicago School of Civics and Philanthropy, and Edward T. Devine of the New York School of Philanthropy (among others), Falconer stressed the importance of finding a director whose approach was applied and who might place the department at the centre of Canada's growing social-work community. 'We wish to secure a person of university training, and, if possible, distinction,' he wrote, 'one also who has had thorough experience in the practical work of social organisation and who will be competent not only to establish a new department or school, but to conduct it in such a way that it may realise what seems to us to be the great possibility of such a school in this Dominion.' Falconer explained that he was contacting American authorities because the committee preferred to find an American candidate, believing that, as he had put it, 'in many ways the social conditions of the United States are more similar to our own than English conditions would be.'[67]

Considering the committee's stated objectives, Franklin Johnson was an unlikely candidate, as he possessed neither practical experience in social work nor a background in applied sociology. He first was recommended by Edward T. Devine of the New York School of Philanthropy, who claimed that Johnson's moral attributes as a former minister in the Baptist church made up for the fact that he had done little teaching and had no social-work training. 'He has an attractive and forceful personality, exceptional intellectual capacity, and genuine interest in social problems,' Devine urged.[68] Emphasizing Johnson's character and religious work, Devine merely skimmed over his academic record, and assured the committee that his recommendation was supported by Franklin H. Giddings at Columbia University, where Johnson was enrolled in the doctoral program in sociology.[69]

Under Giddings's direction, students in sociology at Columbia were trained to approach their research using an objective, statistical method of quantitative measurement. Compared to the work of Albion W. Small and the other members of the early Chicago school, the study of sociology at Columbia was much less oriented towards reform.[70] The difference between the approaches of Small and Giddings had been demonstrated in the contributions of the two sociologists to a discussion at the annual meeting of the American Economic Association in 1894. Small had submitted a paper on 'The Relation of Sociology to Economics,' in which he had asked that sociology be considered an applied science, directed towards moral ends. 'The final work of sociology,' he had argued, 'is to derive from social facts knowledge of available means for realizing social improvement, and of the necessary methods of applying the means.' By contrast, during the discussion of the paper Giddings had responded that sociology was a 'concrete science,' like chemistry or biology, which could coordinate all other social sciences by uncovering the 'fundamental facts and universal principles' explaining the historical evolution of society.[71]

Franklin Johnson's academic background and lack of experience in applied sociology initially troubled Falconer. 'The record of Mr. Johnson,' he pointed out to Edward Devine in May 1914, 'seems to be in some respects excellent, though it occurs to me that possibly his practical experience has been confined rather much to one side of social training.'[72] The following month, the director of the Russell Sage Foundation, John M. Glenn, wrote to warn Falconer against appointing an academic who had no vocational training in social work. 'When a man has not had close enough contact with some particular line or lines of work to learn method and technique, it is not easy for him to understand and sympathize with such work. He is likely to emphasize the theoretical side and teaching of a general nature rather than professional training and discipline. His school is likely to lean to the side of inspiration and information and not to lay enough stress on method.'[73] In light of the committee's own perspective on social-work education, however, Glenn's warning probably would have come more as a recommendation than otherwise, as the possibility that Johnson might esteem academic principles over technique, and inspiration over method, would have strengthened his claim to the position.

Johnson himself, despite his 'objective' training at Columbia, reassured the committee that he regarded his work from a moral perspective. As a Baptist minister, he seems to have been drawn to sociology by the influence of the social gospel. In a somewhat pompous letter to Falconer in July 1914, Johnson stated that he had turned down a much more lucrative and distinguished position in order to accept the task offered by Toronto. He claimed that he did so because he believed in the great importance and usefulness of an undertaking that linked 'the work of the Christian ministry with the equally Christian work of social ministry.' 'I am looking forward with much interest and pleasure to the work in Toronto,' Johnson assured Falconer, 'and shall go into it with enthusiasm, tempered with wisdom, and with the view of building up a great work of far-reaching influence, and so accomplishing much in the service of humanity.'[74] In an address that he delivered in November 1914 to recruit support for University Settlement, Johnson emphasized what he saw as the spiritual foundation of social service. It was reported in The Varsity that he told his audience that social work had grown out of God's work, and was the 'very essence of Christianity.'[75] As before, the members of the committee were swayed by their idealism. 'Apparently [Johnson] does not claim the ripe wisdom of the old practical hand,' Lloyd had written to Falconer in June 1914, 'or the theoretical cocksureness of the school made man. But if he has the human and the intellectual gifts which are here attributed to him in such unstinted measure he has the essential thing for our purpose and I think we should count ourselves fortunate to find such a man.'[76]

Far from asserting moral leadership, however, Franklin Johnson would leave Toronto in disgrace in early 1918. He had been hired on the assumption that he had received his doctoral degree from Columbia University, and for four years the letterhead of the Department of Social Service had advertised its director's possession of a Ph.D. But by 1918 it had been discovered that Johnson did not have his doctorate. Although Falconer tried to avoid scandal by quietly seeking an alternative position for him outside Toronto, rumours circulated in the university that Johnson's academic qualifications had been falsified.[77] In January 1918, Falconer wrote to Graham Taylor of Chicago to inquire about other possible openings, explaining that Johnson wished to secure a more permanent and financially stable appointment than his present one.[78] Forced to give up his position at Toronto, and urged by Falconer to complete his degree, Johnson returned to Columbia University in April. In his final annual report as director of the Department of Social Service, he claimed that he was retiring from the position 'to enter the war service of the American Government.'[79] On Johnson's request, Franklin Giddings sent Falconer a letter to 'go on file,' which stated that Johnson had completed all the work for his doctoral degree 'except the finishing up and publishing of his dissertation.' 'I hope that it will be possible for Johnson to keep on in academic work somewhere,' Giddings wrote. 'But if during the period of the war that should be impossible, he will, I am sure, make good in war activities.'[80] Johnson's replacement, R.M. MacIver, later recalled in his autobiography the humiliating circumstances of Johnson's resignation, which, as he remembered it, had left him 'saddled for a time with the direction of a struggling School of Social Work.' MacIver stated: 'Its director had proved quite unsatisfactory, and on his induced departure no successor could be immediately found to repair the damage and raise the reputation of the school.'[81]

The low standing of the Department of Social Service at the time of Johnson's departure was highlighted in a series of anonymous letters published between November 1917 and March 1918 in a new university magazine, *The Rebel*. The magazine vividly expressed the mood of restlessness among Toronto's faculty and students during the final years of the war. Appearing in February 1917, the introductory issue bravely promised its readers that the journal would offer an 'honest criticism of things as they are.'[82] One of the first areas to come under attack in *The Rebel* was the university's participation in social work, and the program of the fledgling Department of Social Service was ridiculed. Besides showing a general impatience with conservatism, the criticisms in *The Rebel* were an assault on what was seen as the overly academic and theoretical curriculum of the department. More important, however, the letters stand as the first public confrontation between advocates of the university's traditional ideal of service, with its masculine assumptions, and those who supported the belief that social work was a valid profession.

The discussion was launched in November 1917 by a letter from 'Hetairos,' who, pointing out that students taking theology or law at Toronto were especially unequipped to deal with social questions, suggested that they be given the opportunity for practical instruction in the problems they would soon encounter in their careers. 'I take it that any university that would arouse enthusiasm in social problems,' the letter stated, 'and that would fit its students for effective social endeavour, must provide instruction and facilities for practical work.' By asserting the importance of training young professional men in social service, 'Hetairos' was reviving the university's confidence in the superiority of its cultured male graduates, and was expressing the conviction that social problems would finally be given the attention they deserved once male students returned home from the war. In December, a second unsigned letter pursued this point, arguing that even if clergymen and lawyers were properly trained by the university, social reform 'on a grand scale' would be impossible unless other leaders of society cooperated. 'The Social Service Department is probably doing good work for a comparatively small group of women who study for a year or two under its supervision. If, however, this department were enlarged so that it could supply practical demonstrations and supervise field work for students in Arts, Theology, Law, and Medicine, its value would be greatly enhanced.'[83]

In a reply to 'Hetairos' in the December issue, a letter signed by 'Conservative' mockingly defended the curriculum of the Department of Social Service. 'Everyone who knows anything, or near anything, realizes that the University has already established a Department of Social Service that supplies enough theory to deal with any social problem without the slightest reference to field work. Why the necessity of prowling around Juvenile Courts or Settlements, or even Sunday Schools, to learn the practical side of criminality?' 'Conservative' then satirized the voluntaristic and amateur nature of the idealists' approach to service. 'Lawyers need no such training, clergymen can find more inspiration in a sweetly aromatic cup of five o'clock tea than in the excessively disagreeable contents of a slum dive ... Let us stick to the old and tried, rather than experiment with the dynamite of callow and superficial experimenters.' This exchange provoked several enthusiastic responses offering suggestions for improvements. In one letter someone signed as 'P' continued 'Conservative's' satirical defence of the existing program: 'For very many years the University has been content to study the slum from the comfortable arm chairs of its libraries. Why any change?' Although there had been 'romantic radicals' who had envisioned the Department of Social Service as a point of contact between academia and 'real life,' it could be happily reported now that 'conventionality and the status quo' had been regained. Some young students, in fact, had ventured out into the slums, but, 'P' hastened to add, 'Conservative' was to be reassured that they were strictly supervised. 'Don't jump: it is all under the most careful chaperonage. Lights out at ten. No latch keys! The whole atmosphere one of pasteurized propriety which approximates as closely as possible to that of a young "ladies" finishing school.'[84]

The determination of Falconer and Lloyd to institute a broad program in the social sciences, rather than a specialized technical course, had created a curriculum that underemphasized casework methodology and fieldwork, and therefore implicitly devalued the skill that had come to define professional social work. To give the department academic legitimacy, the committee had assumed that the directorship should go to a male academic, instead of to a practising female social worker. In his search for candidates, Falconer had indicated that the committee would only consider a woman if it were unable to find the 'right man.' While he had asked the opinions of men who headed American training centres, he had not requested help from such prominent social workers as Jane Addams of Hull House.[85] Even though male students never did enter the program in any numbers, these gendered assumptions remained incorporated into social-work education at Toronto, and as such they form part of a larger pattern of inequality that was to dominate the development of the profession. The perception that men naturally were better suited to hold social work's executive positions led to discrimination against women in a female-dominated occupation. Despite their superior professional training, by 1950 women were limited primarily to low-paying jobs in the practitioner sector, while men, although a minority in the field of social work, held the higher administrative and planning positions.[86] While other schools of social work in the United States would become more and more preoccupied with teaching casework methodology, the Toronto department would continue to promote an earlier idea of professional education, one which assumed that knowledge, not skill, would provide society's leaders with the power of social amelioration.

6

The Department and Its Graduates, 1918–1928

In 1918, the social scientist R.M. MacIver was placed in charge of a school of social work that, in the words of one critic in *The Rebel*, was perceived to have a reputation comparable to that of a young ladies' finishing school. While preserving the university's original approach to social work, MacIver, and his successor J.A. Dale, attempted to transform the department into an academically rigorous program that could command the respect of the wider university community. In their efforts, both directors found themselves fully supported by the department's graduates, who, through their membership in the Social Service Alumni (SSA) association, formed vital links between the university and the social-work community. According to a survey prepared by the department in 1927, between 1915 and 1926 the university graduated 247 social-work students (229 women and 18 men); 112 of these graduates found positions in social work. Of the 79 graduates who were listed as married or 'detained by home duties,' many were serving as volunteers or as board members in social-service agencies.[1] Seeking professional recognition, these female graduates endorsed the policy of the department as a deliberate strategy to gain prestige for their occupation. By the 1930s, social workers in Canada would become increasingly resistant to discrimination, but during the 1920s, in the early stages of professionalization, it can be argued that social-work organizations made use of male leadership as a necessary way of enhancing their own authority. Although the policy of the department threatened to undermine the importance of casework, the earliest graduates shared their university's belief that membership in a profession required the kind of broad education traditionally acquired by men training for law or medicine. To this extent, the members of the SSA attempted to model their occupation on the older masculine professions, rather than follow other social workers in elevating technique as their claim to professional status.

Throughout the 1920s, the perception that their credibility primarily depended on the academic integrity of the program induced the female graduates to form a close and cooperative relationship with the program's male directors.

In the United States, a pattern had emerged by the 1920s that placed male social scientists with prestigious academic qualifications at the head of schools of social work, while more experienced female social workers managed their daily administrative details.[2] At the University of Toronto, the running of the social-work program from 1915 to 1947 was left in the hands of its longest-serving faculty member, Agnes C. McGregor, who was herself a graduate of the department and an active member of the SSA.[3] MacIver and Dale shaped the program's policy, yet much of the responsibility for the department's continuity of approach essentially belonged to Agnes McGregor. In her formal history of the program, which was published in 1940 to celebrate the school's twenty-fifth anniversary, she glossed over the difficulties in gaining academic status, and stressed instead the progression of the principles laid down by Robert Falconer and G.I.H. Lloyd in 1914. She concluded with the warning that 'the Department must be envisaged and maintained not only as a competent and effective vocational school, but as an educational institution of highest quality.'[4] Dale's successor, E.J. Urwick, recognized her importance, and in his foreword to her anniversary history in 1940 gave her credit for providing the work of the department with 'a marked unity and coherence,' which, he argued, was derived from her unvarying singleness of aim.[5] In both of her roles – as the program's administrator and as an influential member of the SSA – McGregor consistently supported an academic over a technical approach to social-work education. During the 1920s, her intermediary position was crucial in sustaining the harmonious relationship between the directors and the department's professionally active graduates.

R.M. MacIver: A Sociology of Values

In Agnes McGregor's recollections, the real history of the department always began in the spring of 1918, when Franklin Johnson returned to the United States and R.M. MacIver was appointed acting director. MacIver only held the position for two years, yet in McGregor's view his appointment inaugurated a period of intense excitement and progress, when the director's personal convictions and leadership skills perfectly suited the university's impatient postwar mood. 'He brought youth, vigor and broad social idealism to the Department,' she recalled in 1947. 'His students responded eagerly and threw themselves into work in the classroom and in the community, feeling a part of all that was happening, and believing that they were really helping to create a new heaven and a new earth.'[6] While there is no doubt that MacIver injected renewed energy and purpose into social-work education at Toronto, he did not change its orientation; under his direction the curriculum continued to emphasize the importance of the social sciences. At the end of the 1914–15 academic year, G.I.H. Lloyd had resigned from his position at Toronto to return to England. In July, MacIver had been appointed James Mavor's new associate professor of political economy. MacIver had been affiliated with the Department of Social Service since the fall of 1915, having taken over the teaching of Lloyd's course on 'Social Economics.' As Lloyd's successor, he was an obvious choice for the position of acting director, and after Johnson's embarrassing and abrupt departure – according to MacIver – the president 'begged' him to take charge of the department.[7]

Although he had received his formal education in classics at Edinburgh and Oxford, MacIver had become increasingly attracted to the discipline of sociology. When he came to Toronto in 1915, he had recently been awarded his doctoral degree from Edinburgh on the strength of a dissertation analysing social evolution, published two years later as *Community: A Sociological Study*.[8] Compared to its standing in America at this time, in Britain theoretical sociology had failed to gain a significant footing within academia, and by the First World War, with the exception of MacIver himself at the University of Aberdeen, only L.T. Hobhouse at the London School of Economics taught a full program of non-applied sociology.[9] While at Aberdeen, MacIver had written a critical review of the idealist philosopher Bernard Bosanquet's *Philosophical Theory of the State* (1911), which had attacked Bosanquet's theory of political obligation by questioning the assumption that the 'real' or ideal will of the individual harmonized with the general will of the state.[10] This review has led the historian Stefan Collini to maintain that MacIver's sociological theory, like that of L.T. Hobhouse, was primarily shaped by his objection to the teleological aspects of idealism. It would be inaccurate, however, to view MacIver's social thought as representing a break from the ethical tradition that for so many years had influenced social thought at Toronto. For MacIver, as for Hobhouse, sociology was a fundamentally moral discipline – a science dedicated to uncovering the laws of social development and, by extension, to revealing the evolutionary nature of human society.[11]

In MacIver's view, sociology differed in an essential way from such 'physical' sciences as geology, biology, or chemistry, even though, as he argued, the social sciences were equally justified in using the scientific method to discover and formulate universal laws. This crucial difference, he maintained in

Community, was based on the principle that social facts were also values, and that as such they reflected the striving human purpose that shaped them. 'The very existence of society means ethical purpose in its members,' MacIver stated. 'The sociologist who has no ethical interest, no interest in social conditions as relative to values, is a dilettante.' Human community therefore inevitably adopted a developmental character, and the social scientist, alone among those in the field of evolutionary science, could unambiguously introduce the idea of purposeful growth. MacIver wrote: 'When we study community we are studying a world of values, and in the study of values it is impossible to retain the ideal which perhaps inspires the student of external nature. We must speak of better or worse institutions, of higher or lower stages of development, just because it is values we are concerned about.'[12] The standard against which progress could be measured was a community's ability to provide a better common life, an ability gauged by its possession of institutions and customs able to serve a greater number of people. Thus, MacIver believed that the welfare of society and the welfare of the individual were inseparable, and that the individual, in seeking good for others, necessarily found his or her own well-being. 'As all individuality comes to fruition in society, so all individuality must in some way give itself up to society,' he claimed in an article in *The Sociological Review* in 1914. 'A profound sense of final failure accompanies all individuality which detaches itself from social service.'[13]

While *Community* was very well received in Britain, in the United States its moralistic and philosophical approach was out of harmony with the growing popularity of statistical 'objective' sociology.[14] Drawing on the inspiration of the objectivism that Franklin H. Giddings had been promoting at Columbia University since the turn of the century, by the early 1920s many younger American sociologists were adopting an extreme form of scientism, which gave exclusive authority to 'value-free' methodology and statistical technique. There was an increasing division between the applied sociology taught to social workers in such institutions as the Chicago School of Civics and Philanthropy and the theoretical sociology pursued by academics in the college system. At the University of Chicago, the reform interests of the early Chicago school became eclipsed by the appearance of a second generation of sociologists, who directed their attention to the development of social theory based on the principles of human ecology. After 1900, the assumption that academic social science ought to be a masculine area of expertise caused female sociologists to become more and more isolated within the field of vocational social work. The appeal of scientism in the 1920s accentuated this division, as male sociologists could use aggressively 'masculine' scientific language to reinforce the boundaries between academic sociology and female-dominated social work.[15] Throughout the decade, scientific method was elevated to such an extent that one critic later described statistical sociology at this time as 'atomistic raw empiricism.'[16] After leaving Toronto in 1927, MacIver taught sociology at Columbia University for over twenty years, and there he became a vocal opponent of extreme scientism. In his perspective, this over-emphasis on statistics forced sociologists to assume that their purpose was the accumulation, rather than the interpretation, of facts. Like other inheritors of the idealist tradition, MacIver remained suspicious of types of empiricism that were not utilized for moral purposes. 'Measurement is never the end or the goal of science,' he argued in his autobiography, 'but only a way of approach to it.'[17]

In his opinions on social-work education, MacIver shared the view put forth by such British pioneers as E.J. Urwick and W.J. Ashley that students needed much more than simply to acquire skills: they needed to seek out the deeper moral meaning that lay beneath all the facets of social life. For MacIver, education in social work had the potential to bring together what he described as the 'means' of living, the accumulation of skills that resulted in civilization, and the 'ends' of living, the cultural traditions that evolved out of the constant process of human experience. His rejection of a purely vocational approach to social work was based on the same resistance to 'objectivism' that had sparked his criticism of an exclusively statistical sociology. In a 1927 article in the journal of the Social Service Council of Canada, *Social Welfare*, MacIver explained: 'Social [e]ducation, we agree, is the meeting point of culture and civilization. The social worker or the social scientist cannot, like the engineer, think only of the means of living. Social education is not merely a technique. Here the means are too closely related to the ends. The social worker must see his or her relation to a living society, to the things worth while, or the work loses its meaning.' He warned social workers that they risked 'spiritual loss' if they succumbed to the danger of becoming 'engrossed with the means, the technique.'[18] MacIver elaborated his ideas on social-work education in a series of lectures that he delivered at the New York School of Social Work, and that were published in 1931 as *The Contribution of Sociology to Social Work*. Beginning with the statement that the relation of sociology to social work was that of a science to an art, he argued that sociology provided an essential foundation for the development of a social philosophy that could discipline and support the art of the social worker. 'For sociology,' MacIver asserted, 'is the science of social relationships, and social work is an art designed to relieve or remove the definite ailments and maladjustments that beset individuals in specific social situations.'[19]

When MacIver became acting director of Toronto's Department of Social Service in 1918, he left the structure of the curriculum very much as he found it, and focused his attention instead on improving the quality of the teaching and on raising the low academic status of the department. Several instructors were added to the staff, including the political economist S.A. Cudmore, who took over the existing economic courses: 'Labour Problems,' 'Social Economics,' and 'Statistics and Social Research.' MacIver himself taught two new courses, 'Evolution of Modern Industry' and 'Social Evolution,' in which he applied his sociological theory to industrial and social development. In accordance with MacIver's belief that the social sciences provided social workers with an important framework for their daily decisions, the department continued to place little emphasis on the importance of technical training. During MacIver's tenure, as during that of Johnson, only two courses on methodology were incorporated into the curriculum. Arthur H. Burnett had recently left Toronto to work for the Cincinnati Health Department, but his courses on casework technique, 'Charities' and 'Dependents and the Community,' were assumed by F.N. Stapleford of the Neighbourhood Workers' Association and renamed 'The Social Treatment of Poverty' and 'The Essentials of Case Work.'[20] After Agnes McGregor's promotion to director of fieldwork in 1919, the fieldwork program was reorganized and, with an increase in full-time students after the war, was extended to include new affiliations with several Toronto agencies. In an effort to bring the department into closer contact with the university and the city – and perhaps to mitigate the stinging criticisms that had appeared in *The Rebel* – in the fall of 1918 MacIver introduced a special series of lectures open to all students and to the public. The series involved, for example, a course of lectures and addresses on 'Institutions for War Relief and Reconstruction,' given by representatives of such organizations as the Red Cross, the Soldiers' Aid Commission of Ontario, and the Toronto and York Patriotic Society.[21]

After the publication of *Community* in 1917, MacIver had gained considerable recognition as a rising academic. His personal ability to lend prestige to the department, combined with his determination to strengthen the academic basis of the program, finally gave social-work education at Toronto some badly needed status. In addition to promoting the department, MacIver campaigned to have social work accepted as a legitimately professional occupation. Speaking at a conference on 'Opportunities for Women in Social Service,' organized by the university's United Alumnae Association in January 1919, he claimed that there should not be any opposition between 'practical and cultural training,' or between higher education and fitness for practical life. Social service, he urged, had to be recognized as a responsible profession that was passing out of the hands of the amateur and into those of the trained worker.[22]

MacIver's support was eagerly welcomed by the graduates of the department, and from the beginning the Social Service Alumni association was firm in its endorsement of his directorship. The SSA had been formed by the first graduating class in June 1915, and, despite the fact that the association used the designation 'alumni' instead of 'alumnae' in its records, its membership consisted predominantly of female graduates.[23] The identification of the course with an exclusively female program, combined with the circumstances of Franklin Johnson's resignation, had placed the graduates in a disadvantaged position in their search for professional recognition, and MacIver's prominence offered them a way to strengthen the standing of their discipline. In June 1919, the SSA unanimously carried a resolution requesting that MacIver be retained as director, which was signed by forty-five members, including Agnes McGregor, and sent to President Falconer. 'Under Professor MacIver's direction,' the resolution read, 'the Department has developed in a marked degree and we feel strongly that a change at the present time would jeopardize its standing in the community and its possibilities of increased service ... We feel that a continuance of the present directorate would see the development and fruition of valuable plans and would firmly establish the Department of Social Service as an integral part of the University and of the community.'[24] At the end of the year, the SSA members also sent a letter to MacIver himself, expressing their appreciation, as it was later reported to the out-of-town members, 'of his contribution in making the Social Service course a recognized part of the University curriculum.'[25]

By lobbying the university to retain MacIver, the SSA was acting in the capacity of a professional organization, an activity that would soon eclipse its initial role as an alumni group. MacIver's tenure as director ushered in a period of growth and activity for the association that would continue well into the 1920s. The constitution of the SSA had indicated that its objectives were to be both university-oriented and professional: to bring graduates together and keep them in touch with other social workers, to further the aims of the department, and to initiate and promote constructive social action.[26] In the absence of a comparable organized group of social workers, by the fall of 1919 the SSA had started to function as a professional association, shaping its program around short talks or papers by members (which dealt with such topics as a plan for a social workers' exchange) and approving selected provincial legislation. That year, the SSA took what it termed 'the first step in an advance movement,' when it appointed its own representative, Agnes McGregor, to the board of the Toronto Children's Aid Society. In subsequent years, the SSA sought and gained representation on the local boards of other social agencies, including the Protestant Children's Homes, the Big Sister Association, and University Settlement, and its network of connections greatly facilitated the extension of the department's fieldwork program. With members in key positions in social agencies in Toronto, Montreal, Ottawa, and other centres, the SSA increasingly became one of the foremost professional organizations for social workers in the country.[27] During the directorship of MacIver's successor, J.A. Dale, the SSA would continue to identify closely with the department, reinforcing the university's interpretation of social-work education and, in turn, receiving Dale's influential support in its efforts to improve the professional status of social work.

While he vigorously backed the social-work program, MacIver's own interests lay more in the area of political science and theoretical sociology than in the applied sociology taught by the department, and he agreed to serve as acting director for only one more year. In his final annual report, MacIver concluded with a strong statement of support for the department: 'In relinquishing the post of acting director I desire to record my conviction of the growing value of the Department in training students and setting standards for social work throughout Canada.'[28] The degree to which MacIver was successful in elevating the status of social-work education at Toronto is perhaps indicated by the fact that the university decided in February 1920 to establish its first chair of social science. In a significant recognition of the academic orientation of the curriculum, J.A. Dale was appointed both director of the Department of Social Service and professor of social science in the Faculty of Arts.[29]

J.A. Dale: The Pursuit of Professional Standards

J.A. Dale believed that social workers required a liberal education, and he agreed with MacIver and Falconer that this education should unify theory and practice by providing, as he stated in *Social Welfare* in 1924, 'a balance of wise generalization and effective specialization.'[30] For Dale, a well-rounded education ultimately prepared social workers to exercise the responsibility of good citizenship – a duty, he maintained, that should become their life's work. Continuing a tradition of academic importation that soon would include E.J. Urwick as well as Ashley and MacIver, Dale was born in Britain and educated at Oxford. After graduating from Merton College, Oxford, in 1901, he pursued an active interest in adult education, spending periods of time at Toynbee Hall and establishing close connections with the two most significant movements for working-class education: Ruskin College, which was opened at Oxford in 1899, and the Workers' Educational Association, which was started in 1903. He was appointed an Extension Lecturer in the University of Oxford in 1902, and for the following six years lectured throughout England on literary and educational subjects. In 1908 he came to Canada to accept the position of professor of education at McGill University.[31] Through his role as chairman of the committee responsible for McGill's University Settlement,[32] Dale became known to Robert Falconer, who invited him to Toronto in 1912 to give an address on settlement work. In 1919, Dale began corresponding with Falconer concerning a possible appointment in the Department of Social Service.[33] In his inaugural address as director of the department in October 1920, Dale expressed himself in terms that must have reassured Falconer that the Toynbee ethic would continue to determine moral endeavour at Toronto. 'The hope of both education and social service is to bring up a race who shall not impoverish or debase their native land, or the life of a single citizen, and shall leave their country more great, more rich and more beautiful.'[34] In words reminiscent of those used by Arnold Toynbee and Samuel Barnett forty years earlier, Dale articulated the faith in personal contact that was central to the idealist plan for social reintegration. 'It is one of the hardest things,' he explained in an interview quoted in the *Toronto Star Weekly* in January 1921, 'to know your neighbor – really to know him unless he be in your set. Hence misunderstandings and condemnations not only between persons, but between classes and nations, employer and employed, rich and poor ... [The poor] are our neighbors and we do not know them.'[35]

Dale maintained the department's broad focus, and in his first annual report he made a point of praising R.M. MacIver, as both director and teacher, for having given the program 'the tradition of sound learning, whose evidence is in his books.'[36] Under Dale's supervision little was altered. The curriculum continued to offer a number of courses on economics, including two taught by MacIver: 'Social Economics' and 'Industrial Problems.' There were, however, several additional courses for second-year students that reflected the influence of developments in psychiatry. During the 1920s, psychiatric ideas gained considerable popularity among social workers in the United States, and many caseworkers began to shift away from the older emphasis on objective conditions, advocated by Mary Richmond, to look instead at the inner mental process. The view that mental disorders could be responsible for various forms of maladjustment challenged Richmond's assumption that the social worker could manipulate and adjust aspects of the social environment.[37] Canadian social workers also were exposed to new ideas concerning psychological development. In April 1926, at the second annual Social Welfare Conference in Toronto arranged by the Federation for Community Service, two papers that were later printed in *Social Welfare* – 'Some Things the Case Worker Desires from the Psychiatrist' and 'What the Psychiatrist Can Contribute to Case Work' – explored the possibilities of cooperation between these emerging fields of expertise.[38] In the fall of 1920, courses on 'Psychiatry' and 'Occupational Therapy' (changed to 'The Industrial Rehabilitation of the Handicapped' in 1921) were introduced into the curriculum of the Department of Social Service. The following year, a course on 'Mental Testing' was added that specifically discussed the techniques of experimental psychology.[39] Yet even while the curriculum showed evidence of new psychiatric influences, during the 1920s the fieldwork program directed by Agnes McGregor became even more firmly based in the theory of differential casework. By 1927, McGregor had prepared an outline for fieldwork training, adopted from one provided by the American Association for Organizing Family Social Work, that closely followed Richmond's method of diagnosis based on the investigation of social evidence. In her 'Field Work Bulletin' for April 1927 (one of a series that she regularly distributed to supervisors) McGregor presented the new outline, and referred to the need to help students develop 'sound working habits as well as good technique,' a process she described as 'Richmondizing Field Work.'[40]

Despite this increased attention to methodology, under Dale's management the department continued to reinforce its original decision to produce administrators and policy-makers rather than agency workers. To further this goal, new regulations were drawn up for the 1921–2 session that more clearly stressed that the ideal qualification for full-time students was graduation from a university or college. The *Calendar* made the department's reasons explicit: 'This, though not essential, is the most desirable preparation for entrance; both from the point of view of the work itself, and for eventual leadership in social service.'[41] Beginning with the 1923–4 session, the one-year certificate course was eliminated from the program, requiring all full-time students from that point onward to complete the two-year course to qualify for a diploma in social service. In his report to the president in 1922, Dale had explained that the two-year course was designed to train those men and women who, he wrote, 'will have it in their power to influence the policy of institutions, public or private, which are responsible for any phase of social work.'[42] Dale's ambition to see large numbers of postgraduates enrol full-time, however, was not realized during his tenure. In the fall term of 1927, shortly before Dale was forced by ill health to take what would become a permanent leave of absence, only four new students with university degrees registered in the program full-time; the remaining seventeen new students were accepted on the basis of their high-school matriculation work or their experience in social service. Nevertheless, by 1927 it was perceived in the department that the establishment of the two-year course had in fact succeeded in making a clearer line of demarcation between the students seeking professional training and the deaconesses, missionaries, and other part-time students who enrolled out of a general interest in social issues.[43]

Dale himself worked steadily to promote the development of professional standards in the field. In 1922, he initiated discussions among social workers in Winnipeg, Toronto, Montreal, and Halifax concerning the possibility of founding a Canadian association of social workers. At a meeting in Toronto in June 1924, he was appointed chairman of a committee asked to look into the formation of the association. Although he was unable to continue as chairman owing to his always uncertain state of health, Dale remained an active member of the provisional executive after the Canadian Association of Social Workers (CASW) was formally organized in March 1926. In October, *Social Welfare* became the official organ of the new association. Until the creation in 1932 of the CASW's own publication, *The Social Worker*, each issue of *Social Welfare* contained a section controlled by the CASW, which was originally edited by a Toronto graduate, Ethel Dodds Parker. In a pattern that would continue to characterize the development of the profession, all the members of the provisional executive were men. In addition to Dale, it included such leading administrators and educators as Carl A. Dawson, director of the social-work and sociology programs at McGill University; George Basil Clarke, general secretary of the Family Welfare Association of Montreal; John Howard T. Falk, secretary of the Montreal Council of Social Agencies; and Ernest H. Blois, director of Child Welfare in Halifax.[44] Of the two hundred names on the charter membership list, however, over one hundred and fifty were those of women, who, the editors of *The Social Worker* later caustically noted, 'were only moderately kept in the background at the General Meeting and election.'[45] The CASW safeguarded its professional identity, yet in such a way as to favour those engaged in policy-forming positions, and its constitution specified that only those 'professionally occupied with the work of social education, organization, or adjustment' were eligible for membership.[46]

In J.A. Dale's perception, social work was the most effective and selfless expression of true citizenship for both men and women, and he stressed that the elevation of professional standards through the CASW could only facilitate their ability to improve society. This advancement of social workers towards a higher level of organization, he believed, was matched by a community's overall progress towards social betterment. In December 1926, Dale wrote in *Social Welfare*: 'The forms in which society is to evolve depend on the extent to which it succeeds in bringing into clearer consciousness the implications of community, in giving definiteness and warmth to the vague underlying goodwill, in sharpening it into the intelligent direction of social purpose. Not only as social workers but as citizens,' he concluded, 'we shall profit by every opportunity for the union that is strength.' For Dale, the establishment of the CASW meant that social work was entering a stage in which the ideals of service could be realized, and the fundamental link between skill and knowledge could be forged. 'In the faithful doing of their work,' he argued, 'and in the confidence of the help it enables them to bring to distressed men, women and children, [social workers] have seen their ideals more and more expressed in practice, by themselves and by others. They have outgrown the sense of isolation in the consciousness of belonging in a comradeship, whose circle is widening, whose roots go ever deeper into knowledge and humanity.'[47]

Dale's active promotion of professional standards placed him in a position to work even more closely with the department's graduates. The minutes of the SSA reveal a growing unity of interest between its members and the administration. The graduates' degree of loyalty to the department at this time is indicated by their assessment of professional standards according to their university's goals in social-work education. They based their claim to professional status not only on their possession of university training, but more specifically on their ability to combine technical skill with a breadth of cultural knowledge, an ability that allowed them to compare social work to the older male professions of law and medicine.

By the middle of the 1920s, the SSA perceived itself as the principal professional organization for social workers in the city. Its meetings were structured around lectures by guest speakers from across Canada and the United States. The program for 1924–5, for example, included addresses on 'The School and Democracy' by W.D. Bayley of Winnipeg, 'The Unmarried Mother and Her Baby' by Mrs Baylor of the Children's Aid Society in Boston, and 'An Experiment in Community Organization' by Mary Clarke Burnett of Pittsburgh.[48] The SSA also adopted other functions characteristic of a professional body, continuing to secure representation on the boards of social agencies in Toronto, disseminating relevant information to its members, and lobbying for improved standards in social work. In April 1928, proposed changes in provincial child-welfare legislation sparked debate among the members concerning the question of professional qualifications for public positions in social service. At a meeting on 18 April, the SSA formed a resolution that a letter be sent to the premier of Ontario, Howard Ferguson, drawing the attention of the government to the fact that, the minutes recorded,

in the field of Social Welfare, as in that of medicine, of teaching, and of law, technical training and experi[e]nce are of the greatest importance, and that those citizens who are the victims of misfortune, handicapped by unfortunate circumstances, or in need of protection or assistance, through public beneficiary measures, such as the Mothers' Allowance Act, the Children's Protection Act, the Children of Unmarried Parents' Act, etc., are entitled to the best available technical skill and social knowledge as well as personal qualities of understanding, sympathy and insight on the part of those doing the work of investigation, inspection and supervision.

The resolution was passed unanimously, after an amendment was proposed, seconded by Agnes McGregor, that 'technical training' be changed – significantly – to 'professional training.'[49]

In their efforts to promote the claims of the new profession, Toronto's graduates in social work also relied on a moral rationale for their work that owed much to the teaching they had received in the department. At the Social Welfare Conference held in Toronto in 1926, Ethel Dodds Parker, who was then the secretary of the Toronto Child Welfare Council, presented a paper, subsequently published in *Social Welfare*, that attempted to justify the right of social work to professional status. Her article was entitled 'A Code of Ethics for Social Workers,' and she acknowledged that it was influenced by one written by R.M. MacIver, 'The Social Significance of Professional Ethics.' Following MacIver, Parker believed that the social worker was involved in a fundamentally moral activity, and she claimed that a social worker's code therefore was based on the conception of 'duties' rather than of 'rights.' Rooting her argument in the assumption that a profession was distinguished from an occupation by the existence of a code of ethics or 'unity of ideals,' Parker asserted that social work was acquiring most of the characteristics of a profession. She maintained that social workers' strongest qualification in this regard (what she termed their 'keystone of unity') was their conception of 'devoted service,' which placed the interests of the people being served before financial gain. 'Perhaps no other group,' she wrote, 'unless the ministry, has higher qualifications on [this] point.' Like other members of the SSA, Parker associated the cultivation of professional ideals with the need to sustain the education that she herself had experienced at Toronto. In her article she criticized social workers for allowing people to drift into their profession without first undertaking a period of specialized training and discipline. She stated: 'Only when we require training of all, and when that training includes a long drilling on the ethics peculiar to this profession, can we overcome this deficiency.'[50]

The view that professional aims were dependent on the acquirement of a liberal education naturally reinforced the ties between the Department of Social Service and its graduates, and during Dale's tenure the SSA took steps to more actively support the university. In May 1924, Dale addressed the members on developments in the program at the SSA's annual meeting, and at that time he initiated discussions concerning what a growing number began to see as the members' particular responsibility towards the department. The minutes recorded: 'It was pointed out how the Alumni could help to raise the Standard of Social Work by getting the public to understand the need of training.'[51] In January 1925, the SSA executive began to discuss what 'special work' the graduates could undertake, and considered appointing a member to sit in on the meetings of the department. The subject was again brought up at a general meeting of the SSA later that month. After it was suggested that the association's 'first duty should be to the School,' it was proposed that the members sponsor an annual scholarship of one hundred dollars. Sharing Dale's belief in the need to raise the entrance requirements of the program, the SSA members agreed that, rather than award the scholarship to a student who had already entered the course, the aim should be to 'recruit the right type of person.' In selecting a university graduate, Mary Jennison, as the first recipient of their scholarship, the members were satisfied that the requirements of 'previous education, promise of success regarding both practical and theoretical work, as well as financial need' had been met.[52]

Agnes McGregor later looked back on the years of Dale's directorship as a 'happy, carefree era in the history of the School.'[53] After 1925, however, Dale's health became more and more fragile, and by the end of 1927 it was obvious that he was no longer capable of heading the department effectively. In April 1927, R.M. MacIver had decided to leave his position as head of the Department of Political Economy (which he had held since James Mavor's retirement in 1922) to direct the Department of Economics and Sociology at Barnard College in Columbia University.[54] In December, MacIver wrote to Falconer from New York to discuss the situation in the Department of Social Service and to offer a suggestion for Dale's replacement.

MacIver was anxious to warn Falconer against appointing a social worker who did not possess academic qualifications, and his recommendation to the president relied on the gendered assumption that the department ought to be directed, but not necessarily administered, by a male academic. 'What [the Department] needs is someone who has experience and vision,' he advised, 'not merely technical training in social work – which is apt to be very narrow –, someone who can represent it and make decisions on questions of policy but who need not be engrossed in details of administration.' The 'one man' available with these qualifications, MacIver urged, was E.J. Urwick, who had recently been appointed his own successor in heading the Department of Political Economy.[55] MacIver's views were similar to those conveyed in an unsigned memorandum of 1927, found among Falconer's papers, which described the situation in the Department of Social Service and explained that little progress was being made compared with what might be accomplished with a stronger staff. 'The school needs a director with academic and personal prestige,' the memorandum stated, 'and with knowledge of social work. Since social work seriously needs men workers of high ability, the director should be a man. A part time or temporary director such as Professor Urwick would be greatly preferable to the appointment of a less highly qualified and suitable person.'[56] Falconer accepted MacIver's advice, and in January 1928 Urwick agreed to serve without remuneration as acting director of the Department of Social Service, while Dale was granted a leave of absence for the following year, before retiring permanently from the university.[57]

As MacIver had anticipated, under Urwick's guidance the department's moralistic approach to social work was maintained into the years preceding the Second World War. In contrast to that of Dale, however, the period of Urwick's directorship, although initially harmonious, would culminate in dissension between the department and its graduates. After the creation of the CASW in 1926, the SSA would relinquish its role as the city's professional organization, and the department no longer would be so closely linked to the social-work community. During the depression years of the 1930s, the crisis of mass unemployment would force a rapid expansion of Ontario's public-welfare bureaucracy; Toronto graduates would join other social workers in promoting a more specialized view of their role in social adjustment. Urwick's own steadfast determination to return to an earlier ideal of service would become increasingly unacceptable to those who wished to ensure a place for social work in the expanding welfare structure, and who planned to do so by forging a unified professional identity based on efficiency and expertise.

7

A Return to First Principles: E.J. Urwick and the Fight against Machinery, 1928–1937

Although E.J. Urwick stressed the temporary and voluntary nature of his positions, he did not hesitate to exert his influence to shape the policies of the two departments under his control. In 1929, after serving for one year as acting director of the Department of Social Service, he started pressing the university administration to sanction proposals that would have a significant impact at Toronto not only on social-work education but on the development of sociology as an independent discipline. In both areas, Urwick's hostility to all evidence of what he saw as 'machinery' – to bureaucratic structure or to scientific priorities – caused him to set himself against the incursions of social-work specialization, on the one hand, and of theoretical objective sociology, on the other. While at Toronto, he became apprehensive that any form of theoretical sociology, particularly as it was practised in the United States, would inevitably reduce the discipline to a vapid scientific exercise. Like many other late Victorians, he found that the bewildering events of the twentieth century, the Great War and the Depression, only sharpened his desire to return to a world of values and to defend spiritual certainties from the impertinence of scientific presumption.

During his tenure, Urwick successfully prevented theoretical sociology from gaining a foothold at Toronto, and he ensured that when the university did introduce a sociology program, it was in accordance with the standards of applied social research. In 1922, McGill University had created a separate sociology department under the direction of Carl A. Dawson, a sociologist who shared the theoretical perspective that characterized the work of Robert Park and other second-generation members of the Chicago school. Throughout the interwar period, theoretical sociology became firmly established at McGill, as Dawson and his colleagues produced a series of studies that used the principles of Chicago sociology, and particularly the theory of human ecology, to examine Canadian social conditions.[1] In contrast to McGill, at Toronto, E.J. Urwick's authority would continue to prevail long after his retirement in 1937: until 1963 the university would offer sociology only as part of a general program in the social sciences, designed intentionally to prepare students for the postgraduate course in social work.

Regenerating the Toynbee Ethic

By recommending Urwick, it is unlikely that MacIver could have discovered anyone more suited to sustain the Victorian habits of thought that had shaped the Toronto ideal. To understand the philosophy of his directorship, it is important to look at Urwick's early life and academic background in some detail. He attended Wadham College, Oxford, in the late 1880s, taking a first-class degree in 'Greats' in 1890 at the age of twenty-three, and receiving his M.A. in 1892. The British settlement movement was then reaching the peak of its influence, and Urwick, like so many rising young men of his generation, took up residency in London's East End after leaving Oxford. During the 1890s, he explored the reform possibilities of T.H. Green's ethic of personal service: living at Oxford House, a settlement that he had helped to found while at university; serving as a Whitechapel poor-law guardian and as a member of the Port of London Immigration Board; and acting as both a worker and a board member in the London Charity Organisation Society. In October 1897, Urwick became a resident of Toynbee Hall, where, until he left in 1903, he was active in the life of the settlement, holding the position of sub-warden under Samuel Barnett from 1900 to 1902, in addition to other roles as chairman of the Men's Evening Classes Discussion Club, honorary secretary of the Education Committee, and secretary for the Children's Country Holiday Fund.[2] In 1897, the same year that he moved into Toynbee Hall, Urwick also was placed in charge of the newly established School of Ethics and Social Philosophy, which had originated in the London Ethical Society. This position led in 1903 to his appointment as director of the first British program in social work, the London School of Sociology and Social Economics. In 1908, while he continued his work at the School, he was made Tooke Professor of Economic Science at King's College in the University of London. Urwick's two academic affiliations came together in 1912, after the School of Sociology became the Department of Social Science and Administration within the University of London; his title was changed more appropriately to that of Professor of Social Philosophy (a position which he held until he left Britain for Canada in 1924).[3]

While at Toynbee Hall, Urwick demonstrated what would become a life-long commitment to the idealist goals of community reintegration and education. Like Samuel Barnett, he believed that Toynbee Hall should exist not simply to transmit a utilitarian education, but rather to convey those intangible forms of cultural knowledge that led to a higher understanding of life. In January 1900, in his introductory speech as sub-warden, Urwick stated: 'I should like to label the basis of our work at Toynbee Hall as in some sort a Provident Society, – a mental insurance society; the education we aim at is an education which will open our eyes to new and ever increasing interests; true education so training the eyes and ears, and faculties of the mind, that the taste for the things that are permanent shall take the place of the things that are transitory.'[4] For Urwick, as for others influenced by the example of Arnold Toynbee, effective reform was impossible without the establishment of bonds of friendship between those with the advantages of education and affluence, and those in the poorest classes in society. 'Mr. Urwick spoke of the difficulties of work among the 'lowest classes' who were the 'leakage' of the rest,' the *Toynbee Record* reported of the settlement's annual meeting in March 1901, 'and of the necessity for 'stopping the leaks' by which these classes were supplied. The street ruffianism, so much talked of lately, had its origin mainly in bad homes, and bad homes could, in the last resort, only be reformed by personal influence and appeals to conscience.'[5]

Having fully absorbed the tenets of the settlement idea, by 1902 Urwick found himself struggling to make a link between the ideals articulated in the writings of Green and Toynbee and the reality of the settlement movement as it proceeded into the twentieth century. Just as Robert Falconer and G.I.H. Lloyd would later be unable to translate their idealism into the daily workings of Toronto's University Settlement, by 1900 it was beginning to be perceived that even Toynbee Hall embodied a growing discrepancy between the aims of its founders and what its extensive program was actually able to accomplish. Samuel Barnett found himself besieged by challenges from those who dissented from the idealist ethic: by sociologists who emphasized the concepts of family and class over that of community, by socialists who advocated state intervention, and by centralizers who presented a new bureaucratic vision of public service. To a certain extent, Barnett attempted to appease his critics by gradually redirecting Toynbee Hall's activities towards newer methods of sociological investigation, and away from its traditional emphasis on education.[6] Among those who recognized the gap between ideals and reality, Urwick began to cast a critical eye over the activities of Toynbee Hall and other modern settlement houses in Britain and the United States. Urwick's disillusionment with the current manifestation of the settlement movement did not, however, result in his rejection of the idealist convictions that had inspired it, as happened with other critics. Instead, his disappointment prompted him to make an urgent appeal for regeneration – a reform of the settlement movement that he believed would bring it back to the moral confidence and purity of its idealist origins.

In February 1902, while he was still sub-warden of Toynbee Hall, Urwick launched his campaign for reform in a paper read before the Federation of Women's Settlements in London, which was printed the following month as 'The Settlement Ideal' in the British *Charity Organisation Review*. Evoking the optimistic faith of the early 1880s, he argued that the settlement movement had grown out of a revolt against 'machine work of all kinds' and had rested on the premise that lasting influence had to come 'through the action of individual upon individual, not of mass upon mass.' The rich were to imitate the role carried out by the gentry in a country parish, coming to the ignorant poor as educated neighbours rather than patrons and, by living with them, attempting to close up the gap that had so alienated one class from another. The true ideal of 'simple neighbourliness,' Urwick charged, had been abandoned by most of the settlements in Britain, and by almost all in America, and everywhere the settlements had become institutions preoccupied with technique and bureaucracy. 'Founded as a protest against reform by machinery,' he stated, 'they have themselves become centres of machinery, and the machines are running away with the inventors ... Those who should come to be friends too often stay to learn method or manage a piece of machinery, more often still they leave before even a pretence of neighbourliness or friendship can be established.'[7] For Urwick, the duties of citizenship – in T.H. Green's sense of the word – ought to have been a settler's primary responsibility, and their replacement by other, lesser preoccupations rendered the settlement's true goal of social reintegration unattainable.

In order to return back to the earliest intentions of the movement, Urwick suggested a radical change that questioned the institutional structure of all settlements, and, more importantly, challenged the gendered interpretation of service that had made Toynbee Hall an exclusively masculine community. By trying to go back to the ideological origins of Toynbee Hall, Urwick, in fact, was striking at one of the most fundamental elements of the settlement idea: the belief that reform efforts should rightly be the domain of the 'young thinking men' destined to control the country's sources of power. By contrast, like R.M. MacIver and J.A. Dale, Urwick held the view that women had a equal obligation to participate fully in the integral duties of citizenship.[8] Criticizing the artificiality of a settlement life that encouraged single men and women to live in closed, segregated communities, he proposed that small groups of both men and women, married and single, live apart from the central settlement building in scattered homes throughout the area, where they could genuinely 'settle' and come to know their neighbours. 'An hotel has no neighbours, nor has a palace,' he stated.[9] In 1903, Urwick decided to put his own suggestion into practice; with three other Toynbee residents, he established a 'colony' of the settlement in the nearby neighbourhood of Limehouse. From his new vantage point, he continued to urge for reform, hoping that others would follow the initiative of the Limehouse Colony and inaugurate a new era of 'disintegrated' settlements. In February 1904, for example, he opened a debate on 'settlement ideals,' attended by Toynbee residents and others, in which he repeated his argument against institutionalization, insisting that the noun corresponding to the verb 'to settle' was 'settler,' not 'settlement-worker.'[10] As his use of the term settler indicates, however, Urwick's rejection of the masculine exclusivity of Toynbee Hall had only a limited relevance for the large numbers of female social workers who took up settlement work as a career. In Urwick's view, the settlement ideal ought to be voluntaristic; he welcomed women into the movement, but remained apprehensive of what he saw as the dangerous influence of professional ambition.

In his subsequent career as a social philosopher in both Britain and Canada, Urwick refused to allow his recognition of the gap between ideals and reality to discourage him from concentrating on what 'ought to be' rather than what 'was.' In 1912, sixteen years before his appointment at Toronto, he published a determined statement of his social thought, *A Philosophy of Social Progress*, that was at once a condemnation of 'scientific' sociology and a forceful plea to reinstate the spiritual foundations of social reform. In the latter sense, his work owed more to the mid-Victorian tradition of social criticism than to contemporary treatises in the social sciences, and his prose often took on an urgent prophetic quality reminiscent of Carlyle or Ruskin. While granting the sociologist the right to use the scientific method to uncover some knowledge concerning the conditions of social life, he flatly denied that the sociologist had any authority to predict the future of social change, or to offer guidance on how society might best progress. Sociology might claim to be a coordinating science, but the reality of this claim, Urwick argued, was rendered impossible by the fact that the whole of human life was modified and controlled by the forces of a spiritual universe, a universe that completely eluded all attempts at scientific analysis or inquiry.

Like R.M. MacIver in *Community*, Urwick rejected the use of categories borrowed from the physical sciences because he believed that social facts were also social values, and that as such they could never be divorced from their importance in determining the quality of social life. Having proved to his own satisfaction that a science of society was impossible, Urwick offered instead a philosophy of social progress, formulated on the assumption that change resulted from 'life-impulses' in the individual that could neither be calculated nor predicted, and that were dependent on the 'spiritual element' possessed by everyone. Drawing on T.H. Green's assertion that all human beings were able to communicate with the God immanent within them by realizing their higher selves, Urwick maintained that real progress could only be assessed by the extent to which an individual was capable of discovering his or her 'true' or spiritual self through citizenship. 'At this point,' he stated, 'the important thing to realize is that citizenship – as the unifying whole of all social duties – has been lost sight of among the parts, and needs to be restored to its place; and that till it is restored, no real social policy, no true moral advance, no sureness of dealing with any difficulty, is possible.' Since the realization of the true individual was the 'only absolutely good end,' Urwick adopted the extreme idealist position that what ought to be in fact mattered more than what actually was. He concluded his book with a final indictment of materialism in social amelioration: 'And this is the philosopher's final lesson: to learn that what is of importance is not the reform, but the will that prompts it; not the improvement of social machinery, but the resolve that machinery shall be improved until all are helped by it; not the results achieved by our devices, but the effort to achieve something good for the use of our fellow-citizens.'[11]

Written at a time when the idea of state intervention in Britain was beginning to gain acceptance – a Liberal government had recently brought in such very concrete reforms as old-age pensions and unemployment insurance – Urwick's insistence on the supremacy of ideals over actions left him open to the charge of being anachronistic. Reviewing *A Philosophy of Social Progress* in May 1912, the *Toynbee Record* expressed its annoyance with Urwick's disregard for tangible accomplishments, and complained that his philosophical position was 'largely commonplace and no matter of dispute.' 'We cannot agree that the results of reform are not to be counted, but only the will to reform,' the reviewer objected; 'rather we should have said that to the reformer who has realised the purpose of reform, results are everything, for they form the content by which that purpose is brought into fact.'[12] Despite his growing alienation from the new brand of Toynbee Hall men, however, Urwick remained on good terms with Samuel and Henrietta Barnett, who perhaps sympathized with his desire to get back to first principles. In June 1913, he served as one of four casket-bearers at Samuel Barnett's funeral in Whitechapel. Henrietta Barnett would later remember him as one of 'the men we worked with, lived with, and loved,' an 'incomparable host, whose courteous tact hid the will which never forgot its goals reached by self-forgetting labour.'[13] Urwick also maintained his connections with Toynbee Hall, and, in his career at the University of Toronto, he used his personal contacts at both the settlement and the London School of Economics to benefit several of his Canadian students while they were studying overseas.[14]

In 1924, at the age of fifty-seven, Urwick uprooted himself and his family from their life in Britain and settled in a neighbourhood of Toronto near the university, restless in what he then thought would be an early retirement. He had been pursued by poor health throughout his career, and his self-appointed exile in Canada, in his view, was a drastic attempt to avoid the dangers of London's damp climate. 'You can imagine what a grief it was to me,' he wrote later to a friend in England, 'to have to abandon all my work in London, in order to get the benefit of better health in another country.'[15] Once in Toronto, Urwick established tentative contacts with the university. Although he was anxious to be of use, it ran contrary to his Toynbee principles to actually seek out anything beyond disinterested service.[16] In November 1925, he undertook to lead a study group of the SSA, which throughout the following academic year would meet every two weeks to discuss – appropriately – 'the Social Good.'[17] In January 1926, Urwick was, in MacIver's words, 'at hand' to fill in during the sudden illness of C.R. Fay, a professor in the Department of Political Economy. At MacIver's request, he was appointed a special lecturer in economic history for the remainder of the term. By this point MacIver almost certainly had an eye to the future; in November he arranged to have Urwick (who still retained the title of Professor of Social Philosophy in the University of London) become an honorary member of the staff, without salary.[18] When MacIver resigned in April 1927, he indicated to Falconer that Urwick was intending to remain in Toronto for the following year, and the president, taking the hint and hoping to avoid a nightmare of infighting among the political economists, requested Urwick to serve as acting head of the Department of Political Economy.[19] It was important to Urwick that his affiliation with the University of Toronto had been unsolicited on his part. Even though he directed the departments of both political economy and social service for over ten years, he consistently maintained the modest position that he was just temporarily doing 'a little useful work' during his enforced retirement. 'Quite by accident I fell into some delightful work here,' he characteristically wrote in a letter of 1930. 'Its only drawback is that it is increasing so fast that I can hardly keep up with it. But I intend to go on until senility becomes too obvious.'[20]

Urwick's years as a settler in the East End had left him permanently disenchanted with the ability of organized reform efforts to transcend what he saw

as the corrupting influence of public subscriptions and institutional struc-
tures. Although he continued to involve himself in reform issues, such as the
housing problem in Toronto, his personal experience during the early part of
his career caused him always to remain wary of the difficulty involved in
successfully incorporating ethical ideals into the practical policy of any organization. While living in Toronto, he agreed to serve as an active member of
the board of directors of University Settlement from 1927 to 1940 (and was
ex-officio honorary chairman as head of the Department of Social Service),
but the board's minutes for this period reveal that he consistently advocated
the need for the other members to adapt or recast their ideals to suit the
changing times.[21] At a special meeting of both the staff and the board held in
December 1937, the purpose and future policy of the settlement were discussed, and Urwick, the minutes recorded, took the opportunity once again to
question 'the whole movement at present both here and in England.'[22] His
recognition of the limitations of the settlement idea, however, seems only to
have increased his determination to carry the idealist message to younger
generations of social reformers. Through his role in social-work education in
Canada, as in Britain, Urwick sustained his campaign against the evil effects
of 'machinery' on attempts at social amelioration.

Sociology and Social Work

Urwick's goal was to make the Department of Social Service into an academically rigorous postgraduate program, and to provide a four-year undergraduate course in the social sciences as a prerequisite, which would channel
talented students directly into the department. In January 1929, he prepared
the first of several strongly worded reports containing his recommendations
for the future of social work. 'For some years past,' he informed Falconer,
'the Department of Social Service has merely marked time.' After pointing
out that the department was in no way able to satisfy the current demand for
qualified social workers, he criticized the 'internal defects' of the 'present
patch-work course,' which, since its establishment in 1914, had attempted to
mix courses in the social sciences with highly specialized skills-oriented
courses such as 'Recreation,' 'Case Work Methods,' or 'settlements.' Com-
plaining that the curriculum had little coherence, he argued that the association between the two groups of courses was by no means clear, and that no
real attempt had been made to bring them into relation. Like Dale, Urwick
stressed the need for the department to attract university graduates, and he
suggested that the course should be able to draw in the type of men and
women who were capable, as he put it, 'of becoming leaders in the social

work of the country.' As a solution to the problems of the curriculum, Urwick proposed that its academic orientation be strengthened, and that primacy be given to the academic basis of social-work education rather than to balancing theory and technique in an uneasy alliance. He wrote: 'The better method – and the only successful method – is to plan first the essential ground work of a course which shall furnish the knowledge and induce the viewpoint necessary to all social work; and then to build upon this foundation whatever specialisms may seem advisable.' For Urwick, as for MacIver and Dale before him, the academic authority of the program required the presence of a well-respected male social scientist on the staff. In his January report, Urwick recommended strengthening the program by appointing two new staff members, 'of whom one should be a man.' As he had wished, in April 1929 a young social scientist, Harry M. Cassidy, was given the newly created position of assistant professor in the Department of Social Service.[23]

A first step towards the fulfilment of Urwick's plan was accomplished in October 1929, when the university senate approved his request to have the name of the department changed to what he considered to be the more suitable title of 'Social Science.'[24] That same month, he submitted a second, more detailed report to the president, in response to unidentified opposition from among the members of the senate's committee on social science, which at that time was considering his proposals. Fearing that social philosophy would be rejected as being insufficiently 'objective,' Urwick explained his conviction that students in social work needed to be made aware of the 'supreme importance' of moral and spiritual influences.[25]

After assuming the directorship, Urwick had been troubled by the specialized approach taken by many social workers in Toronto. 'I find one of the great dangers here is intense concentration upon the technique of case work etc. rather than upon the principles underlying it,' he had written to a colleague in Britain in January 1929. 'And there is a danger of even the best workers losing any vision of the wider social facts of their work and the possibilities of putting prevention before treatment.'[26] While Urwick supported the desire of social workers to gain professional status, his faith in the importance of ideals over actions made him suspicious of the corrupting effect of administration and technique on the social worker's will to achieve good. 'It must not be forgotten,' he warned in his October report to the president, 'that there is, a real danger – very pronounced at the present time – of social workers drifting into a materialistic attitude which is certainly not counteracted by exclusive attention to objective scientific method.' The most potent hazard, he believed, was the increasing tendency among social workers to overemphasize the value of psychological insight in casework, and to elevate

psychiatric technique as the profession's primary claim to 'scientific' expertise. Arguing that the subject was in any case too complex to be undertaken
by students of social work, Urwick also protested that psychiatry was 'apt to
excite a slightly morbid over-interest in the student's mind.'[27] In common
with other late-nineteenth-century idealists, Urwick was unable to accept the
psychologist's supposition that social organization was affected by forces that
were fundamentally irrational.[28] As a philosopher, his search for meaning
within the patterns of social life depended on the conviction that human
activity was guided by an ethical purpose, a unifying spiritual force that had
an existence apart from the normal or abnormal powers of the mind.

By 1932, Urwick had succeeded in realizing his plans for both sociology
and social work. In 1930, he had made his campaign public when he submitted two articles to *Social Welfare*, 'The Training of Social Workers' and 'First
Principles First,' outlining his views on the changes needed in social-work
education.[29] His arguments had been accepted by the standing senate's committee on social science, which had recommended in May 1931 that President
Falconer appoint a special committee of the senate to consider implementing
his proposals. Beginning in the 1932–3 session, the university instituted a
four-year honour course in social science – called the 'sociology' course
despite Urwick's protests – which was directed by a committee under his
chairmanship and was designed to provide those students entering the social-
work program with a more intensive academic background.[30] It was therefore
proposed that a graduate in the sociology course could receive a diploma in
social work after completing only one additional year of more practical training in the Department of Social Science. As expected, in October 1932 *The
Varsity* reported that most of the ten students registered in the sociology
program intended to go on and take the social-work diploma. With the
exception of two new courses in the actual discipline of sociology, the program was in reality a composite of existing courses taught in the Faculty of
Arts, including economics, psychology, history, and philosophy, and, like the
program in social work, was intended to provide students with a general
grounding in the social sciences.[31] Addressing the criticism that the proposed
course might look 'rather thin' from the point of view of 'certain American
universities,' Urwick wrote to Falconer that the members of the committee
were fully justified in pursuing their own interpretation of sociology and
that he did not think it was, as he expressed it, 'necessary for us to contem-
plate at present a development of Sociological teaching along the lines usually adopted in American universities.'[32]

The introduction of the new program was in many ways a culmination of
the plans for social-work training first introduced by Robert Falconer in

1914, and as such it marked an appropriate conclusion to his long tenure as president. Troubled by poor health, Falconer resigned in 1932. (Until 1945, the presidency of the university would be held by the prominent Anglican church leader Henry J. Cody.) By 1935, Urwick was able to report that over two-thirds of those students currently enrolled in the Department of Social Science held a B.A. Beginning in the 1936–7 session, the condition of entry to the course was changed to require the possession of a university degree, although the *Calendar* noted that exceptions were to be made in cases of special experience or 'proved capacity' in other fields. As Urwick had outlined in his proposals of 1929, the department's curriculum, which included such courses as 'Philosophical Aspects of Social Theory' and 'Economic Basis of Social Life,' was designed to emphasize the unity of the principles underlying social education, and to minimize the importance of technical expertise, particularly that of psychiatric casework.[33]

Although he and MacIver shared the basic assumption that the study of society must necessarily involve the moral participation of the sociologist, Urwick's battle against non-applied sociology eventually led him to quarrel openly with MacIver over the degree to which scientific method could be used to analyse society. In public addresses throughout the 1930s, Urwick repeatedly expressed his opposition to what he saw as the estrangement of the social sciences from philosophy, warning his audiences of the danger of following the American example and separating 'religion and sentiment' from the study of human actions.[34] Maintaining that sociology merely became 'ludicrous' when it attempted to be objective, he wrote in February 1935: 'The first condition of objectivity is that all the objects to be observed shall be devoid of any meaning whatever, or any appeal to your and my interests and purposes. And that is a sorry method to apply to life.'[35] Even though MacIver himself had for many years been fighting against the influence of scientism on theoretical sociology, in May 1938 Urwick published a highly critical review of MacIver's *Society: A Textbook of Sociology* in the *Canadian Journal of Economics and Political Science.*

In the twenty years since *Community* first had appeared, MacIver had developed a more comprehensive approach to the study of social relationships, but his opinions on the essential principles of sociology remained substantially unaltered. Derived from earlier material that he had rewritten, *Society* was MacIver's attempt to provide undergraduates with 'certain primary concepts' to use in the study of sociology.[36] While he acknowledged the importance of many of MacIver's philosophical insights, Urwick was deeply offended by what he saw as the misleading presumption that sociology, or any other form of social study, actually possessed the body of universally accepted facts and principles that would entitle it to textbook treatment. He dismissed MacIver's attempts to establish exact definitions as creating a 'mass of sociological schematizations and classifications,' and cautioned that an over-attention to the structure of a discussion – to the limits set by definitions – would prevent the discovery of the essential meaning that existed within that structure. Urwick's strong disapproval, however, was not really aimed at what MacIver had actually written, but rather at what Urwick feared his work might lead to and promote: a complete abandonment of ethical principles in favour of excessive American objectivism. 'Surely it is time to drop this futile but meaningless talk about the necessary disinterest of the student of social life,' Urwick argued. 'What use is it to ask us to select our material without bias and deal with this value-impregnated realm without any care about values?'[37] MacIver had not, in fact, suggested that the sociologist remain unconcerned with values, and in a response to the review, published in November 1938, he protested that Urwick had misrepresented his position. Yet after restating his belief in the moral involvement of the sociologist on certain key ethical questions, MacIver concluded with the assertion that Urwick's separation of science and philosophy was unsound and, he implied, antiquated. He wrote: 'I would maintain ... that unless philosophy seeks to build on the data and the conclusions of science it becomes a kind of dilettante theology, supporting our interests or our prejudices, but offering neither the enlightenment of science nor the sustenance of religion.'[38]

By the late 1930s, Urwick's tenacious allegiance to idealist principles had weakened the bonds of cooperation that had previously existed between the department and its professional graduates, and had caused him to enter into a public dispute with leading members of the SSA. During the first few years of his directorship, Urwick had enjoyed the same confidence and support that had characterized the relationship in the time of MacIver and Dale. At a meeting of the SSA in April 1928, Urwick had confided his views on the current inadequacy of the department, and had requested the members' support by tactfully pointing out that, as graduates, their professional standing to a great extent depended upon the status of the program. The minutes had summarized the message in his address: 'Social work status rises and falls with the standard of training which is being given, therefore unconsciously the Alumni shares in the responsibility.' On Urwick's suggestion, an alumni advisory committee had been formed to counsel the department on matters of policy. Fourteen members had been appointed – including Ethel Dodds Parker, by then the director of the city's Division of Social Welfare – who all held prominent positions in public or private welfare agencies.[39]

For the SSA, Urwick's request for help had come at exactly the right time.

With the establishment of the Toronto chapter of the CASW in the spring of
1928, the SSA had worried that its functions were being duplicated by the
new organization, and it had attempted to redefine its mandate in relation to
the aims of the department. After considerable debate among the members,
in November 1928 the SSA had resolved to surrender its professional activities to the CASW, and to limit its activities to bringing graduates together
and to supporting the department through recruiting, training, and scholarship work.[40] As they had ten years earlier with MacIver, the SSA members
had recognized the value of Urwick's 'academic standing and prestige,' and in
April 1929, the new advisory committee had sent a letter to Falconer requesting that Urwick be allowed to continue as acting director of the department.[41]
This collaboration had been sustained throughout Urwick's campaign to
reorganize the social-work program. He had received the endorsement of
Toronto graduates through both the Community Welfare Council of Ontario
(formerly the Social Service Council of Ontario) and the CASW, which was
at that time under the presidency of Ethel Dodds Parker. In February 1932,
Parker had written to Falconer on behalf of the CASW to indicate the association's recognition of 'the importance of both educational background and
special training for Social work.' She had assured Falconer that 'the whole
Canadian Membership is behind the policy which, we understand, is under
consideration by the University of Toronto, namely – the establishment
within the Faculty of Arts of a selective course which specializes in the subjects which are considered to be a pre-requisite to professional training.'[42]

Since the early 1930s, however, Urwick had been concerned over what he
saw as the spread of a 'materialistic attitude' among Canadian social workers.
The economic collapse of the depression years had forced an unprecedented
number of Canadian families onto state relief. In the absence of any federal
welfare program, provincial and municipal authorities attempted to create an
administrative structure that could distribute the urgently needed public
funds. Anticipating a sudden growth in welfare bureaucracy, after 1930
prominent social workers (including Charlotte Whitton, then the director of
the Canadian Council on Child and Family Welfare) began to campaign for a
recognition of their unique skills, which, they argued, would be indispens-
able in the development and administration of the emerging public system.[43]
For graduates of the Department of Social Service, the crisis of the Depression provided them with a renewed confidence in the value of their skills, and
some began to look critically at the university's traditional approach to professional education. This confidence was strengthened by the general popularity during the 1930s of ideas concerning the importance of 'efficiency' and
'expertise' in all forms of work, ideas that were derived from theories of sci-

entific management and Progressive era Pelmanism.[44] One of the strongest advocates of a special role for social work was Frieda Held, a graduate of Toronto who had been hired by the new provincial Department of Public Welfare established in 1930. Held had long been affiliated with the university: an active member of the SSA since her graduation in 1920, she had been one of the first to be appointed to the alumni advisory committee in 1928, and had been teaching in the department as a special lecturer throughout the 1930s.[45] In February 1936, an article by Frieda Held appeared in *The Social Worker* in which she argued that education for social work ought to be changed to reflect the new specialized requirements of public-welfare administration. If social workers were to fill public-welfare positions, she urged, then their training must include 'technical studies in the principles of administration, interpretation, organization and business management.' 'The development of public welfare has come upon us with a rush,' Held wrote. 'There is a large gap between the content of social work training that is in practice and the practical and vital needs of Public Welfare.'[46]

This new emphasis on the importance of administrative technique revived Urwick's deep suspicion of bureaucratic organization. In the fall of 1936, he shattered his peace with the SSA by openly criticizing the CASW's policy. In August 1936, *The Social Worker* had published the first part of a report, written by a special committee of the CASW, on 'What Is a Social Worker?' To Urwick's dissatisfaction, the report had concluded: 'A social worker is one who, having acquired certain professional technique, is qualified to treat, and if possible prevent, social maladjustments in the area of human and environmental relationships.' Believing that the definition conveyed an inadequate picture of a social worker's goals and responsibilities, Urwick wrote 'An Alternative View'; although he did not have it published in *The Social Worker*, he discussed it with the second-year students in the department.[47] Frieda Held was one of the authors of the report, and she reacted angrily to Urwick's criticisms. The result, Agnes McGregor later explained to Harry Cassidy, was 'INDIGNATION – HURT FEELINGS – RUMBLINGS and a Deputation of Protest.' Shortly afterward, hostility increased between the department and the CASW (and by extension many of the SSA members) when the CASW's committee on recruiting and training, convened by Frieda Held, formally protested against the university's recent decision to restrict admission to the social-work program to university graduates.[48]

In June 1937, Urwick retired, but being reluctant to completely sever his connection with the university, he continued to teach in the Department of Social Science until 1940. While his retirement from the directorship eased the tensions with the CASW, Urwick himself remained convinced that Canadian social workers were overvaluing the importance of specialization and technique, and therefore were succumbing to the pernicious influences of 'machinery.'[49] After 1940, when he was forced by ill health to leave Toronto for British Columbia, he continued to worry over the direction of the social-work program, writing to Harold Innis, his successor as head of the Department of Political Economy, in September 1942 that he thought 'there was too much of a tendency to acquiesce in some of the questionable aims of the dominant social workers.'[50]

In 1927, MacIver had recommended the appointment of E.J. Urwick to the directorship of the Department of Social Service because he had assumed, correctly, that Urwick would carry on the work that he himself had initiated in 1918, and that Dale had sustained throughout the early 1920s. As MacIver indicated in his reply to Urwick's criticisms in 1938, however, Urwick's appointment ultimately had the effect of introducing an intellectually para-lysing influence into the development of both social work and sociology at Toronto. Like that of W.J. Ashley half a century before, Urwick's social thought was shaped by his strong affinity for the tenets of idealism, and his empirical training as an academic allowed him to approach social problems with that blend of 'science and sentiment' typically cultivated at the University of Toronto. In contrast to Ashley, however, Urwick's growing suspicion of materialism in all its manifestations caused him finally to reject the claims of the scientific method to truly illuminate any aspect of social life. For social workers attempting to define their role in Canada's emerging welfare system, Urwick's insistence on preserving the high moral ground of the disinterested volunteer struck at the foundations of their claim to professional status. While Urwick believed – unlike Samuel Barnett – that women had a central role to play in social service, he could only look with distaste on those who placed professional aspirations over altruistic goals in social work. By the beginning of the Second World War, Urwick would find himself alienated from the mood of students and graduates alike, and, from his retirement home in Vancouver, he would watch anxiously for signs that his work at Toronto was disintegrating.

Conclusion: Expertise, Efficiency, and the Bureaucratic Spirit

In December 1942, E.J. Urwick wrote one of many troubled letters that he sent to his friend Harold Innis at Toronto, expressing his fear of the changes accelerated by the war. 'We talk about the militarism of Germany and Japan, but is it not the case that the real enemy of human progress is the militarism in the hearts of men of all nations?' he asked. 'I am afraid the academic mind ... harbours these wrong attitudes almost as much as financiers and exploiters in the market-place.' By 1944, Urwick had become convinced that all of war-time society was driven by a mindless respect for order and authority, a form of 'machinery' that, in his view, fundamentally threatened the idealist and empirical basis of the social-science curriculum at the University of Toronto. In April 1944, less than a year before his death, he wrote to Innis: 'I despair of a return to the sane atmosphere in which Adam Smith quite naturally combined the moral sentiments with his scientific thought about economic forces. The whole trend to-day is to exalt the rationalist scientific approach and to discard the philosophical. I am not thinking only of the worship of the physical and mechanical sciences, but rather of the attempt to make ethics, philosophy, sociology, etc. conform in method and language to the physical sciences – with disastrous results.'[1]

Sensitive to the forces that gradually were eroding the values of the Toynbee generation, Urwick's instincts were essentially correct. His apprehensions of the effect of the wartime environment on academic life were to prove well founded in light of the declining status of the liberal-arts curriculum after 1940 and the corresponding growth of the modern bureaucratic university.[2] During the 1940s, the Toronto ideal would be confronted by significant challenges that questioned the foundations of its ethical assumptions and increasingly exposed its inability to satisfy the changing priorities of the postwar era. In the curriculum of the School of Social Work and in the policy of University Settlement, ideas on the centrality of technical expertise and efficiency in social work took on a new importance, and a bureaucratic ideal threatened to displace the university's traditional deference for the goals of personal connection and community reintegration. At Toronto, however, idealism was embedded too deeply in the curriculum to allow it to be easily subject to change, and throughout the decade the social sciences would retain their close ties to the humanities. Even while idealist convictions steadily lost their relevance for many faculty members and students, Urwick's influence – and that of Ashley, Falconer, MacIver, and Dale before him – would continue to dominate the disciplinary structure of both social work and sociology for a decade after his retirement in 1937. Until the early 1950s, Urwick's objectives would be maintained most fiercely by two men who themselves held divergent opinions: by the economic historian Harold Innis in the Department of Political Economy, and by the biochemist Hardolph Wasteneys on the board of University Settlement.

Harold Innis was Urwick's most forceful, if perhaps least likely, ally. The political economist Vincent Bladen later remembered that Urwick initially had been unable to understand either Innis's manners or his economic theories, but gradually had recognized the talent of 'this raw Ontario farm boy,' and had refused to retire until he was certain that Innis would follow him as head of the department.[3] Innis's ambition to eradicate all traces of moral bias from the 'science' of economic history would not seem at first glance to endear him to Urwick. Yet in their mutual dislike of bureaucracy and authoritarianism, and in their desire to sustain what they both saw as the purity of their university's task, Innis and Urwick could, and did, find common ground. As Carl Berger has suggested, Innis's very recognition of the existence of personal bias made him reject the view that the social scientist could ever be entirely detached and objective. Although Innis refused to mistake what 'ought to be' for what was, and therefore resented the pressure put on economists during the Depression to advocate immediate remedies, he nevertheless believed that the social scientist had a moral responsibility to uncover the long-term forces that determined social and economic conditions.[4]

Between the late 1930s and his early death in 1952, Innis opposed the kind of commercial orientation that the Department of Political Economy had reflected under James Mavor, but he did not repudiate the moral imperative upon which that attitude had been based. In an address to members of the United Church of Canada in 1947, he warned that 'skill and discipline' in social service were of little value unless, in his words, 'the practitioners of good works are selected for their integrity and the high quality of their characters.' He shared Urwick's fear that the university's liberal values were being endangered by restless materialism, and his address frequently echoed the concerns that Urwick had conveyed in his final letters. 'Modern civilization, characterized by an enormous increase in the output of mechanized knowledge with the newspaper, the book, the radio and the cinema,' Innis claimed, 'has produced a state of numbness, pleasure, and self-complacency perhaps only equalled by laughing-gas ... The demands of the machine are insatiable.'[5] In 1944, he resigned as chairman of the School of Social Work council when he heard that the social scientist Harry Cassidy was to be the new director, objecting to the appointment, he explained to President Cody, on the basis that Cassidy contaminated his scholarship by combining it with political advocacy.[6] For Innis, the proper role of the university was to protect the integrity of academic research from such corrupting demands and, by doing so, to encourage the development of an independent Canadian identity.

In 1939, Harold Innis had been made responsible for sociology when the four-year honour program was attached officially to the Department of Political Economy.[7] During his retirement, Urwick corresponded regularly with Innis regarding departmental matters. His letters often referred uneasily to the future of sociology, cautioning Innis to avoid the dangers of American statistical sociology, on the one hand, and the hazards of non-academic Christian sociology – taught by 'a half-baked sociologist-parson' – on the other. Writing from British Columbia in September 1940, Urwick expressed his relief that Innis was in charge of sociology, and urged him to keep a close eye on the program. 'Like you,' he told Innis, 'I care more for the ultimate values than for any of the intermediate ones with which we are so much occupied in Economics and Political Science. You have always managed to keep the torch burning, even though unobtrusively, but that is the best way, if, as I believe, what is felt is much more potent than what is grasped by the reason.'[8] As Urwick had hoped, under Innis's direction during the 1940s the curriculum retained its original focus, incorporating a broad range of courses in the social sciences and continuing to prepare students for postgraduate study in social work. It was not until 1963, when an independent Department of Sociology was established at Toronto, that the program was able to escape from under the wing of political economy. With the notable exception of McGill University, which created a separate Department of Sociology in 1922, before the early 1960s other Canadian universities paralleled Toronto by forming interdisciplinary departments where sociology was subordinated in importance to economics and political science. It has been contended, therefore, that the influence of Toronto's Department of Political Economy, and that of Innis in particular, was crucial in preventing English-Canadian sociology from developing as an autonomous, objective discipline on the American model.[9]

Though Harold Innis was able to exert his authority over sociology, the School of Social Work was placed beyond his control when, in spite of his protest, Harry Cassidy was appointed to the directorship in January 1945. Cassidy would sustain and even strengthen the original structure of the social-work program, yet he exemplified a new type of social scientist; a public-welfare expert whose very existence depended on a rejection of the aim of personal connection that had formed the core of the idealist reform movement. Cassidy belonged to the postwar age in a way that Urwick and other followers of T.H. Green never could. Under his leadership, social-work education at Toronto incorporated the efficient bureaucratic spirit that both Urwick and Innis so feared in the final years of their lives. Urwick himself had been responsible for first bringing Cassidy to Toronto in 1929 as a junior professor in the Department of Social Science. In 1934, Cassidy had resigned to accept the position of director of social welfare for the province of British Columbia, and then in 1939 had moved to the United States to head the School of Social Welfare at the University of California, Berkeley. While he had wished to return to Toronto to direct the Department of Social Science in the late 1930s, Urwick had resisted any attempt to appoint Cassidy as his replacement. Urwick's negative attitude towards him was a great disappointment to Agnes McGregor, then the assistant director, who continued to campaign for his appointment after Urwick's retirement, and finally secured Cassidy's return in January 1945.[10] In an address to the School of Social Work Alumni Association in November 1947, shortly after her own retirement, McGregor asserted her confidence that Cassidy's appointment would guarantee the continuation of the principles introduced by Falconer and Lloyd. 'I feel strongly,' she stated, 'that at the end of each chapter of its history, whether the story was bright or dark those values implicit in the life of the School from the very first were still its animating force, and will continue to be so as the School grows great in prestige and influence.'[11]

In terms of the structural continuity of the program, McGregor's faith was not misplaced. Harry Cassidy agreed with the school's previous directors that social-work education should be primarily academic rather than vocational, and, like them, he modelled its curriculum on the kind of course created by Sophonisba Breckenridge and Edith Abbott at the University of Chicago. Following Breckenridge and Abbott, Cassidy believed that social workers should be given a broadly based preparation in the social sciences that could teach them to conduct independent research into social problems and that, in general, could train them to be welfare policy-makers. In July 1941, the Department of Social Science had gained the status of a professional school when it was renamed the School of Social Work and its council was formed to link it directly to the senate of the university.[12] As director between 1945 and his death in 1951 (shortly before that of Harold Innis), Cassidy took steps to reinforce the school's academic and professional standing, and he built upon the changes that Urwick had introduced during the early 1930s. Beginning in the 1945–6 session, the admission standards were tightened to limit even further the number of non-graduates; applicants were required to have a strong background in the social sciences – a requirement that prompted undergraduates to take the four-year sociology course as a prerequisite to social-work training. In the fall of 1947, Urwick's vision of the program as a postgraduate course was fully realized with the establishment of the professional degrees of B.S.W. and M.S.W. for those completing one or two years of graduate study respectively. Throughout his tenure, Cassidy encouraged research among both students and faculty, and under his direction studies in social policy and housing became an important part of the school's curriculum.[13]

Although Harry Cassidy fortified the existing structure of the social-work program, his influence had a corrosive effect on the idealist values that in the past had injected the course with its quality of moral certitude. Cassidy's biographer, Allan Irving, has described him as a 'Canadian Fabian,' possessing an attitude of mind that sought social reform through the administrative expertise of enlightened welfare bureaucrats. Like the early British Fabians Sidney and Beatrice Webb, Cassidy believed that reform could be stimulated by public education and factual research, and he placed his faith for social progress in the efficiency of experts with highly specialized skills.[14] During the 1900s in Britain, the Fabians had presented a serious challenge to the tradition of reform epitomized by the young men at Toynbee Hall. Toynbee Hall's educational program had been constructed on the belief that the development of connections between university men and their working-class neighbours inevitably would recreate the bonds of local community destroyed by industrialization. Standish Meacham has argued that the Fabians – and other advocates of centralization – redefined the idealist goal of community in national rather than local terms and, by substituting the work of bureaucratic experts for the one-to-one service of individuals, dismissed as irrelevant T.H. Green's primary emphasis on the importance of personal contact.[15] For an idealist like E.J. Urwick, Harry Cassidy's promotion of the Fabians' bureaucratic state was an exhibition of 'machinery' at its most distasteful extreme. Although Toronto's program from the beginning had been designed to produce policy-makers, the curriculum had been based on the assumption that social work was not to be seen as a demonstration of professional expertise, but rather as an expression of self-negating service. Cassidy's determination to create a class of public-welfare bureaucrats linked professionalism in social work to a quality of detachment that was in every way antithetical to the idealist tenets incorporated into the program in 1914.

After the war, the profession of social work in Canada became increasingly dominated by those who shared Cassidy's views on efficiency and economic planning.[16] During the 1940s, this spirit gained support among the social workers at University Settlement and caused a growing alienation of opinion to form between the largely female staff and the predominantly male faculty members on the board of directors. Since 1915, when Sara Libby Carson had been placed in charge of its program, University Settlement had been managed by female social workers, and its fortunes had been closely linked to those of the Department of Social Service. Like the department, the settlement had drifted during the years of the First World War, and then had discovered renewed support for its mandate during the directorships of J.A. Dale and E.J. Urwick. In 1920, Dale had dissuaded the board of directors from closing down the settlement, and throughout his tenure he had promoted its program as a continuation of what he called the university's 'tradition of sane wholesome service.'[17] Although both Dale and Urwick had acted on the settlement's board of directors, however, Dale's frequent absences from illness and Urwick's disenchantment with its organizational structure had caused them to exert only an indirect influence on its policy. The academic most responsible, therefore, for the preservation of idealist convictions on the board was Hardolph Wasteneys. As a prominent member during the late 1920s and 1930s, and as chairman from 1940 to 1953, Wasteneys remained determined to defend the priorities of the Toronto ideal from the incursions of modern social work.

Born in Britain, Wasteneys came to Toronto to teach biochemistry after receiving his doctorate from Columbia University in 1916, and he served as head of the Department of Biochemistry from 1928 until his retirement in 1951. Although his research in biochemistry was not directly applicable to social problems, Wasteneys perceived his work to be broadly defined in moral terms, and he believed that advancements in science led inevitably to social progress. In a public lecture in January 1923, he urged: 'The really great scientists of all ages have been conscious that the main object to be obtained by science is service to humanity.'[18] Outside his academic responsibilities, he exhibited the same commitment to active citizenship that earlier in the century had been demonstrated by such academics as E.J. Kylie and S.A. Cudmore, and his involvement in University Settlement was matched by his interest in many similar reform projects in Toronto. In his view of settlement work, Wasteneys was inspired by the writings of Arnold Toynbee and Samuel Barnett. As a strong presence on the board for over twenty-five years, he ensured that their vision of community reintegration would continue to dominate the policy of University Settlement well into the 1950s.[19] In 1928, for example, Wasteneys, who was then the board's vice-chairman, prepared a statement that explained that the purpose of the settlement was to facilitate understanding and contact between the members of the university and the inhabitants of its neighbourhood. 'It is like a hand stretched out to give and to receive,' he maintained; 'to give because any member of a University has something vital to offer; to receive, because no member of a University can be educated unless his sympathy and thought are stimulated by contact with the lives and thoughts of all sorts and conditions of men.' At a meeting in May, the statement was adopted for use in the settlement's new publicity pamphlet because, as the minutes reported, the other board members thought it was 'such an happy expression of what they felt the Settlement should stand for in relation to the University and the Community.'[20]

Beginning in the early 1940s, the management of University Settlement began to be disrupted by conflict between the professional aspirations of its staff and the idealist views of Wasteneys and other faculty members on the board. In May 1943, the head resident, Frances Crowther, submitted a confidential report to Wasteneys as chairman, in which she pointed out the staff's difficulty in transforming the board's sanguine faith in nineteenth-century precepts into the kind of verifiable projects demanded by their more sophisticated professional training. She wrote: 'There is a difference between the policy as outlined by the Board which is largely English in its outlook and the actual working out of Settlement program by the influence of American thinking. A new Staff and changed conditions in the neighbourhood have pointed up the ineffectiveness and lack of vitality of some of the work that we are doing. If the Settlement is to play the role in the University and neighbourhood which it should our whole policy and organization should be reviewed and redefined.'[21] Reconciling the gap between ideals and actions had always been difficult for the residents of University Settlement. In some ways, Crowther's problems were no different from those experienced by J.M. Shaver in 1910. Her report, however, reflected the fact that the staff members were sensitive to the new priorities that were affecting their profession, and that these influences were distancing them still further from the view of settlement work sustained by the board.

Throughout the decade, the staff members of University Settlement became more and more impatient with what they saw as the directors' ineffective and amateur approach to the agency's program, and the board meetings frequently involved clashes of opinion over issues relating to professional status.[22] The tensions reached a climax in April 1948, when Hardolph Wasteneys tendered his resignation as chairman in protest of the board's decision to consider a report stipulating personnel standards for the staff. During the annual meeting that month, Wasteneys explained that he felt the existence of personnel standards to be 'contrary to the spirit [of] the Settlement.'[23] To support his perspective, Wasteneys referred to E.J. Urwick – whom he considered along with Toynbee and Barnett to be one of the 'pioneers' of the settlement movement – and he repeated Urwick's concern that a 'materialistic attitude' among social workers would destroy their fragile bond of connection with those they served. According to Wasteneys, Urwick had 'pleaded with social workers to remain ever "amateurs" not, of course, in the sense in which the word is used in the field of sport, but devoted, self-sacrificing, selfless servants of their fellow man.' Following the meeting, the staff members presented a statement of their own views to the board, which asserted that their wish to have the agency set up high personnel standards was not inconsistent with their desire, as social workers, to serve humanity. 'We see nothing unreasonable,' they argued, 'in recording, in the interests of efficiency and clarity, what has already been accepted in practice.'[24] While Wasteneys eventually agreed to continue as chairman in response to protests from the board and the settlement's clubs, his determination to cling to an elite and voluntaristic view of service was out of harmony with the definition of professional social work put forth by the staff members. His retirement five years later was merely an affirmation of the fact that the policy of University Settlement had to accommodate the changing objectives of both the university and the social-work community. In 1956, the board acceded to the staff's recommendation that the settlement be converted from an educational institution into a neighbourhood recreation centre. In cooperation with the City of Toronto, a new building was constructed in 1958 to house such necessary modern facilities as a swimming pool and a gymnasium.[25]

This book has explored the influence of an ethic that for over fifty years determined the nature of social service at the University of Toronto. The distinctive combination of 'science and sentiment' that constituted the Toronto ideal looked back to the late nineteenth century for its inspiration, to the work of Arnold Toynbee and T.H. Green at Oxford University and to the example of social activism epitomized by the first university settlement, Toynbee Hall. Since the appointment of W.J. Ashley to the chair of political economy in 1888, the University of Toronto had established a tradition which insisted that the empirical analysis of social conditions be shaped by the moral sensibilities of British philosophical idealism. After the retirement of E.J. Urwick in 1937, this tradition lost its most determined and persuasive advocate, and the Toronto ideal steadily declined in relevance for the postwar generation.

In 1910, the young residents of University Settlement had been faced with a considerable challenge: how to translate into effective action the social thought that inspired the settlement or, more simply, how to put an idea into practice. Years later, J.M. Shaver remembered his period at the settlement as a time of great difficulty, when he and his wife embarked on a venture for which neither had any previous experience. Throughout their year at University Settlement, the Shavers continued to be daunted by the challenge of fulfilling the vague aspirations of the settlement's board of directors. For the next decade the work remained hesitant as the board members searched for a model that would embody their social ideal. The struggle to realize that ideal was complicated by the fact that from the beginning the directors and the resident workers did not agree on exactly how the settlement would achieve its objective, nor did they always possess a common vision of what their goal should be.

While not inharmonious in theory, in practice the linking of fact to ideal produced quite different goals. As the University Settlement board soon discovered, the idealist pursuit of a reintegrated community actually was irrelevant to the empirical examination of local social conditions. Forming bonds of friendship between the settlement's residents and their neighbours was not so much incompatible with statistical research as completely unrelated to it. By the end of the first year, the directors seemed to be faced with a choice: either they could make University Settlement a laboratory for social study, and by doing so associate it with the network of applied sociologists at the Hull House settlement in Chicago, or they could continue to pursue idealist ambitions within the parameters of the original British settlement movement. The decision eventually taken by the board to preserve the initial idealist rationale for the settlement, while simultaneously affiliating it with the emerging profession of social work, was a compromise that had a significant impact on the disciplinary development of both social work and sociology at the University of Toronto.

While they inspired social action, idealist tenets, by their very nature, were difficult to establish in the practical organization of any project. The social thought that stimulated the creation of University Settlement and the Department of Social Service was anchored in the optimistic assumption that society could progress towards an ideal. In their plans for a better world, idealist thinkers characteristically failed to distinguish between this abstract ideal and the realities of modern society, or between 'what ought to be' and what actually was. The confusion originated in an idealist philosophical tradition that described reality in prescriptive terms, and that confidently assumed that the essence of a thing – either political or social – was what it in fact had the potential to become. This prescriptive tendency permitted Victorians to assert the importance of the intellect in organizing reality and, for many of them, made it possible to reconcile the results of scientific research with the principles of their religious faith.[26] Yet the same flexibility that allowed philosophical idealism to have such a profound effect on late-nineteenth-century thought actually limited its ability, as a popular belief, to provide reformers with a workable agenda for social change. Although the idealist ethic supplied the intellectual basis for the British settlement movement, the goals of personal connection and local community relied on an ideal vision of society that could not, realistically, be reached through the educational classes operated by the middle-class residents of Toynbee Hall.[27] All the Toronto academics discussed in this study shared to some degree that fundamental inability to separate 'ought' from 'is,' and consequently they all were obliged to seek compromises in their pursuit of an ideal community. This book has attempted not only to connect ideas to actions, but to account for the disillusionment experienced by idealist reformers when they themselves tried to bridge the gap between social thought and practice.

In 1910, Robert Falconer had entreated Toronto students to seek the 'highest good,' and the university's young men had come to believe that the ultimate expression of their own citizenship could be found in self-denying service to others. The establishment of University Settlement and the Department of Social Service had been attempts to institutionalize that Victorian ideal of service within the expanding structure of the twentieth-century university. The construction of social service as a distinctly masculine obligation had initially functioned to exclude women. Even though university women from the beginning had greatly outnumbered men both in volunteer settlement work and in the enrolment of the department, the gendered assumptions at the root of the Toronto ideal had continued to shape the development of academic social work well into the 1940s. Throughout the 1920s and 1930s, successive directors had ensured that the program retain its resolute focus on the broad moral principles underlying social work, a policy that, by devaluing casework technique and specialization, ultimately challenged the place of professional social work in Canada's emerging welfare bureaucracy.

After the Second World War, social welfare could no longer be perceived simply as a voluntary masculine responsibility worked out at the community level. The growing complexity of public-welfare services administered by the federal, provincial, and municipal governments required trained women and men who could efficiently organize resources in a bureaucratic system. The goal of social progress still dominated the university's mandate, but during the 1940s the very idea of progress had been infused with an admiration for order and technological expertise, a new preoccupation that effectively undermined the altruistic spirit central to the Toronto ideal. 'We so readily think of civilization in terms of equipment,' Urwick had protested wistfully in 1940, 'of bigger and better pots and pans in fact ... rather than in the plain terms of the qualifications of the good citizen, and of the good society, whose marks will be universal trust in the goodwill of all, and security for the onward march of each towards a fuller life in conscious co-operation with all.'[28] While many Toronto academics after the war continued to look hopefully towards an ideal society, the conviction of moral rightness that had encouraged the men of Urwick's generation no longer had the authority to prescribe what that society ought to be.

Notes

Abbreviations

AO   Archives of Ontario
NAC   National Archives of Canada
TFRB Thomas Fisher Rare Book Library, University of Toronto
UCA   United Church / Victoria University Archives
UTA   University of Toronto Archives
UTL   University of Toronto Library

Introduction

1 *The Varsity* 30, no. 3 (11 October 1910), 1.
2 Greg Kealey, ed., *Canada Investigates Industrialism* (Toronto 1973); Herbert Brown Ames, *The City below the Hill* (Toronto 1972).
3 Mariana Valverde, *The Age of Light, Soap, and Water: Moral Reform in English Canada, 1885–1925* (Toronto 1991), 129–54.
4 For histories of the development of public welfare in Canada, see Dennis Guest, *The Emergence of Social Security in Canada* (Vancouver 1985), and James Struthers, *The Limits of Affluence: Welfare in Ontario, 1920–1970* (Toronto 1994).
5 UTA, Office of the Registrar, A73-0051/244(06), file: Settlement Work 1910–42, clipping: *Toronto Mail*, 22 March 1910.
6 See, for example, Linda M. Shires, *Rewriting the Victorians: Theory, History, and the Politics of Gender* (New York 1992); Michael Roper and John Tosh, eds, *Manful Assertions: Masculinities in Britain since 1800* (London 1991); Mary Poovey, *Uneven Developments: The Ideological Work of Gender in Mid-Victorian England* (Chicago 1988); Joan Wallach Scott, *Gender and the Politics of History*

(New York 1988); J.A. Mangan and James Walvin, eds, *Manliness and Morality: Middle-class Masculinity in Britain and America, 1800–1940* (Manchester 1987).

1: British Roots

1 Beatrice Webb, *My Apprenticeship* (New York 1926), 173.
2 Henrietta O. Barnett, 'What Has the C.O.S. to Do with Social Reform?' in Samuel A. Barnett and Henrietta O. Barnett, *Practicable Socialism: Essays on Social Reform* (London 1888), 169. For an analysis of the public interest in London's East End during the 1880s, see Judith R. Walkowitz, *City of Dreadful Delight: Narratives of Sexual Danger in Late-Victorian London* (Chicago 1992).
3 Standish Meacham, *Toynbee Hall and Social Reform, 1880–1914: The Search for Community* (New Haven, Conn., 1987), 1–23.
4 Melvin Richter, *The Politics of Conscience: T.H. Green and His Age* (London 1964), 19–30; Andrew Vincent and Raymond Plant, *Philosophy, Politics and Citizenship: The Life and Thought of the British Idealists* (Oxford 1984), 94; Meacham, *Toynbee Hall*, 12–16.
5 Mrs Humphry Ward, *A Writer's Recollections* (London 1918), 133, 119–20.
6 Rosemary Ashton, introduction to *Robert Elsmere*, by Mrs Humphry Ward (Oxford 1987), vii; John Sutherland, *Mrs. Humphry Ward: Eminent Victorian, Pre-eminent Edwardian* (Oxford 1990), 147–8.
7 Quoted in Ward, *Recollections*, 249.
8 Arnold Toynbee, 'Industry and Democracy,' in *Lectures on the Industrial Revolution in England: Popular Addresses, Notes and Their Fragments* (London 1884), 201–2.
9 'Arnold Toynbee,' *Toynbee Record* 7, no. 4 (January 1895), 51–6; Meacham, *Toynbee Hall*, 17; Alon Kadish, *Apostle Arnold: The Life and Death of Arnold Toynbee, 1852–1883* (Durham, NC, 1986), 202–12.
10 Henrietta O. Barnett, 'The Beginnings of Toynbee Hall,' quoted in Henrietta O. Barnett, *Canon Barnett: His Life, Work, and Friends* (London 1918), vol. 1, 302–3. Throughout their married life, Samuel and Henrietta Barnett worked in close collaboration. A collection of their essays is introduced with the statement: 'Each Essay is signed by the writer, but in either case they represent our common thought, as all that has been done represents our common work.' Samuel A. Barnett and Henrietta O. Barnett, introduction to *Practicable Socialism*, vi.
11 Arnold Toynbee, '"Progress and Poverty": A Criticism of Mr. Henry George,' quoted in Webb, *My Apprenticeship*, 177.
12 Samuel A. Barnett, 'University Settlements in East London,' quoted in J.A.R. Pimlott, *Toynbee Hall: Fifty Years of Social Progress, 1884–1934* (London 1935), 272.
13 Quoted in H.O. Barnett, *Canon Barnett*, vol. 1, 312.
14 Asa Briggs and Anne Macartney, *Toynbee Hall: The First Hundred Years* (London

1984), 8–22; 'The Early History of Toynbee Hall,' *Toynbee Record* 5, no. 1 (October 1892), 2–4; Kadish, *Apostle Arnold*, 226.

15 Jane Lewis, *Women and Social Action in Victorian and Edwardian England* (Stanford 1991), 24–82.

16 H.O. Barnett, 'The Beginnings of Toynbee Hall,' quoted in *Canon Barnett*, vol. 1, 302.

17 Monthly Calendars, *Toynbee Record* (1888–1906); Martha Vicinus, *Independent Women: Work and Community for Single Women, 1850–1920* (Chicago 1985), 215–18.

18 Samuel Barnett to Francis G. Barnett, 4 April 1897, quoted in H.O. Barnett, *Canon Barnett*, vol. 2, 50–1.

19 H.O. Barnett, *Canon Barnett*, vol. 1, 98.

20 F.C. Montague, *Arnold Toynbee* (Baltimore 1889); Alfred Milner, *Arnold Toynbee: A Reminiscence* (London 1895); Gertrude Toynbee, *Reminiscences and Letters of Joseph and Arnold Toynbee* (London 1911). For an examination of the Toynbee myth, see Kadish, *Apostle Arnold*, 213–46.

21 'Arnold Toynbee,' *Toynbee Record* 7, no. 4 (January 1895), 53.

22 Mrs Humphry Ward, *Marcella* (New York 1985), 45.

23 N. Burwash, 'The Development of the University, 1887–1904,' in W.J. Alexander, ed., *The University of Toronto and Its Colleges, 1827–1906* ([Toronto] 1906), 57–60; other histories include W. Stewart Wallace, *A History of the University of Toronto, 1827–1927* (Toronto 1927), and Claude T. Bissell, ed., *University College: A Portrait, 1853–1953* (Toronto 1953).

24 Quoted in Douglas Richardson, *A Not Unsightly Building: University College and Its History* (Toronto 1990), 74.

25 Richardson, *A Not Unsightly Building*, 134. For a history of women at Toronto, see Anne Rochon Ford, *A Path Not Strewn with Roses: One Hundred Years of Women at the University of Toronto, 1884–1984* (Toronto 1985).

26 *The Varsity* 8, no. 11 (4 February 1888), 132; *The Varsity* 9, no. 1 (3 November 1888), 4–5; *The Varsity* 9, no. 3 (17 November 1888), 23.

27 UTA, James Loudon, B72-0031/010(W20), pamphlet: *Address at the Convocation of the University of Toronto and University College, October 19, 1888, by Sir Daniel Wilson.*

28 Quoted in Anne Ashley, *William James Ashley: A Life* (London 1932), 54.

29 W.J. Loudon, *Studies of Student Life* (Toronto 1923–8).

30 UTA, John Langton Family, B65-0014/003(01), Sir Daniel Wilson's Journal; William E. Lingelbach, B73-1124/001; Bessie Mabel Scott Lewis, B80-0033/001; University College Council, A69-0016/001(02), University College Council Minutes; University College, A69-0011/002, University College Literary and Scientific Society Minutes. For an analysis of student behaviour, see Keith Walden, 'Respectable Hooligans: Male Toronto College Students Celebrate Hallowe'en,

1884–1910,' *Canadian Historical Review* 68, no. 1 (March 1987), 1–34, and 'Hazes, Hustles, Scraps, and Stunts: Initiations at the University of Toronto, 1880–1925,' in Paul Axelrod and John G. Reid, eds, *Youth, University and Canadian Society: Essays in the Social History of Higher Education* (Kingston, Ont., 1989), 94–121.

31 UTL, William Lyon Mackenzie King Diaries, 1893–1931, Microfiche, Manuscript Version, G6463, 5 October 1894, and G6469, 25 October 1894.

32 *The Varsity* 9, no. 3 (18 November 1888), 23; A. Ashley, *William James Ashley*, 46–7.

33 See, for example, *The Varsity* 8, no. 11 (4 February 1888), 132. The debate in *The Varsity* was animated by the fact that one of the Canadian candidates, William Houston, was the province's legislative librarian and had been embroiled in university politics for years. The president, Daniel Wilson, had continually opposed Houston's claims to the new position, noting in his journal in 1885 that the college could secure money for better purposes 'than feeing a broken-down Grit political hack to teach what he calls "Political Science."' UTA, John Langton Family, B65-0014/003(01), Sir Daniel Wilson's Journal (10 November 1885), 96.

34 A. Ashley, *William James Ashley*, 11–23; UTA, Pamphlets: *Testimonials in Favour of W.J. Ashley, M.A.: A Candidate for the Drummond Professorship of Political Economy in the University of Oxford*, Lujo Brentano to W.J. Ashley, 2 November 1890.

35 W.J. Ashley, review of *Arnold Toynbee*, by F.C. Montague, in *Political Science Quarterly* 4, no. 3 (September 1889), 533–4.

36 W.J. Ashley, *Surveys Historic and Economic* (London 1900), ix.

37 UTL, King Diaries, Microfiche, Transcript Version, G652, 14 December 1897.

38 W.J. Ashley, 'The Present Position of Political Economy,' *Economic Journal* 17, no. 68 (December 1907), 475. Ashley dedicated his first major work, *An Introduction to English Economic History and Theory* (London 1888), to the memory of Arnold Toynbee.

39 W.J. Ashley, 'Present Position of Political Economy,' 482.

40 W.J. Ashley, *What Is Political Science? An Inaugural Lecture Given in the Convocation Hall of the University of Toronto, 9th November, 1888* (Toronto 1888), 17, 11.

41 Robert L. Church, 'The Economists Study Society: Sociology at Harvard, 1891–1902,' in Paul Buck, ed., *Social Sciences at Harvard, 1860–1920: From Inculcation to the Open Mind* (Cambridge, Mass., 1965), 18–90; Kadish, *Apostle Arnold*, 98–154, 238–46.

42 W.J. Ashley, *What Is Political Science?*, 16, 19, 21, 23.

43 Vincent and Plant, *Philosophy, Politics and Citizenship*, 1–2.

44 Quoted in A. Ashley, *William James Ashley*, 36, 34. Church, in 'The Economists Study Society,' 66–7, misleadingly describes Ashley as a 'socialist.'

45 Quoted in A. Ashley, *William James Ashley*, 36, 40, 105–6.

46 *The Varsity* 11, no. 15 (9 February 1892), 174–5.

47 UTA, James Loudon, B72-0031/001(A19), pamphlet: *Address at the Convocation of the University of Toronto, June 10th, 1890 by the Chancellor, the Hon. Edward Blake*. For an account of the positive reaction by the Toronto press to W.J. Ashley's work, see C.A. Ashley, 'Sir William Ashley and the Rise of Schools of Commerce,' *Commerce Journal*, March 1938, 41.

48 Samuel A. Barnett, 'Practicable Socialism,' in *Practicable Socialism*, 194.

49 Webb, *My Apprenticeship*, 200.

50 Meacham, *Toynbee Hall*, 31.

51 Quoted in A. Ashley, *William James Ashley*, 37, 38.

52 Ward, *A Writer's Recollections*, 162–70.

53 AO, RG 2, Department of Education, Series D-7, box 1, file: W.J. Ashley, 'Syllabus of new Political Science Department by W.J. Ashley, October 1888'.

54 W.J. Ashley, 'On the Study of Economic History,' *Quarterly Journal of Economics* 7, no. 2 (January 1893), 22.

55 NAC, William Lyon Mackenzie King Papers, MG 26, J 1, vol. 5, 4349–56, microfilm, reel C-1904, W.J. Ashley to W.L.M. King, 27 February 1906.

56 UTA, William James Ashley, B65-0033(02), Minute Book of the Economic Seminary, University College, Toronto, 1889–92.

57 UTA, P78-0321(01), *Toronto University Studies in Political Science*, 1st ser., no. 1–4 (Toronto 1889–95), 5.

58 AO, RG 2, Department of Education, Series D-7, box 1, file: W.J. Ashley, W.J. Ashley to G.W. Ross, 17 July 1892; UTA, John Langton Family, B65-0014/003(01), Sir Daniel Wilson's Journal (26 June 1892), 210.

59 UTA, Edward Blake, B72-0013/001(11), G.W. Ross to Edward Blake, 30 June 1892; B72–0013/001(12), G.W. Ross to Edward Blake, 22 July and 8 August 1892.

60 UTA, Edward Blake, B72-0013/001(12), W.J. Ashley to G.W. Ross, 31 August 1892.

61 University of Toronto, TFRB, James Mavor Papers, Ms. Coll. 119, box 1A, file 59, W.J. Ashley to James Mavor, n.d.

62 UTA, Vincent Wheeler Bladen, B74-0038, interview by C. Roger Myers, 4 January 1974, transcript, University of Toronto Oral History Project, 44. For a modern fictional portrait that makes the most of Mavor's image, see James Reaney, *The Dismissal: or Twisted Beards and Tangled Whiskers* (Erin, Ont., 1978).

63 UTA, Pamphlets: *Letter of Application and Testimonials [of] James Mavor [for the] Lectureship in Political Economy, University College, Liverpool* [1888]; UTA, Edward Blake, B72-0013/001(13), W.P. Byles, M.P. to Edward Blake, 10 September 1892; B72-0013/001(13), Edward Blake to R. Harcourt, 27 September 1892.

64 James Mavor, *My Windows on the Street of the World*, vol. 1 (London 1923), 156, 217.

65 Mavor, *My Windows*, vol. 1, 176–81.

66 S.E.D. Shortt, *The Search for an Ideal: Six Canadian Intellectuals and Their Convictions in an Age of Transition, 1890–1930* (Toronto 1976), 118–35; Paul Craven, *'An Impartial Umpire': Industrial Relations and the Canadian State, 1900–1911* (Toronto 1980), 44. For a critique of Shortt, see A.B. McKillop, 'Moralists and Moderns,' *Journal of Canadian Studies* 14, no. 4 (Winter 1979–80), 144–50.

67 Mavor, *My Windows*, vol. 1, 59.

68 Ibid., 172.

69 TFRB, Mavor Papers, Ms. Coll. 119, box 58A, file 14A, 'On Social Progress and Spiritual Life,' TMs, 14 November 1900.

70 For examples of the content of 'Political Philosophy' under James Mavor, see UTA, Examinations 021 (1894) and 035 (1910).

71 Alan Franklin Bowker, 'Truly Useful Men: Maurice Hutton, George Wrong, James Mavor and the University of Toronto, 1880–1927' (Ph.D. diss., University of Toronto, 1975), 316; Ian M. Drummond, *Political Economy at the University of Toronto: A History of the Department, 1888–1982* (Toronto 1983), 38; Shortt, *Search for an Ideal*, 123–4; TFRB, Mavor Papers, Ms. Coll. 119, box 70, special subjects: living conditions in Toronto, 1897–1906.

72 UTA, Department of Graduate Records, A73-0026/75(02), Sedley Anthony Cudmore; A73-0026/128(33–4), Hamar Greenwood; and A73-0026/288(16), Simon James McLean. These graduates form part of the group identified by Doug Owram as Canada's first 'government generation.' Doug Owram, *The Government Generation: Canadian Intellectuals and the State, 1900–1945* (Toronto 1986)..

2: Evangelism and the Limits of Social Action

1 UTA, James Loudon, B72-0031/010(W21), pamphlet: *Address at the Convocation of Faculties of the University of Toronto, and University College, October 1st, 1889, by the President, Sir Daniel Wilson*.

2 Phyllis D. Airhart, 'Ordering a New Nation and Reordering Protestantism, 1867–1914,' in George A. Rawlyk, ed., *The Canadian Protestant Experience, 1760–1990* (Montreal and Kingston 1990), 116–25; Marilyn Barber, 'Nationalism, Nativism and the Social Gospel: The Protestant Church Response to Foreign Immigrants in Western Canada, 1897–1914,' in Richard Allen, ed., *The Social Gospel in Canada* (Ottawa 1975), 222.

3 Richard Allen, 'The Background of the Social Gospel in Canada,' in Allen, ed., *Social Gospel in Canada*, 2–34; Brian J. Fraser, *The Social Uplifters: Presbyterian*

Progressives and the Social Gospel in Canada, 1875–1915 (Waterloo, Ont., 1988), 77–98.

4 TFRB, Toronto Social Welfare Agencies, Ms. Coll. 12, box 2, file: The Fred Victor Mission, 'From One Room to the Six Floor Building.'

5 Executive minutes of the Board of Moral and Social Reform and Evangelism, Presbyterian Church in Canada, 16 November 1910, quoted in Ethel Dodds Parker, 'The Origins and Early History of the Presbyterian Settlement Houses,' in Allen, ed., *Social Gospel in Canada*, 95.

6 Airhart, 'Ordering a New Nation,' 124–5.

7 Parker, 'Origins and Early History,' 89, 113.

8 UTA, University of Toronto, Student Christian Movement, B79-0059/002, YMCA Executive Minutes, 1871–91 (29 March 1873); Murray G. Ross, *The Y.M.C.A. in Canada: The Chronicle of a Century* (Toronto 1951), 114–22; John Webster Grant, *A Profusion of Spires: Religion in Nineteenth-Century Ontario* (Toronto 1988), 173.

9 UTA, Student Christian Movement, B79-0059/002, YMCA Executive Minutes, 1871–91 (17 December 1887).

10 UTA, Sir Daniel Wilson, B77-1195, pamphlet: *Sir Daniel Wilson*, by H.H. Langton, 13.

11 UTA, James Loudon, B72-0031/010(W20), pamphlet: *Address at the Convocation of the University of Toronto and University College, October 19, 1888, by Sir Daniel Wilson.*

12 UTA, Student Christian Movement, B79-0059/002, YMCA Executive Minutes, 1871–91.

13 UTA, Student Christian Movement, B79-0059/002, YMCA Executive Minutes, 1871–91, Report of City Mission Committee, 11 December 1890, submitted by E.A. Henry, Convener, inserted into minute book.

14 UTA, Pamphlets: *University of Toronto Young Men's Christian Association, Annual Report, 1890–91.*

15 For discussions of the continuity of evangelical belief in the Methodist and Presbyterian church colleges, see Michael Gauvreau, *The Evangelical Century: College and Creed in English Canada from the Great Revival to the Great Depression* (Montreal 1991), 191–201; and Marguerite Van Die, *An Evangelical Mind: Nathanael Burwash and the Methodist Tradition in Canada, 1839–1918* (Montreal 1989), 12.

16 UTA, James Loudon, B72-0031/010(W21), pamphlet: *Address at the Convocation of Faculties of the University of Toronto, and University College, October 1st, 1889, by the President, Sir Daniel Wilson*; A.B. McKillop, *A Disciplined Intelligence: Critical Inquiry and Canadian Thought in the Victorian Era* (Montreal 1979), 200–1. An indication of the direction of James Gibson Hume's teaching is

given in the 1898–99 program for local lectures, where he is listed as offering such courses as 'Faith and Doubt in Modern Controversy' and 'Problems of Social Reform.' See UTA, James Loudon, B72-0031/003(D10), 'Programme for Local Lectures, 1898–99, University of Toronto.'

17 UTA, James Loudon, B72-0031/011, James Loudon, 'Memoirs of James Loudon: President of the University of Toronto, 1892–1906,' TMs, 34a.

18 UTA, Edward Blake, B72-0013/001(12), James Loudon to Edward Blake, 28 July 1892; James Loudon, B72-0031/001(A43), James Loudon, 'The Universities in Relation to Research,' address to the Royal Society of Canada, [1902]; James Loudon, B72-0031/002(C22), pamphlet: *Address at the Convocation of the University of Toronto, October 14, 1898, by James Loudon*.

19 Hamar Greenwood had a long parliamentary career in Britain, holding several positions in David Lloyd George's government, and was the last chief secretary for Ireland from 1920 to 1922. He was made a viscount in 1937. UTA, Department of Graduate Records, A73-0026/128(33–4), Hamar Greenwood.

20 *The Varsity* 11, no. 7 (17 November 1891), 82; UTA, James Loudon, B72-0031/003(D21), program of the Political Science Club, 1894–5. Another 'Political Science Club' had existed at the university since 1886, and was the project of William Houston, a graduate of Toronto and the legislative librarian for Ontario. See UTA, John Langton Family, B65-0014/003(01), Sir Daniel Wilson's Journal (21 April and 20 May 1886), 104–5.

21 UTA, James Loudon, B72-0031/oversized, clipping: *Toronto World*, 28 January 1895.

22 UTA, Edward Blake, B72-0013/002(03), G.W. Ross to the Lieutenant Governor in Council, 14 February 1895; UTL, William Lyon Mackenzie King Diaries, 1893–1931, Microfiche, Transcript Version (Toronto 1973), G211, 9 February 1895.

23 For example, see UTA, James Loudon, B72-0031/011(01), J.W. McLaughlin to James Loudon, 22 January 1895; ibid., B72-0031/oversized, clipping: *Toronto World*, 19 February 1895. The details of the 1895 student strike can be found in the *Report of the Commissioners on the Discipline in the University of Toronto* (Toronto 1895).

24 On a slip of paper enclosed in an envelope entitled 'list of bastards,' Loudon's nephew, W.J. Loudon named the 'malcontents' among the faculty 'in order of magnitude,' placing A.T. DeLury, William Dale, and F.B.R. Hellems at the top. UTA, James Loudon, B72-0031/003(C), envelope: 'List of bastards by W.J. Loudon,' 1895.

25 Ramsay Cook, *The Regenerators: Social Criticism in Late Victorian English Canada* (Toronto 1985), 197; R. MacGregor Dawson, *William Lyon Mackenzie King: A Political Biography, 1874–1923* (Toronto 1958), 57.

26 UTL, King Diaries, Microfiche, Transcript Version, G324, 17 December 1895; G235, 27 April 1895.

27 Ibid., G321, 9 December 1895; G323, 15 December 1895; G320, 7 December 1895.

28 Paul Craven, 'An Impartial Umpire': Industrial Relations and the Canadian State, 1900–1911 (Toronto 1980), 31–73.

29 UTL, King Diaries, Microfiche, Transcript Version, G89, 12 April 1894; G198, 2 January 1895.

30 Ibid., G416, 25 July 1896; G494, 7 January 1897; G567, 13 July 1897.

31 Ibid., G1214, 11 October 1899.

32 Mrs Humphry Ward, Robert Elsmere (Oxford 1987), 549–56.

33 Mrs Humphry Ward, A Writer's Recollections (London 1918), 289–90.

34 Quoted in John Sutherland, Mrs. Humphry Ward: Eminent Victorian, Pre-eminent Edwardian (Oxford 1990), 219.

35 UTL, King Diaries, Microfiche, Transcript Version, G1240, 12 November 1899; G1246, 20 November 1899; 1243–4, 1318, 16 November 1899.

36 Ibid., G809, 30 May 1898; G1365, 24 February 1900.

37 Ibid., G790, 6 May 1898.

38 Quoted in William Lyon Mackenzie King, The Secret of Heroism: A Memoir of Henry Albert Harper (New York 1906), 134, 110–12, 102–3, 44, 85.

39 NAC, William Lyon Mackenzie King Papers, MG 26, J 1, vol. 5, 4349–56, microfilm, reel C-1904, W.J. Ashley to W.L.M. King, 27 February 1906.

3: Science and Sentiment

1 'The University Settlement,' University of Toronto Monthly 11, no. 4 (February 1911), 115.

2 J.M. Shaver's wife, E.C. Shaver (née Asselstine), was a university graduate, having received her M.A. from Queen's in 1907. Her contribution to the settlement – unfortunately unspecified in the records – was considered important enough for the board to pay her an independent salary of $6.25 a week. By comparison, the two other residents, E. Murray Thomson and W.A. Scott, each received $10.00 a week. UCA, Biographical file: James M. Shaver; UTA, Office of the President (Falconer), A67-0007/016, file: University Settlement, 1911, Analysis of Accounts, 31 January 1911.

3 Terry Copp, The Anatomy of Poverty: The Condition of the Working Class in Montreal, 1897–1929 (Toronto 1974); Michael J. Piva, The Condition of the Working Class in Toronto, 1900–1921 (Ottawa 1979).

4 James Pitsula, 'The Emergence of Social Work in Toronto,' Journal of Canadian Studies 14, no. 1 (Spring 1979), 37–9; Stephen A. Speisman, 'Munificent Parsons and Municipal Parsimony: Voluntary vs Public Poor Relief in Nineteenth Century Toronto,' Ontario History 65, no. 1 (March 1973), 47–8; Piva, Condition of the Working Class, 72–4; Paul Adolphus Bator, '"The Struggle to Raise the Lower

Classes": Public Health Reform and the Problem of Poverty in Toronto, 1910 to 1921,' *Journal of Canadian Studies* 14, no. 1 (Spring 1979), 43–9; Jacquelyn Gale Wills, 'Efficiency, Feminism and Cooperative Democracy: Origins of the Toronto Social Planning Council, 1918–1957' (Ph.D. diss., University of Toronto, 1989), 98.

5 TFRB, James Mavor Papers, Ms. Coll. 119, box 70, special subjects: living conditions in Toronto, 1897–1906; 'In the Slums of "Toronto the Good,"' *Christian Guardian* 80, no. 21 (26 May 1909), 3; UTA, Department of Graduate Records, A73-0026/212(15), Edward Joseph Kylie; City of Toronto Archives, Reports, RG 001, box 002, *Report of the Medical Health Officer Dealing with the Recent Investigation of Slum Conditions in Toronto*, 1911.

6 University of Toronto, *Torontonensis* 4 (1902), 205.

7 Diana Pedersen, '"The Call to Service": The YWCA and the Canadian College Woman, 1886–1920,' in Paul Axelrod and John G. Reid, eds, *Youth, University and Canadian Society: Essays in the Social History of Higher Education* (Kingston, Ont. 1989), 189–200; Wendy Mitchinson, 'The YWCA and Reform in the Nineteenth Century,' *Histoire sociale/Social History* 12, no. 24 (November 1979), 383.

8 Allen F. Davis, *Spearheads for Reform: The Social Settlements and the Progressive Movement, 1890–1914* (Toronto 1967), 12.

9 Mary Jo Deegan, *Jane Addams and the Men of the Chicago School, 1892–1918* (New Brunswick, NJ, 1988), 33–69; Rosalind Rosenberg, *Beyond Separate Spheres: Intellectual Roots of Modern Feminism* (New Haven, Conn., 1982), 33–6; Ellen Fitzpatrick, *Endless Crusade: Women Social Scientists and Progressive Reform* (New York 1990), 10. For revisionist studies of Hull House and the American settlement movement, see Ruth Hutchinson Crocker, *Social Work and Social Order: The Settlement Movement in Two Industrial Cities, 1889–1930* (Chicago 1992); Rivka Shpak Lissak, *Pluralism and Progressives: Hull House and the New Immigrants, 1890–1919* (Chicago 1989).

10 Jane Addams, *Twenty Years at Hull-House* (New York 1961), 225.

11 Addams, *Twenty Years*, 239–56; Lillian D. Wald, *The House on Henry Street* (New York 1915), v–vi, 179–83.

12 'University Settlement Movement,' *Acta Victoriana* 21, no. 1 (October 1897), 4–5.

13 Alice A. Chown, 'The Social Settlement Movement,' *Acta Victoriana* 23, no. 3 (December 1899), 208.

14 Beverly Boutilier, 'Gender, Organized Women, and the Politics of Institution Building: Founding the Victorian Order of Nurses for Canada, 1893–1900' (Ph.D. diss., Carleton University, 1993), 45–95; Veronica Strong-Boag, *The Parliament of Women: The National Council of Women of Canada, 1893–1929* (Ottawa 1976), 10–55, 109–11. At the University of Toronto, the Faculty of Household Science and the Faculty of Education were established in 1906 and 1907 respectively.

W. Stewart Wallace, *A History of the University of Toronto, 1827–1927* (Toronto 1927), 219, 224.

15 UTA, University College, A69-0011/013, Alumnae Association of University College, Annual Minutes, 1898–1928, Report of the Occupations Committee (20 April 1900); A69-0011/014, Alumnae Association of University College, General and Executive Minutes, 1898–1927 (20 April and 2 June 1900); A69-0011/013, Alumnae Association of University College, Annual Minutes, 1898–1928 (12 April 1901).

16 'The College Girl,' *The Varsity* 24, no. 8 (1 December 1904), 131; Metropolitan Toronto Central Library, Baldwin Room, S 54, Mary Jennison, 'A History of Canadian Settlements,' TMs [photocopy], 1965.

17 Patricia A. Palmieri, 'Here Was Fellowship: A Social Portrait of Academic Women at Wellesley College, 1895–1920,' in Alison Prentice and Marjorie R. Theobald, eds, *Women Who Taught: Perspectives on the History of Women and Teaching* (Toronto 1991), 246.

18 Ethel Dodds Parker, 'The Origins and Early History of the Presbyterian Settlement Houses,' in Richard Allen, ed., *The Social Gospel in Canada* (Ottawa 1975), 96–7.

19 'Sara Libby Carson,' *Social Welfare* 11, no. 5 (February 1929), 113; UTA, Office of the President (Falconer), A67-0007/028, file: Evangelia Settlement 1913, 'Summary of Ten Months Work from 1st January to 1st November, 1913'.

20 UTA, University College, A69-0011/014, Alumnae Association of University College, General and Executive Minutes, 1898–1927 (29 November 1902); UCA, Young Women's Christian Association, 90.135V, box 1, file 1, Victoria College YWCA Minutes, 1895–1905 (13 March 1902).

21 'The College Girl,' *The Varsity* 24, no. 8 (1 December 1904), 131.

22 UTA, University College, A69-0011/014, Alumnae Association of University College, General and Executive Minutes, 1898–1927 (5 November 1904 and 11 February 1905); Metropolitan Toronto Central Library, Baldwin Room, S 54, Mary Jennison, 'A History of Canadian Settlements,' TMs [photocopy], 1965.

23 UTA, Mossie May Waddington Kirkwood, B74-0020, interview by Elizabeth Wilson, 27 March 1973, transcript, University of Toronto Oral History Project, 56–8. Kirkwood received her B.A. from Trinity College in 1911, and later became Principal of St Hilda's College from 1936 to 1953. UTA, Department of Graduate Records, A73-0026/488(41), Mossie May Waddington (Kirkwood).

24 UTA, Waddell Family, B73-0028/001, pamphlet: *Eighth Annual Report of the Alumnae Association of University College, Toronto, 1905–1906*, 6.

25 Standish Meacham, *Toynbee Hall and Social Reform, 1880–1914: The Search for Community* (New Haven, Conn., 1987), 18–20.

26 E.J. Kylie, 'Oxford Education,' *The Varsity* 24, no. 8 (1 December 1904), 127–8.

27 UTA, Department of Graduate Records, A73-0026/212(15), Edward Joseph Kylie, clipping: *Toronto Star*, 21 October 1905.

28 Ibid., Edward Joseph Kylie; Hortense Catherine Fardell Wasteneys, 'A History of the University Settlement of Toronto, 1910–1958: An Exploration of the Social Objectives of the University Settlement and of Their Implementation' (Ph.D. diss., University of Toronto, 1975), 52.

29 UTA, Department of Graduate Records, A73-0026/212(15), file: Edward Joseph Kylie, clipping: *Toronto Globe*, 16 May 1916.

30 UTA, James Loudon, B72-0031/001(A6), S.J. McLean to James Loudon, 5 September 1905; B72-0031/001(A5), James Mavor to James Loudon, 5 October 1905.

31 UTA, Department of Graduate Records, A73-0026/288(16), Simon James McLean. See also, UTA, Department of Alumni Affairs, A72-0024/021, pamphlet: *University of Toronto, Faculty of Arts, Class 1894*.

32 S.J. McLean, 'Social Amelioration and the University Settlement: With Special Reference to Toynbee Hall,' *The Canadian Magazine* 8, no. 6 (April 1897), 469–70, 473.

33 UTA, Department of Graduate Records, A73-0026/75(02), Sedley Anthony Cudmore.

34 C.F.G. Masterman, *The Condition of England* (London 1909).

35 S.A. Cudmore, 'The Condition of England,' *University of Toronto Monthly* 10, no. 2 (December 1909), 71, 77–8.

36 UTA, Office of the Registrar, A73-0051/244(06), file: Settlement Work 1910–42, clipping: *Toronto Mail*, 22 March 1910.

37 James G. Greenlee, *Sir Robert Falconer: A Biography* (Toronto 1988), 24–6.

38 Robert Alexander Falconer, 'Inaugural Address,' *University of Toronto Monthly* 8, no. 1 (November 1907), 7, 10, 12.

39 *The Varsity* 30, no. 3 (11 October 1910), 1.

40 Keith Walden, 'Hazes, Hustles, Scraps, and Stunts: Initiations at the University of Toronto, 1880–1925,' in Axelrod and Reid, eds, *Youth, University and Canadian Society*, 104.

41 UTA, University College Council, A69-0016/001(03), University College Council Minutes, 1890–1958 (18 January 1907).

42 E. Brecken, 'Religious Life in Oxford,' *Acta Victoriana* 31, no. 7 (April 1908), 463.

43 S.G. Tallents, 'Toynbee Hall,' *University of Toronto Monthly* 10, no. 4 (February 1910), 201. S.G. Tallents is listed as a visitor from Balliol College, Oxford, in the *Toynbee Record* 21, no. 6 (March 1909), 90.

44 'The Settlement Movement,' *University of Toronto Monthly* 11, no. 2 (December 1910), 38.

45 A.M. Goulding, 'An University Settlement,' *The Arbor* 1, no. 1 (February 1910), 32–7.

46 Pedersen, '"The Call to Service,"' in Axelrod and Reid, eds, *Youth, University and Canadian Society*, 206, 199–200; Murray G. Ross, *The Y.M.C.A. in Canada: The Chronicle of a Century* (Toronto 1951), 172–5, 220–5.

47 UTA, University of Toronto, Student Christian Movement, B79-0059/008, file: YMCA Annual Report, 1907–8, 1908–9; Office of the President (Falconer), A67-0007/004, file: YMCA 1908.

48 UCA, Biographical file: James M. Shaver, 'Life Sketch of Mr. J.M. Shaver,' [1923], 3. For an analysis of late-nineteenth-century evangelical revival meetings, see David B. Marshall, *Secularizing the Faith: Canadian Protestant Clergy and the Crisis of Belief, 1850–1940* (Toronto 1992), 89–98.

49 UTA, Department of Graduate Records, A73-0026/409(16), James M. Shaver, clipping: *The Christian Guardian*, 1 April 1925.

50 Thunder Bay Historical Museum Society, Biographical file: Cecil King, interview by Olga Jagodnik, 16 February 1977, transcript, 5–7; J.M. Shaver, 'The Immigrant in Industry,' *Social Welfare* 3, nos. 10–11 (July–August 1921), 275–7. For a discussion of J.S. Woodsworth's struggle with the secular implications of the social gospel, see Ramsay Cook, *The Regenerators: Social Criticism in Late Victorian English Canada* (Toronto 1985), 213–23.

51 UCA, Biographical file: James M. Shaver, 'Life Sketch,' 6.

52 'In the Slums of "Toronto the Good,"' *Christian Guardian* 80, no. 21 (26 May 1909), 3.

53 UCA, Methodist Church (Canada), Toronto Conference, Methodist Union of Toronto, 84.050C, file 2–5, Fred Victor Mission Board Minutes, 1907–13 (20 May and 22 June 1909); Biographical file: James M. Shaver, 'Life Sketch,' 5.

54 'The Students' Christian Social Union,' *Acta Victoriana* 33, no. 1 (October 1909), 37.

55 UCA, Local Church Records Collection, Fred Victor Mission, Annual Report: *Forward: The Story of Our Work by Our Workers, 1909*, 24; Fred Victor Mission, Annual Reports, pamphlet: *Making History, 1886–1911*, 43–7.

56 UTA, Office of the President (Falconer), A67-0007/026, file: University Settlement, 1912–13, Arthur H. Burnett to Robert Falconer, 20 March and 5 April 1913; University of Toronto, *Torontonensis* 14 (1912), 183.

57 'The Social Union Programme,' *Acta Victoriana* 33, no. 4 (January 1910), 292–3.

58 NAC, John Joseph Kelso Papers, MG 30, C 97, vol. 1, file: University Training Courses, TMs, 'Address at Victoria College,' n.d., and file: Reform Causes, TMs, n.d..

59 NAC, Kelso Papers, MG 30, C 97, vol. 1, file: Reform Causes, clipping: *Toronto Mail*, n.d.

60 'YMCA Notes,' *The Varsity* 29, no. 15 (26 November 1909).

61 UTA, Student Christian Movement, B79-0059/008, file: YMCA Annual Report, 1909–10, 7, 13; *Torontonensis* 12 (1910), 13 (1911).
62 NAC, Kelso Papers, MG 30, C 97, vol. 33, file 187, J.M Shaver to J.J. Kelso, 24 April 1934.
63 *The Varsity* 29, no. 40 (15 March 1910).
64 *The Varsity* 31, no. 15 (1 November 1911).
65 The first permanent board of directors appointed in October 1910 was headed by Robert Falconer and consisted of the following members: J.J. Kelso, provincial superintendent of neglected and dependent children; G.A. Warburton, secretary of the City of Toronto YMCA; three Toronto businessmen (R.J. Clark, J.S. McLean, and T.A. Russell); and eight University of Toronto faculty members (W.B. Hendry, G.I.H. Lloyd, R.W. Angus, M.W. Wallace, H.T.J. Coleman, H.C. Griffith, E.M. Walker, and E.F. Burton). NAC, Kelso Papers, MG 30, C 97, vol. 6, file: Social Settlements, Central Neighbourhood House, pamphlet: *The University Settlement, 1910–1911: Telling of the Opening up of the Settlement with Plans for the Winter Sessions*; 'The University Settlement,' *University of Toronto Monthly* 11, no. 4 (February 1911), 113–14.
66 UTA, Office of the President (Falconer), A67-0007/009, file: G.I.H. Lloyd, 1909–10, pamphlet: *Letter of Application, Accompanied by Names of Referees, and Testimonials, from Godfrey I.H. Lloyd* [1909]; *Toynbee Record* 11, no. 7 (April 1899), 107.
67 NAC, Kelso Papers, MG 30, C 97, vol. 6, file: Social Settlements, Central Neighbourhood House, pamphlet: *The University Settlement, 1910–1911*.

4: The Search for a Model

1 UTA, Office of the President (Falconer), A67-0007/011, file: Malcolm W. Wallace, 1910, Robert Falconer to M.W. Wallace, 24 June 1910.
2 NAC, John Joseph Kelso Papers, MG 30, C 97, vol. 1, file: Reform Causes, clipping: *Toronto Mail*, n.d.; 'The University Settlement,' *University of Toronto Monthly* 11, no. 4 (February 1911), 112–16.
3 UTA, Office of the President (Falconer), A67-0007/045b, file: University Settlement, 1916, Report of the Organizing Committee, n.d. The committee consisted of six men: R.W. Angus, G.A. Warburton, E.F. Burton, J.J. Kelso, W.B. Hendry, and Harry McGee. All but McGee also served on the first board of directors.
4 NAC, Kelso Papers, MG 30, C 97, vol. 33, file 187, J.M. Shaver to J.J. Kelso, 24 April 1934.
5 Ibid., vol. 6, file: Social Settlements, Central Neighbourhood House, pamphlet: *The University Settlement, 1910–1911*.
6 'The University Settlement,' 115; UTA, Student Christian Movement, B79-0059/

002, Faculty of Applied Science and Engineering, YMCA Minutes, 1905–17 (17 November 1910).

7 'The University Settlement,' *University of Toronto Monthly* 11, no. 8 (June 1911), 379–80.

8 UTA, Office of the President (Falconer), A67-0007/012, file: R.J. Clark, 1910–11, Robert Falconer to R.J. Clark, 19 January 1911.

9 *The Varsity* 30, no. 6 (21 October 1910); ibid., no. 21 (6 January 1911); ibid., no. 24 (17 January 1911); ibid., no. 28 (31 January 1911).

10 For example, see an article requesting volunteers for Central Neighbourhood House in *The Varsity* 32, no. 4 (7 October 1912).

11 UTA, Office of the President (Falconer), A67-0007/026, file: University Settlement, 1912–13, Arthur H. Burnett to Robert Falconer, 5 April 1913; *Torontonensis* 14 (1912), 183; Andrew Jones and Leonard Rutman, *In the Children's Aid: J.J. Kelso and Child Welfare in Ontario* (Toronto 1981), 129.

12 UTA, Office of the President (Falconer), A67-0007/006, file: J.J. Kelso, 1909, J.J. Kelso to Robert Falconer, 17 March 1909; NAC, Kelso Papers, MG 30, C 97, vol. 1, file: Reform Causes, TMs, n.d.

13 Jones and Rutman, *In the Children's Aid*, 129–31.

14 UTA, United Alumnae Association, B65-0030/001, United Alumnae Committee, 1909–13, TMs, proposal, 'A Neighborhood House for Central Toronto,' n.d.; Patricia J. O'Connor, *The Story of Central Neighbourhood House, 1911–1986* (Toronto 1986), 17–18.

15 Ethel Dodds Parker, 'The Origins and Early History of the Presbyterian Settlement Houses,' in Richard Allen, ed., *The Social Gospel in Canada* (Ottawa 1975), 118.

16 Arthur H. Burnett, 'The Conservation of Citizenship: A Critique on Settlement Service,' *Acta Victoriana* 35, no. 2 (November 1911), 62.

17 *The Varsity* 31, no. 13 (25 October 1911).

18 UTA, University Settlement (Ephemera), B78-1395, pamphlet: *Some Facts About the University Settlement* [1911]; UCA, Biographical file: James M. Shaver; UTA, Office of the President (Falconer), A67-0007/013, file: Milton B. Hunt, 1911, Milton B. Hunt to M.W. Wallace, 3 June 1911.

19 UTA, Ross Family, B83-0031/001, file: Student Handbooks, 1913–14, pamphlet: *University of Toronto Students' Handbook, 1913–14*; Student Christian Movement, B79-0059/002, Faculty of Applied Science and Engineering, YMCA Minutes, 1905–17 (16 October 1913); Will T. Kennedy, 'The University of Toronto YMCA,' *Torontonensis* 16 (1914).

20 *Torontonensis* 15 (1913); UTA, Student Christian Movement, B79-0059/004, file: YMCA Handbook, 1914–15, pamphlet: *University of Toronto Students' Handbook, 1914–15*; *Torontonensis* 18 (1916); UTA, Office of the Registrar,

A73-0051/240(30), file: University College YWCA, clipping: *The Varsity*, 1 February 1918.

21 *Torontonensis* 18 (1916).

22 Diana Pedersen, '"The Call to Service": The YWCA and the Canadian College Woman, 1886–1920,' in Paul Axelrod and John G. Reid, eds, *Youth, University and Canadian Society: Essays in the Social History of Higher Education* (Kingston, Ont.: 1989), 201–7; Richard Allen, *The Social Passion: Religion and Social Reform in Canada, 1914–28* (Toronto 1971), 219–23.

23 UTA, Student Christian Movement, B79-0059/017, file: YWCA, Toronto District Committee, Reports, 1919–20, 'Report to the Toronto District Committee, November 18, 1919'.

24 Ibid., B79-0059/001, file: Clarkson Setting Up Conference, 1918, R.B. Ferris to J.E. Nunn, [1918].

25 Ibid. B79-0059/049, file: Student Secretaries Conference, Lake Couchiching, [1919], 'Seminar for Student Secretaries Conference, Lake Couchiching, August 20–29 [1919]'.

26 Ibid., B79-0059/049, file: SCA Canada, 'Report of the Findings Committee, Central Women's Student Conference, June 16, 1920'.

27 UTA, Office of the President (Falconer), A67-0007/081, file: YMCA, 1923, R.B. Ferris to Robert Falconer, 25 April 1923; 'Constitution of the Student Christian Association of the University of Toronto (As Amended March 1923).'

28 UTA, Student Christian Movement, B79-0059/002, YMCA Executive Minutes, 1919–22, Report on Present Condition of YMCA Activities in the University, [December 1920].

29 Dorothy Ross, *The Origins of American Social Science* (Cambridge, Eng., 1991), 122–38, 226–7; Mary Jo Deegan, *Jane Addams and the Men of the Chicago School, 1892–1918* (New Brunswick, NJ, 1988), 74–83; Ellen Fitzpatrick, *Endless Crusade: Women Social Scientists and Progressive Reform* (New York 1990), 54–5, 173–200; Rosalind Rosenberg, *Beyond Separate Spheres: Intellectual Roots of Modern Feminism* (New Haven, Conn., 1982), 33–6.

30 Thunder Bay Historical Museum Society, Biographical file: Cecil King, interview by Olga Jagodnik, 16 February 1977, transcript, 7; UTA, Office of the President (Falconer), A67-0007/015, file: Graham Taylor, 1911, Robert Falconer to Graham Taylor, 9 March 1911.

31 UTA, Office of the President (Falconer), A67-0007/015, file: Graham Taylor, 1911, Robert Falconer to Graham Taylor, 9 March 1911.

32 Ibid., A67-0007/013, file: Milton B. Hunt, 1911, Robert Falconer to Milton B. Hunt, 2 June 1911.

33 *The Varsity* 31, no. 8 (13 October 1911).

34 UTA, Office of the President (Falconer), A67-0007/013, file: Milton B. Hunt, 1911, Milton B. Hunt to M.W. Wallace, 3 June 1911.

35 UTA, University Settlement (Ephemera), B78-1395, pamphlet: *Some Facts About the University Settlement* [1911].

36 *The Varsity* 31, no. 13 (25 October 1911).

37 Ibid. 32, no. 22 (20 November 1912); ibid. 31, no. 9 (16 October 1911); UTA, Office of the President (Falconer), A67-0007/018, file: Mrs Lloyd, 1912, Robert Falconer to Mrs Lloyd, 25 April 1912; NAC, Kelso Papers, MG 30, C 97, vol. 6, file: Social Settlements, Central Neighbourhood House, pamphlet: *The University Settlement* [1912]; UTA, University of Toronto, Faculty of Social Work, A85-0002/015, Enrolment Cards, 1914–15.

38 NAC, Kelso Papers, MG 30, C 97, vol. 6, file: Social Settlements, Central Neighbourhood House, pamphlet: *The University Settlement* [1912].

39 UTA, Office of the President (Falconer), A67-0007/025, file: Mrs V. Simkhovitch, 1913, Robert Falconer to V. Simkhovitch, 10 April 1913.

40 Ibid., A67-0007/026, file: University Settlement, 1912–13, Arthur H. Burnett to Robert Falconer, 20 March 1913; NAC, Kelso Papers, MG 30, C 97, vol. 6, file: Social Settlements, Central Neighbourhood House, pamphlet: *The 'Futurist' Number: University Settlement Review* [1913].

41 Fitzpatrick, *Endless Crusade*, 58–60; Deegan, *Jane Addams*, 18–19, 83–9; Ross, *Origins of American Social Science*, 226.

42 NAC, Kelso Papers, MG 30, C 97, vol. 6, file: Social Settlements, Central Neighbourhood House, pamphlet: *The 'Futurist' Number*.

43 UTA, Office of the President (Falconer), A67-0007/026, file: University Settlement, 1912–13, Norman J. Ware to J.J. Kelso, 9 May [1913].

44 Ibid., A67-0007/025, file: Norman J. Ware, 1913, Robert Falconer to Norman J. Ware, 25 June 1913.

45 NAC, Kelso Papers, MG 30, C 97, vol. 6, file: Social Settlements, Central Neighbourhood House, pamphlet: *The 'Futurist' Number*.

46 UTA, Student Christian Movement, B79-0059/034, file: YMCA University Settlement, 1913–14, pamphlet: *The University Settlement*, December 1913; *The Varsity* 34, no. 19 (13 November 1914).

47 UTA, Office of the President (Falconer), A67-0007/032, file: University Settlement, 1914, Robert Falconer to the Mayor of Toronto, 26 March 1914; A67-0009/002(20-2), Mabel F. Newton to Robert Falconer, 25 November 1914.

48 UTA, Office of the President (Falconer), A67-0007/036, file: J.G. Shearer, 1915, Robert Falconer to J.G. Shearer, 8 April 1915.

49 After the appointment of Sara Libby Carson in 1915, University Settlement was not directed by a man until 1955, when Harry Morrow was given the position of

head resident. Hortense Catherine Fardell Wasteneys, 'A History of the University Settlement of Toronto, 1910–1958: An Exploration of the Social Objectives of the University Settlement and of Their Implementation' (Ph.D. diss., University of Toronto, 1975), 91–4, 224–5.

50 *The Varsity* 35, no. 16 (5 November 1915). For a study of University Settlement during the interwar years, see Wasteneys, 'A History of the University Settlement.'

51 UTA, Faculty of Social Work, A85-0002/001–019, Enrolment Cards, 1914–16. The three graduates were Ethel Dodds Parker, who graduated in 1915, and Marjorie Sypher and Josie G. Saunders, of the class of 1916.

52 UTA, Office of the President (Falconer), A67-0007/040a, file: University Settlement, 1915–16, Robert Falconer to Harry Edwards, 6 January 1916; *The Varsity* 36, no. 32 (11 December 1916); UTA, University College, A69-0011/014, Alumnae Association of University College, General and Executive Minutes, 1898–1927 (12 November 1915); ibid., Dean of Women, B74-0011/001(11), Annual Report, 1921–2.

5: Skill or Knowledge?

1 R.D. Gidney and W.P.J. Millar, *Professional Gentlemen: The Professions in Nineteenth-Century Ontario* (Toronto 1994), 3–25, 210–11, 354–9, 380–3.

2 Ibid., 8, 239, 332.

3 Kathryn McPherson, 'Science and Technique: Nurses' Work in a Canadian Hospital, 1920–1939,' in Dianne Dodd and Deborah Gorham, eds, *Caring and Curing: Historical Perspectives on Women and Healing in Canada* (Ottawa 1994), 71–101.

4 Mary Jo Deegan, *Jane Addams and the Men of the Chicago School, 1892–1918* (New Brunswick, NJ, 1988), 313–17; Martha Vicinus, *Independent Women: Work and Community for Single Women, 1850–1920* (Chicago 1985), 211–46; Rosalind Rosenberg, *Beyond Separate Spheres: Intellectual Roots of Modern Feminism* (New Haven, Conn., 1982), 50; Mary Jo Deegan, 'Early Women Sociologists and the American Sociological Society: The Patterns of Exclusion and Participation,' *American Sociologist* 16, no. 1 (February 1981), 14–24.

5 Recent scholarship has shown that the devaluing of technique and its separation from academic theory also shaped the development of two other predominantly female professions, nursing and teaching. See, for example, McPherson, 'Science and Technique,' 71–101; Susan Gelman, 'The "Feminization" of the High School: Women Secondary Schoolteachers in Toronto: 1871–1930,' in Ruby Heap and Alison Prentice, eds, *Gender and Education in Ontario: An Historical Reader* (Toronto 1991), 71–102.

6 McPherson, 'Science and Technique,' 87–8.

7 John H. Ehrenreich, *The Altruistic Imagination: A History of Social Work and*

Social Policy in the United States (Ithaca, NY, 1985), 64–5; Roy Lubove, *The Professional Altruist: The Emergence of Social Work as a Career, 1880–1930* (Cambridge, Mass., 1965), 20–49; James Leiby, *A History of Social Welfare and Social Work in the United States* (New York 1978), 121–4, 178–90.

8 Mary E. Richmond, *Social Diagnosis* (New York 1917), 62. See also Mary E. Richmond, *What Is Social Case Work? An Introductory Description* (New York 1922).

9 Lubove, *Professional Altruist*, 86, 113–15.

10 Paul Adolphus Bator, '"The Struggle to Raise the Lower Classes": Public Health Reform and the Problem of Poverty in Toronto, 1910 to 1921,' *Journal of Canadian Studies* 14, no. 1 (Spring 1979), 45–7; for a history of Toronto's Department of Health, see Heather MacDougall, *Activists and Advocates: Toronto's Health Department, 1883–1983* (Toronto 1990).

11 Jacquelyn Gale Wills, 'Efficiency, Feminism and Cooperative Democracy: Origins of the Toronto Social Planning Council, 1918–1957' (Ph.D. diss., University of Toronto, 1989), 96–8; Ethel Dodds Parker, 'The Origins and Early History of the Presbyterian Settlement Houses,' in Richard Allen, ed., *The Social Gospel in Canada* (Ottawa 1975), 118–20; James Pitsula, 'The Emergence of Social Work in Toronto,' *Journal of Canadian Studies* 14, no. 1 (Spring 1979), 38–40.

12 Parker, 'Origins and Early History,' 102; UTA, Office of the President (Falconer), A67-0007/028, file: Evangelia Settlement, 1913, 'Summary of Ten Months Work from 1st January to 1st November, 1913'; Patricia J. O'Connor, *The Story of Central Neighbourhood House, 1911–1986* (Toronto 1986), 15.

13 Jean Palmer and Florence Philpott, 'The Story of the Toronto Association of Neighbourhood Services, 1918–1985,' in O'Connor, *Story of the Toronto Settlement House Movement*, 56.

14 NAC, John Joseph Kelso Papers, MG 30, C 97, vol. 6, file: Social Settlements, Central Neighbourhood House, pamphlet: *The 'Futurist' Number: University Settlement Review* [1913].

15 Parker, 'Origins and Early History,' 89–121; Brian J. Fraser, *The Social Uplifters: Presbyterian Progressives and the Social Gospel in Canada, 1875–1915* (Waterloo, Ont., 1988), 94.

16 NAC, Kelso Papers, MG 30, C 97, vol. 1, file: University Training Courses, TMs, 'Setting Forth the Need,' n.d.; Parker, 'Origins and Early History,' 103; Fraser, *Social Uplifters*, 71.

17 Kenneth McNaught, *A Prophet in Politics: A Biography of J.S. Woodsworth* (Toronto 1959), 59–60; Ramsay Cook, *The Regenerators: Social Criticism in Late Victorian English Canada* (Toronto 1985), 219–20.

18 J.S. Woodsworth, 'Social Work as a Profession,' *Acta Victoriana* 38, no. 6 (March 1914), 293, 292.

19 UTA, Office of the President (Falconer), A67-0007/036, file: J.S. Woodsworth, 1914, President's Secretary to J.S. Woodsworth, 30 June 1914; Robert Falconer to J.S. Woodsworth, 14 September 1914.

20 *The Varsity* 32, no. 18 (11 November 1912); UCA, Local Church Records Collection, Fred Victor Mission, Annual Reports, pamphlet: *Programme of Social Studies, Season 1913–1914.*

21 NAC, Kelso Papers, MG 30, C 97, vol. 1, file: University Training Courses, T.R. Robinson to J.J. Kelso, 12 March 1913; J.J. Kelso to T.R. Robinson, 15 March 1913. For information on T.R. Robinson, see UTA, Department of Graduate Records, A73-0026/383(70), Thomas Rutherford Robinson.

22 UTA, Office of the President (Falconer), A67-0007/003, file: S. Morley Wickett, 1908, Robert Falconer to S. Morley Wickett, 3 January 1908.

23 Ibid., A67-0007/032, file: Social Service, 1913–14, AN, n.d.

24 It is probable that the membership of both the Social Science Study Club and the Social Workers' Club reflected the numerical dominance of women in the field of social work. Agnes McGregor writes that the Social Science Study Club was launched with 'a membership of about 275 prominent women.' UTA, Pamphlets, box 6: Agnes C. McGregor, 'The Department of Social Science, University of Toronto, 1914–1940,' in *Training for Social Work in the Department of Social Science, University of Toronto, 1914–1940* (1940), 12.

25 UTA, University of Toronto, Senate, A68-0012/roll 6, vol. 12, Senate Minutes, 1913–17, 82–4 (13 March and 17 April 1914); Board of Governors, A70-0024/015, vol. 3, Board of Governors Minutes, 1911–14, 367 (14 May 1914).

26 UTA, Office of the President (Falconer), A67-0007/032, file: Edmund Walker, 1913–14, Sarah T. Warren to Edmund Walker, 19 June 1914.

27 In an interview years later, Falconer emphasized Lloyd's integral role in establishing the Department of Social Service, particularly in drawing up the original resolution presented to the board of governors. UTA, Pamphlets, box 6: McGregor, 'Department of Social Science,' in *Training for Social Work*, 12.

28 UTA, Office of the President (Falconer), A67-0007/032, file: Social Service, 1913–14, TMs, 'Proposed School of Social Service,' n.d.

29 *University of Toronto Calendar*, 1915–16, 637.

30 Reba N. Soffer, *Ethics and Society in England: The Revolution in the Social Sciences, 1870–1914* (Berkeley, Calif., 1978), 58.

31 Marjorie J. Smith, *Professional Education for Social Work in Britain: An Historical Account* (London 1965), 15–47.

32 E.J. Urwick, 'Social Education of Yesterday and Today,' quoted in Smith, *Professional Education*, 50.

33 Janet Beveridge, *An Epic of Clare Market: Birth and Early Days of the London School of Economics* (London 1960), 65.

34 *London School of Economics and Political Science Calendar,* 1913–14, 85; 1914–15, 92.

35 Ibid., 1912–13 to 1920–1. From 1916–17 through 1918–19 the course was entitled 'Preparatory Class in Casework and Methods of Charitable Administration.'

36 Reba N. Soffer, 'Why Do Disciplines Fail? The Strange Case of British Sociology,' *English Historical Review* 97, no. 385 (October 1982), 774–81. For an examination of the sociological thought of L.T. Hobhouse, see Stefan Collini, *Liberalism and Sociology: L.T. Hobhouse and Political Argument in England, 1880–1914* (Cambridge, Eng., 1979).

37 Smith, *Professional Education,* 58–65.

38 Quoted in J.H. Muirhead, 'University of Birmingham: Social Study,' in Anne Ashley, *William James Ashley: A Life* (London 1932), 107–8.

39 UTA, Pamphlets, box 6: McGregor, 'Department of Social Science,' in *Training for Social Work,* 10–11; Leiby, *History of Social Welfare,* 122, 187–9; Lubove, *Professional Altruist,* 19, 143–5; Ellen Fitzpatrick, *Endless Crusade: Women Social Scientists and Progressive Reform* (New York 1990), 173–200, 212.

40 *University of Toronto Calendar,* 1915–16, 636.

41 'Universities and the Social Problem,' *University of Toronto Monthly* 15, no. 5 (March 1914), 234.

42 UTA, Office of the President (Falconer), A67-0007/009, file: G.I.H. Lloyd, 1909–10, pamphlet: *Letter of Application, Accompanied by Names of Referees, and Testimonials, from Godfrey I.H. Lloyd* [1909]; Pamphlets, box 6: McGregor, 'Department of Social Science,' in *Training for Social Work,* 12. In 1899 Lloyd was a visitor at Toynbee Hall for several months, at which time E.J. Urwick was also a resident. *Toynbee Record* 11, no. 7 (April 1899), 107.

43 UTA, Office of the President (Falconer), A67-0007/032, file: Social Service, 1913–14, TMs, 'Proposed School of Social Service,' n.d.

44 UTA, Pamphlets, box 6: McGregor, 'Department of Social Science,' in *Training for Social Work,* 12–14; Office of the President (Falconer), A67-0007/032, file: Social Service, 1913–14, TMs, 'Proposed School of Social Service,' n.d.

45 UTA, Office of the President (Falconer), A67-0007/032, file: Social Service, 1913–14, TMs, 'Proposed School of Social Service,' n.d.

46 Ibid., A67-0007/148, file: A32/2, Social Service, 1914–15, TMs, 'Report of the Director of the Department of Social Service,' [1914–15]; ibid., A67-0007/031, file: Social Service, 1914, TMs, 'Report regarding Courses of Training for Social Workers,' 14 May 1914.

47 UTA, Dorothy W. Eddis, B76-1037, University of Toronto, Department of Social Service, Annual Examination in Social Ethics, 1916; Essays, 1915–16.

48 UTA, Office of the President (Falconer), A67-0007/042, file: Franklin Johnson, Jr,

1916–17, Robert Falconer to Franklin Johnson, Jr, 13 March 1917; *University of Toronto Calendar, 1917–18*, 15.

49 Ibid., A67-0007/148, file: A32/2, Social Service, 1914–15, TMs, 'Report of the Director of the Department of Social Service,' [1914–15]. After 1915 the name of the required course was changed to 'Dependents and the Community.'

50 Lubove, *Professional Altruist*, 144–5.

51 *University of Toronto Calendar*, 1915–16, 643–4; UTA, Office of the President (Falconer), A67-0007/032, file: Social Service, 1913–14, TMs, 'Proposed School of Social Service,' n.d.

52 *University of Toronto Calendar*, 1915–16, 639, and 1917–18, 17–18; UTA, Office of the President (Falconer), A67-0007/149, file: A32/2, Social Service, 1915–17, TMs, 'Report of the Director of the Department of Social Service,' 1915–16, 1916–17.

53 Lubove, *Professional Altruist*, 23–49; Bator, '"Struggle to Raise,"' 43–9.

54 UTA, Pamphlets, box 6: McGregor, 'Department of Social Science,' in *Training for Social Work*, 14; Office of the President (Falconer), A67-0007/034, file: Franklin Johnson, Jr, 1914, Franklin Johnson, Jr, to Robert Falconer, 11 November 1914; Faculty of Social Work, A85-0002/007–19, Student Enrolment Cards, 1914–15.

55 UTA, Faculty of Social Work, A85-0002/007–19, Student Enrolment Cards, 1914–15. For information on Ethel Dodds Parker, see Metropolitan Toronto Central Library, Baldwin Room, Ethel (Dodds) Parker Papers.

56 UTA, Office of the President (Falconer), A67-0007/149, file: A32/2, Social Service, 1915–17, TMs, 'Report of the Director of the Department of Social Service,' 1915–16, 1916–17.

57 Quoted in *University of Toronto Roll of Service, 1914–1918* (Toronto 1921), xi.

58 Quoted in James G. Greenlee, *Sir Robert Falconer: A Biography* (Toronto 1988), 219.

59 Ibid., 219, 221.

60 *Roll of Service*, 529.

61 *University of Toronto Calendar*, 1915–16, 1917–18; UTA, Faculty of Social Work, A85-0002/007–19, Student Enrolment Cards, 1914–15.

62 UTA, Office of the President (Falconer), A67-0007/149–50, file: A32/2, Social Service, 1915–18, TMs, 'Report of the Director of the Department of Social Service,' 1915–16, 1916–17, 1917–18.

63 UTA, Pamphlets, box 6: McGregor, 'Department of Social Science,' in *Training for Social Work*, 30.

64 *University of Toronto Calendar*, 1921–22, 596; UTA, Ephemera, B84-1089, pamphlet: *University of Toronto, Department of Social Service, Special Course in Work with Boys*, n.d.

65 UTL, Agnes C. McGregor, 'Memories,' TMs [photocopy], 1959, 27–8.

66 NAC, Kelso Papers, MG 30, C 97, vol. 6, file: School of Social Work, University of Toronto, J.J. Kelso to T.R. Robinson, 7 July 1932.

67 UTA, Office of the President (Falconer), A67-0007/032, file: Sarah Warren, 1914, Robert Falconer to Charles R. Henderson, Graham Taylor, Gaylord White, Hastings H. Hart, and Edward T. Divine, 16 May 1914.

68 Ibid., A67-0007/036, file: Byron Edmund Walker, 1914–15, Edward T. Devine to Robert Falconer, 27 May 1914.

69 Ibid., A67-0007/036, file: Byron Edmund Walker, 1914–15, Edward T. Devine to Robert Falconer, 2 June 1914; ibid., A67-0007/033, file: Edward T. Devine, 1914, Robert Falconer to Edward T. Devine, 11 September 1914; ibid., A67-0007/047b, file: Franklin Johnson, Jr, 1918, Transcript of Franklin Johnson, Jr, from Columbia University, 22 March 1918.

70 Dorothy Ross, *The Origins of American Social Science* (Cambridge, Eng., 1991), 224–9, 369; Robert C. Bannister, *Sociology and Scientism: The American Quest for Objectivity, 1880–1940* (Chapel Hill, NC, 1987), 75–86.

71 William James Ashley, Simon N. Patten, Franklin H. Giddings, Lester F. Ward, 'Discussion' of Albion W. Small's paper, 'The Relation of Sociology to Economics,' in *Abstracts in Publications of the American Economic Association* 10, no. 3 (March 1895), 106–17.

72 UTA, Office of the President (Falconer), A67-0007/028, file: Edward T. Devine, 1914, Robert Falconer to Edward T. Devine, 29 May 1914.

73 Ibid., A67-0007/036, file: Byron Edmund Walker, 1914–15, J.M. Glenn to Robert Falconer, 24 June 1914.

74 Ibid., A67-0007/034, file: Franklin Johnson, Jr, 1914, Franklin Johnson, Jr, to Robert Falconer, 31 July 1914.

75 *The Varsity* 34, no. 17 (9 November 1914).

76 UTA, Office of the President (Falconer), A67-0007/036, file: Byron Edmund Walker, 1914–15, G.I.H. Lloyd to Robert Falconer, 27 June [1914].

77 UTA, University Historian, A83-0036/014, file: Faculty of Social Work, 1914–32, TMs, Lorna F. Hurl, 'Building a Profession: The Origin and Development of the Department of Social Service in the University of Toronto, 1914–1928,' December 1981, 13–14, 51–2. Hurl writes that she was told of this rumour in a personal interview with Elsie Lawson, a student in the department from 1918 to 1919.

78 UTA, Office of the President (Falconer), A67-0007/049b, file: Graham Taylor, 1918, Robert Falconer to Graham Taylor, 21 January 1918.

79 Ibid., A67-0007/150, file: A32/2, Social Service, 1917–18, TMs, 'Report of the Director of the Department of Social Service,' 1917–18.

80 Ibid., A67-0007/047a, file: Franklin H. Giddings, 1918, Franklin H. Giddings to Robert Falconer, 30 April 1918; A67-0007/047a, file: Franklin H. Giddings, 1918, Robert Falconer to Franklin H. Giddings, 2 May 1918.

81 R.M. MacIver, *As a Tale That Is Told: The Autobiography of R.M. MacIver* (Chicago 1968), 89.

82 UTA, P78-0712(01), *The Rebel* 1, no. 1 (February 1917), 3. *The Rebel* was published anonymously by 'members of the University of Toronto,' and ran from February 1917 to March 1920, at which time it indicated its intention in September to become a general political and literary magazine under a new name, *The Canadian Forum*. UTA, P78-0712(01), *The Rebel* 4, no. 6 (March 1920), 230.

83 UTA, P78-0712(01), Hetairos, 'The University and Social Service I,' *The Rebel* 2, no. 2 (November 1917), 72–4; 'The University and Social Service II,' *The Rebel* 2, no. 3 (December 1917), 114–16.

84 UTA, P78-0712(01), Conservative, 'The University and Social Service,' *The Rebel* 2, no. 3 (December 1917), 120–2; P., 'The University and Social Service,' *The Rebel* 2, no. 6 (March 1918), 266–7.

85 UTA, Office of the President (Falconer), A67-0007/032, file: Social Service, 1913–14, Gaylord White to Robert Falconer, 22 May 1914.

86 James Struthers, '"Lord give us men": Women and Social Work in English Canada, 1918 to 1953,' *Canadian Historical Association Historical Papers* (1983), 111–12; Wills, 'Efficiency, Feminism and Cooperative Democracy,' 321–2.

6: The Department and Its Graduates, 1918–1928

1 UTA, Office of the President (Falconer), A67-0007/112, file: Social Service, 1927, TMs, 'List of Graduates in Each Year Since Inception.'

2 Penina Migdal Glazer and Miriam Slater, *Unequal Colleagues: The Entrance of Women into the Professions, 1890–1940* (New Brunswick, NJ, 1987), 175, 191.

3 In 1915 McGregor enrolled in the program while also working part-time in the department as an office assistant. After graduating from the course with first-class standing in 1916, she was appointed secretary to the faculty. Between 1915 and her retirement in 1947, she was promoted to director of fieldwork under MacIver, and then to assistant director under E.J. Urwick. UTA, Faculty of Social Work, A85-0002/013, Student Enrolment Cards, 1915–16; UTA, Department of Graduate Records, A73-0026/270(86), file: Agnes Christine McGregor, clipping: *Toronto Telegram*, 4 May 1960; *Torontonensis* 18 (1916), 207; UTA, Office of the President (Falconer), A67-0007/042, file: Franklin Johnson, Jr, 1916–17, Franklin Johnson, Jr, to Robert Falconer, 27 September 1916; UTL, Agnes C. McGregor, 'Memories,' TMs [photocopy], 1959, 27–8.

4 UTA, Pamphlets, box 6: Agnes C. McGregor, 'The Department of Social Science, University of Toronto, 1914–1940,' in *Training for Social Work in the Department of Social Science, University of Toronto, 1914–1940*, 1940, 14.

5 UTA, Pamphlets, box 6: E.J. Urwick, 'Foreword,' in *Training for Social Work*, 8.

6 UTA, Ephemera, B81-1020, Agnes C. McGregor, 'Reminiscences,' TMs [photo-copy], 1947, 1–2.

7 UTA, Office of the President (Falconer), A67-0007/034, file: W.T. Layton, 1915, Robert Falconer to W.T. Layton, 5 April 1915; UTA, Office of the President (Falconer), A67-0007/037, file: Appointments, 1914–15, Robert Falconer to R.M. MacIver, 6 July 1915; R.M. MacIver, *As a Tale That Is Told: The Autobiography of R.M. MacIver* (Chicago 1968), 89.

8 UTA, Office of the President (Falconer), A67-0007/035, file: James Mavor, 1915, Robert Falconer to James Mavor, 17 April 1915; MacIver, *As a Tale*, 64–5.

9 Reba N. Soffer, 'Why Do Disciplines Fail? The Strange Case of British Sociology,' *English Historical Review* 97, no. 385 (October 1982), 768.

10 R.M. MacIver, 'A Criticism of the Neo-Hegelian Identification of "Society" and "State,"' appendix B in *Community: A Sociological Study: Being an Attempt to Set out the Nature and Fundamental Laws of Social Life*, 4th ed. (London 1970), 425–33. This appendix was an excerpt of MacIver's article 'Society and State,' *Philosophical Review* 20 (January 1911), 30–45.

11 Stefan Collini, 'Sociology and Idealism in Britain, 1880–1920,' *Archives européennes de sociologie* 19, no. 1 (1978), 27–9; Collini, *Liberalism and Sociology: L.T. Hobhouse and Political Argument in England, 1880–1914* (Cambridge, Eng., 1979), 198–9, 235.

12 MacIver, *Community*, 57, 170.

13 R.M. MacIver, 'Society and "the Individual,"' *Sociological Review* 7, no. 1 (January 1914), 63.

14 MacIver, *As a Tale*, 87.

15 Dorothy Ross, *The Origins of American Social Science* (Cambridge, Eng., 1991), 394, 404–5; Mary Jo Deegan, *Jane Addams and the Men of the Chicago School, 1892–1918* (New Brunswick, NJ, 1988), 313–17.

16 Harry Alpert, 'Robert M. MacIver's Contributions to Sociological Theory,' in Morroe Berger, Theodore Abel, and Charles H. Page, eds, *Freedom and Control in Modern Society* (New York 1954), 289.

17 MacIver, *As a Tale*, 128.

18 R.M. MacIver, 'Education and Life,' *Social Welfare* 10, no. 2 (November 1927), 24.

19 R.M. MacIver, *The Contribution of Sociology to Social Work* (New York 1931), 1, 9.

20 *University of Toronto Calendar*, 1918–19, 5–20; UTA, Office of the President (Falconer), A67-0007/150, file: A32/2, Social Service, 1918–19, TMs, 'Report of the Acting Director of the Department of Social Service,' 1918–19; UTA, Pamphlets, box 6: McGregor, 'Department of Social Science,' in *Training for Social Work*, 16–17; *University of Toronto Calendar*, 1918–19, 5–20.

21 *University of Toronto Calendar*, 1918–19, 14; UTA, Office of the President

(Falconer), A67-0007/151, file: A32/2, Social Service, 1919–20, TMs, 'Report of the Acting Director of the Department of Social Service,' 1919–20; ibid., A67-0007/150, file: A32/2, Social Service, 1918–19, TMs, 'Report of the Acting Director of the Department of Social Service,' 1918–19.

22 UTA, Department of Graduate Records, A73-0026/274(88), file: Robert M. MacIver, clipping: *Toronto Globe*, 31 January 1919.

23 The SSA membership list of May 1922, for example, includes only one male name in a list of ninety-four paid members. TFRB, John Joseph Kelso, Ms. Coll. 115, box 1, file: School of Social Work Alumni, TMs, 'Social Service Alumni, University of Toronto, list of paid members,' May 1922.

24 UTA, Office of the President (Falconer), A67-0007/053a, file: Robert Morrison MacIver, 1919, TMs, resolution enclosed with letter from Margaret K. Nairn and Ethel Lovell to Robert Falconer, 2 June 1919.

25 TFRB, Toronto Social Welfare Agencies, Ms. Coll. 12, box 2, file: School of Social Work, letter to out-of-town members, 21 July 1920.

26 UTA, Social Service Alumni, B89-0004/001(01), TMs, 'Constitution of the Social Service Alumni of the University of Toronto,' n.d.

27 TFRB, Toronto Social Welfare Agencies, Ms. Coll. 12, box 2, file: School of Social Work, letters to out-of-town members, 21 July 1920 and n.d. [1922]; UTA, Ephemera, B81-1020, McGregor, 'Reminiscences,' 3; TFRB, John Joseph Kelso, Ms. Coll. 115, box 1, file: School of Social Work Alumni, TMs, 'Social Service Alumni, University of Toronto, list of paid members,' May 1922; UTA, Office of the President (Falconer), A67-0007/112, file: Social Service, 1927, TMs, 'Department of Social Service, List of Graduates in Each Year Since Inception,' n.d.

28 UTA, Office of the President (Falconer), A67-0007/151, file: A32/2, Social Service, 1919–20, TMs, 'Report of the Acting Director of the Department of Social Service,' 1919–20.

29 Ibid., A67-0007/058a, file: James Alfred Dale, 1919–20, Robert Falconer to J.A. Dale, 13 February 1920.

30 J.A. Dale, 'The Training of Social Workers,' *Social Welfare* 6, no. 10 (July 1924), 201.

31 Barbara M. Finlayson, 'Professor Dale,' *Social Welfare* 9, no. 3 (December 1926), 234–5; UTA, Department of Graduate Records, A73-0026/077(24), file: James A. Dale, clippings: *The School*, April 1920, and *Toronto Telegram*, 29 November 1951; UTA, Office of the President (Falconer), A67-0007/108b, file: Robert M. MacIver, 1927–8, Robert Falconer to R.M. MacIver, 14 December 1927; *Toynbee Record* 18, no. 4 (January 1906); ibid., 26, nos. 2–5 (November 1913–February 1914).

32 For a history of the University Settlement of Montreal, which was incorporated into McGill University in 1910, see Marlene Shore, *The Science of Social*

Redemption: McGill, the Chicago School, and the Origins of Social Research in Canada (Toronto 1987), 48–9.

33 UTA, Office of the President (Falconer), A67-0007/022, file: James A. Dale, 1912, Robert Falconer to J.A. Dale, 24 and 30 October 1912; *The Varsity* 32, no. 22 (20 November 1912), 4–5; UTA, Office of the President (Falconer), A67-0007/058a, file: James A. Dale, 1919–20, Robert Falconer to J.A. Dale, 30 October 1919.

34 UTA, Department of Graduate Records, A73-0026/077(24), file: James A. Dale, clipping: *The Varsity*, 6 October 1920.

35 Ibid., James A. Dale, clipping: *Toronto Star Weekly*, 29 January 1921.

36 UTA, Office of the President (Falconer), A67-0007/151, file: A32/2, Social Service, 1920–1, TMs, 'Report of the Director of the Department of Social Service,' 1920–1.

37 John H. Ehrenreich, *The Altruistic Imagination: A History of Social Work and Social Policy in the United States* (Ithaca, NY, 1985), 64–77; Roy Lubove, *The Professional Altruist: The Emergence of Social Work as a Career, 1880–1930* (Cambridge, Mass., 1965), 86, 108–15; Glazer and Slater, *Unequal Colleagues*, 183–4.

38 E.P. Lewis, 'What the Psychiatrist Can Contribute to Case Work,' *Social Welfare* 8, no. 8 (June–July 1926), 187; Mae Fleming, 'Some Things the Case Worker Desires from the Psychiatrist,' *Social Welfare* 8, no. 8 (June–July 1926), 188–9.

39 UTA, Division of University Extension, P78-0055/003, pamphlet: *Statement and Reports Presented to the University Commission by the Board of Governors and Senate of the University of Toronto*, 6 December 1920; *University of Toronto Calendar*, 1921–2, 601–2.

40 UTA, Office of the President (Falconer), A67-0007/100, file: James A. Dale, 1927, TMs, Agnes C. McGregor, 'Field Work Bulletin,' 1 April 1927. Ruth Hill, the associated executive secretary of the American Association for Organizing Family Social Work, presented a paper to the Toronto Conference in 1926 that encouraged an approach to casework similar to that recommended by McGregor. See Ruth Hill, 'The Spirit of Case Work as a Philosophy for Life,' *Social Welfare* 8, no. 8 (June–July 1926), 181–4.

41 *University of Toronto Calendar*, 1921–2, 594; UTA, Office of the President (Falconer), A67-0007/151, file: A32/2, Social Service, 1920–1, TMs, 'Report of the Director of the Department of Social Service,' 1920–1.

42 'Report of the Director of the Department of Social Service,' in *University of Toronto President's Report*, 1923–4, 62; 'Report of the Director of the Social Service Department,' in ibid., 1921–2, 61.

43 UTA, Office of the President (Falconer), A67-0007/112, file: Social Service, 1927, TMs, Agnes C. McGregor, 'Field Work Bulletin,' October 1927; ibid., A67-0007/112, file: Social Service, 1927, TMs, 'Department of Social Service, List of Graduates in Each Year Since Inception,' n.d.

44 'Report of the Director of the Social Service Department,' in *University of*

Toronto President's Report, 1921–2, 61; R.W. Hopper, 'Official Announcement in Respect to the Organization of the Canadian Association of Social Workers,' *Social Welfare* 9, no. 1 (October 1926), 284–6; 'As We Grew,' *The Social Worker* 3, no. 10 (August–September 1935), 1–7; 'Charter Membership List,' *Social Welfare* 9, no. 2 (November 1926), 303.

45 'As We Grew,' 2.

46 Hopper, 'Official Announcement,' 284.

47 J.A. Dale, 'Social Work's Coming of Age,' *Social Welfare* 9, no. 3 (December 1926), 324.

48 UTA, Social Service Alumni, B89-0004/001(03), Social Service Alumni Minutes, 1924–5.

49 Ibid., B89-0004/001(05), Social Service Alumni Minutes, 1926–7 (15 November 1926); B89-0004/001(06), Social Service Alumni Minutes, 1927–8 Report of the Committee Regarding the Mothers' Allowance Commission (18 April 1928).

50 Ethel Dodds Parker, 'A Code of Ethics for Social Workers,' *Social Welfare* 8, no. 8 (June–July 1926), 196–9.

51 UTA, Social Service Alumni, B89-0004/001(03), Social Service Alumni Minutes, 1924–5 (29 May 1924).

52 Ibid., Social Service Alumni Minutes, 1924–5 (15, 26 January and 22 April 1925); ibid., B89-0004/001(05), Social Service Alumni Minutes, 1926–7 (18 October 1926 and 21 February 1927).

53 UTA, Ephemera, B81-1020, McGregor, 'Reminiscences,' 3.

54 UTA, Office of the President (Falconer), A67-0007/102, file: Robert Morrison MacIver, 1926–7, R.M. MacIver to Robert Falconer, 11 April 1927.

55 Ibid., A67-0007/108b, file: Robert Morrison MacIver, 1927–8, R.M. MacIver to Robert Falconer, 6 December 1927.

56 Ibid., A67-0007/112, file: Social Service, 1927, TMs, unsigned, 'Memo. Regarding Social Service Department,' n.d.

57 Ibid., A67-0007/108b, file: Robert Morrison MacIver, 1927–8, Robert Falconer to R.M. MacIver, 7 December 1927; A67-0007/110a, file: Edward Johns Urwick, 1927–8, Robert Falconer to E.J. Urwick, 19 December 1927 and 13 January 1928; A67-0007/107a, file: James Alfred Dale, 1927–8, Robert Falconer to J.A. Dale, 7 June 1928.

7: A Return to First Principles

1 Marlene Shore, *The Science of Social Redemption: McGill, the Chicago School, and the Origins of Social Research in Canada* (Toronto 1987), 68–120.

2 *Toynbee Record* 11, no. 7 (April 1899), 103; 12, no. 1 (October 1899), 16; 12, no. 5 (February 1900), 62; 15, no. 1 (October 1902), 2–3; 18, no. 1 (October 1905), 6;

Henrietta O. Barnett, *Canon Barnett: His Life, Work, and Friends* (London 1918), vol. 1, 179.

3 *Toynbee Record* 21, no. 1 (October 1908), 5; Reba N. Soffer, *Ethics and Society in England: The Revolution in the Social Sciences, 1870–1914* (Berkeley 1978), 58. For biographical information on E.J. Urwick, see UTA, Department of Graduate Records, A73-0026/482(66), Edward Johns Urwick; Agnes C. McGregor, 'Professor Urwick,' *The Social Worker* 13, no. 3 (April 1945), 16; and Harold A. Innis, 'Edward Johns Urwick, 1867–1945,' *Canadian Journal of Economics and Political Science* 11, no. 2 (May 1945), 265–8.

4 *Toynbee Record* 12, no. 5 (February 1900), 63.

5 Ibid. 13, no. 6 (April 1901), 79.

6 Standish Meacham, *Toynbee Hall and Social Reform, 1880–1914: The Search for Community* (New Haven, Conn., 1987), 87–110.

7 E.J. Urwick, 'The Settlement Ideal,' *Charity Organisation Review* (March 1902), 119, 121.

8 E.J. Urwick, *A Philosophy of Social Progress*, 2d ed., rev. (London 1920), 154–6.

9 Urwick, 'The Settlement Ideal,' 126.

10 *Toynbee Record* 16, no. 6 (March 1904), 83–4.

11 Urwick, *A Philosophy of Social Progress*, 1–25, 52–9, vi, 153, 198, 240. Urwick presented a similar argument concerning sociology in 'Sociology and Social Progress,' *Sociological Review* 3, no. 2 (April 1910), 137–49.

12 *Toynbee Record* 25, no. 8 (May 1912), 118–19.

13 Ibid., no. 10 (July–September 1913), 150; Barnett, *Canon Barnett*, vol. 2, 26, 27.

14 See, for example, UTA, Department of Political Economy, A65-0005/001(04), E.J. Urwick to J.J. Mallon, 15 September 1928; ibid., L. Rasminsky to E.J. Urwick, 18 October 1928; UTA, Department of Political Economy, A69-0007/001(07), F.A. Haight to E.J. Urwick, 1 November 1929.

15 UTA, Department of Political Economy, A69-0007/001(03), E.J. Urwick to C.I. Brennand, 4 June 1930. In October 1902, Urwick's health had also caused him to resign his position as sub-warden of Toynbee Hall. *Toynbee Record* 15, no. 1 (October 1902), 2–3; 15, no. 8 (May 1903), 107.

16 In 1936, Urwick's emphasis on disinterested service contributed to his rejection of a proposal by Harry M. Cassidy to create a Canadian Institute of Social-Economic Research at Toronto. Urwick told the president (then H.J. Cody) that he was suspicious that Cassidy wished to make a place for himself as director of the new institute. 'I do not like any scheme based on self-interest,' he confessed. UTA, Office of the President (Cody), A68-0006/029(03), file: Correspondence, T-V, E.J. Urwick to H.J. Cody, 21 August 1936. For Cassidy's proposal, see UTA, Department of Political Economy, A76-0025/001(07), TMs, H.M. Cassidy, 'A Canadian Institute of Social-Economic Research: A Preliminary Plan,' 30 July 1936.

17 UTA, Social Service Alumni, B89-0004/001(04), Social Service Alumni Minutes, 1925–6 (24 November 1925).

18 UTA, Office of the President (Falconer), A67-0007/095, file: Robert Morrison MacIver, 1925–6, R.M. MacIver to Robert Falconer, 9 February 1926; UTA, Department of Political Economy, A65-0005/001(25), TMs, R.M. MacIver, 'Report on the Department of Political Economy for the year 1925–6,' 24 April 1926; UTA, Office of the President (Falconer), A67-0007/102, file: Robert Morrison MacIver, 1926–7, R.M. MacIver to Robert Falconer, 29 October 1926; A67-0007/104, file: E.J. Urwick, 1926–7, Robert Falconer to E.J. Urwick, 12 November 1926.

19 UTA, Office of the President (Falconer), A67-0007/104, file: E.J. Urwick, 1926–7, Robert Falconer to E.J. Urwick, 25 April 1927. Vincent Bladen, who was then a junior member of the Department of Political Economy, later recalled that it was lucky Urwick was available, to prevent the two most senior professors, G.E. Jackson and W.T. Jackman, from bitterly competing for the headship. UTA, Vincent Wheeler Bladen, B74-0038, interview by C. Roger Myers, 4 January 1974, transcript, University of Toronto Oral History Project, 97–9. For another inside view of fighting within the department, see UTA, Office of the President (Falconer), A67-0007/115, file: Harold Adams Innis, 1929, Harold A. Innis to Robert Falconer, [15 April 1929].

20 UTA, Office of the President (Falconer), A67-0007/104, file: E.J. Urwick, 1926–7, E.J. Urwick to Robert Falconer, 15 November 1926; UTA, Department of Political Economy, A69-0007/001(03), E.J. Urwick to C.I. Brennand, 4 June 1930.

21 City of Toronto Archives, University Settlement House Collection, SC 24, series B, box 001, Board of Directors of University Settlement Minutes, 1925–4 (12 March 1931, 11 June 1931, 16 April 1931); and 1935–43 (10 March 1938).

22 Ibid., Board of Directors of University Settlement Minutes, 1935–43 (2 December 1937).

23 UTA, Office of the President (Falconer), A67-0007/129, file: Social Service, 1929–31, TMs, E.J. Urwick, 'Report on the Present Needs of the Department of Social Service,' 17 January 1929; UTA, Harry Morris Cassidy, B72-0022/016, file: Urwick, E.J. Urwick to Harry Cassidy, 24 January and 19 April 1929.

24 UTA, University of Toronto, Senate, A68-0012/roll 7, vol. 16, Senate Minutes, 1929–32, 49 (11 October 1929).

25 UTA, Office of the President (Falconer), A67-0007/123, file: E.J. Urwick, 1929–30, TMs, E.J. Urwick, 'The Education of Social Workers,' 4 October 1929.

26 UTA, Department of Political Economy, A69-0007/001(11), E.J. Urwick to H.M. Kelly, 31 January 1929.

27 UTA, Office of the President (Falconer), A67-0007/123, file: E.J. Urwick, 1929–30, TMs, E.J. Urwick, 'The Education of Social Workers,' 4 October 1929.

28 Meacham, *Toynbee Hall*, 107–9.

29 E.J. Urwick, 'The Training of Social Workers,' *Social Welfare* 12, no. 8 (May 1930), 176–7; Urwick, 'First Principles First,' *Social Welfare* 13, no. 2 (November 1930), 29–30, 32.

30 UTA, Office of the President (Falconer), A67-0007/129, file: Social Service, 1929–31, TMs, 'Memorandum on the Department of Social Science, Summarizing points in the discussion of the Senate's Committee held on Friday, December 19th,' n.d.; ibid., A67-0007/128a, file: E.J. Urwick, 1930–1, Robert Falconer to E.J. Urwick, 14 May 1931; UTA, Office of the Registrar, A73/0051/135, file: SW, 1930–2, A.B. Fennell to E.J. Urwick, 19 December 1932; UTA, University of Toronto, Senate, A68-0012/roll 8, vol. 16, Senate Minutes, 1929–32, 446 (12 February 1932); UTA, University of Toronto, Board of Governors, A70-0024/023, vol. 12, Board of Governors Minutes, 1931–3, 141 (10 March 1932).

31 UTA, Office of the Registrar, A73-0051/230(01), file: Sociology, 1932–6, clipping: *The Varsity*, 4 October 1932; UTA, Office of the President (Falconer), A67-0007/135a, file: Social Science, 1932, A.B. Fennell to Robert Falconer, 16 February 1932; W.G. Martin to Robert Falconer, 23 February 1932.

32 UTA, Office of the President (Falconer), A67-0007/135a, file: Social Science, 1932, E.J. Urwick to Robert Falconer, 19 February 1932.

33 'Report of the Acting Director of Department of Social Science,' in *University of Toronto President's Report*, 1934–5, 99; 1935–6, 98; *University of Toronto Calendar*, 1937–38, 14–17.

34 UTA, Department of Graduate Records, A73-0026/482(66), Edward Johns Urwick, clippings: *The Varsity*, 20 November 1935 and 17 February 1937; UTA, Office of the Registrar, A73-0051/230(01), file: Sociology, 1932–6, clipping: *The Varsity*, 22 January 1936.

35 E.J. Urwick, 'The Role of Intelligence in the Social Process,' *Canadian Journal of Economics and Political Science* 1, no. 1 (February 1935), 73.

36 R.M. MacIver, *Society: A Textbook of Sociology* (New York 1937), 3.

37 E.J. Urwick, 'Is There a Scientific Sociology?' *Canadian Journal of Economics and Political Science* 4, no. 2 (May 1938), 240, 233–5, 239.

38 R.M. MacIver, 'Science and Sociology: A Reply to Professor Urwick,' *Canadian Journal of Economics and Political Science* 4, no. 4 (November 1938), 551.

39 UTA, Social Service Alumni, B89-0004/001(06), Social Service Alumni Minutes, 1927–8 (18 April 1928); ibid., Minutes, 1927–8, Report of the Formation of an Alumni Advisory Committee to the Social Service Department of the University of Toronto, n.d. [April 1928].

40 'Report of the Director of the Department of Social Service,' in *University of Toronto President's Report*, 1922–3, 60; UTA, Social Service Alumni, B89-0004/001(03), SSA Minutes, 1924–5 (25 November 1924); B89-0004/001(06), SSA

Minutes, 1927–8 (8 June 1928); B89-0004/001(07), SSA Minutes, 1928–9 (29 October and 6 November 1928).

41 UTA, Office of the President (Falconer), A67-0007/117, file: E.J. Urwick, 1928–9, Jean McTaggart to Robert Falconer, 10 April 1929.

42 Ibid., A67-0007/133, file: Mrs G. Cameron Parker, 1932, A. Ethel Parker to Robert Falconer, 8 February 1932. See also UTA, Office of the Registrar, A73-0051/135, file: SW, 1930–2, E.D. MacPhee and D.B. Harkness to Robert Falconer, 26 October 1931.

43 James Struthers, *The Limits of Affluence: Welfare in Ontario, 1920–1970* (Toronto 1994), 77–108, 130. For a biography of Charlotte Whitton, see Patricia T. Rooke and R.L. Schnell, *No Bleeding Heart: Charlotte Whitton, a Feminist on the Right* (Vancouver 1988).

44 Kathryn McPherson, 'Science and Technique: Nurses' Work in a Canadian Hospital, 1920–1939,' in Dianne Dodd and Deborah Gorham, eds, *Caring and Curing: Historical Perspectives on Women and Healing in Canada* (Ottawa 1994), 80; Struthers, *Limits of Affluence*, 82.

45 TFRB, John Joseph Kelso, Ms. Coll. 115, box 1, file: School of Social Work Alumni, TMs, 'Social Service Alumni, University of Toronto, list of paid members,' May 1922; UTA, Office of the President (Cody), A68-0006/012(03), file: T-V, TMs, List of Special Lecturers, 1933–4; A68-0006/018(02), file: TO-WA, TMs, List of Special Lecturers, 1934–5; A68-0006/024(03), file: U-WA, TMs, List of Special Lecturers, 1935–6; A68-0006/029(03), file: T-V, TMs, List of Special Lecturers, 1936–7.

46 Frieda Held, 'For What Shall We Train Students of Social Work?' *The Social Worker* 4, no. 5 (February 1936), 3.

47 'What Is a Social Worker?' *The Social Worker* 4, no. 10 (August–September 1936), 7; UTA, Harry Morris Cassidy, B72-0022/014, file: Agnes McGregor, Agnes C. McGregor to Harry Cassidy, 28 March 1937.

48 UTA, Harry Morris Cassidy, B72-0022/014, file: Agnes McGregor, Agnes C. McGregor to Harry Cassidy, 28 March 1937.

49 AO, F 980, H.J. Cody Papers, Series A-3, MU 4965, file 1, E.J. Urwick to H.J. Cody, 8 June 1937; UTA, Office of the President (Cody), A68-0006/033(05), file: T-V, H.J. Cody to E.J. Urwick, 14 June 1937; UTA, Department of Political Economy, A76-0025/001(07), E.J. Urwick to G.E. Jackson, 1 May 1937.

50 UTA, Harold Adams Innis, B72-0025/011(12), E.J. Urwick to Harold Innis, 15 September 1942.

Conclusion

1 UTA, Harold Adams Innis, B72-0025/011(12), E.J. Urwick to Harold Innis, 30 December 1942 and 24 April 1944.

2 Patricia Jasen, '"In Pursuit of Human Values (or Laugh When You Say That)":
The Student Critique of the Arts Curriculum in the 1960s,' in Paul Axelrod and
John G. Reid, eds, *Youth, University and Canadian Society: Essays in the Social
History of Higher Education* (Kingston, Ont., 1989), 247–71.

3 UTA, Vincent Wheeler Bladen, B74-0038, interview by C. Roger Myers,
4 January 1974, transcript, University of Toronto Oral History Project, 95–100.

4 Carl Berger, 'Harold Innis: The Search for Limits,' in *The Writing of Canadian
History: Aspects of English-Canadian Historical Writing: 1900 to 1970* (Toronto
1976), 100–11.

5 Harold A. Innis, 'The Church in Canada,' in Mary Q. Innis, ed., *Essays in
Canadian Economic History* (Toronto 1956), 393, 383.

6 Allan Irving, 'A Canadian Fabian: The Life and Work of Harry Cassidy' (Ph.D.
diss., University of Toronto, 1982), 441–2.

7 UTA, Office of the President (Cody), A68-0006/039(03), file: U, E.J. Urwick to
H.J. Cody, 5 May 1939.

8 UTA, Harold Adams Innis, B72-0025/011(12), E.J. Urwick to Harold Innis,
24 September 1940 and 30 December 1942.

9 Harry H. Hiller, *Society and Change: S.D. Clark and the Development of Canadian Sociology* (Toronto 1982), 12–16; S.D. Clark, 'Sociology in Canada: An Historical Over-view,' *Canadian Journal of Sociology* 1, no. 2 (Summer 1975), 226–
7. For a history of the development of sociology at McGill, see Marlene Shore, *The
Science of Social Redemption: McGill, the Chicago School, and the Origins of
Social Research in Canada* (Toronto 1987).

10 UTA, Harry Morris Cassidy, B72-0022/014, file: Agnes C. McGregor, Agnes C.
McGregor to Harry Cassidy, 29 July 1939, 15 August 1939, 13 and 31 December
1939, 1 February 1941.

11 UTA, Ephemera, B81-1020, Agnes C. McGregor, 'Reminiscences,' TMs [photo-
copy], 1947, 5.

12 Irving, 'A Canadian Fabian,' 328, 350–2, 442–5; UTA, Ephemera, B81–1020,
McGregor, 'Reminiscences,' 5; Agnes C. McGregor, 'Memories,' TMs [photo-
copy], 1959, 28.

13 Irving, 'A Canadian Fabian,' 421–5, 445.

14 Ibid., 490–5.

15 Standish Meacham, *Toynbee Hall and Social Reform, 1880-1914: The Search for
Community* (New Haven, Conn., 1987), 88–96.

16 Jacquelyn Gale Wills, 'Efficiency, Feminism and Cooperative Democracy: Origins
of the Toronto Social Planning Council, 1918–1957' (Ph.D. diss., University of
Toronto, 1989), 321.

17 UTA, Office of the President (Falconer), A67-0007/058a, file: James A. Dale,
1919–20, Robert Falconer to J.A. Dale, 21 April 1920, and J.A. Dale to Robert
Falconer, 24 April 1920; UTA, Department of Graduate Records, A73-0026/

077(24), James A. Dale, clipping: *The Varsity*, 26 February 1925.

18 UTA, Department of Graduate Records, A73-0026/497(05), Hardolph Wasteneys, clipping: *Toronto Globe and Mail*, 3 February 1965; clipping: *Toronto Mail*, 11 January 1923.

19 Hortense Catherine Fardell Wasteneys, 'A History of the University Settlement of Toronto, 1910–1958: An Exploration of the Social Objectives of the University Settlement and of Their Implementation' (Ph.D. diss., University of Toronto, 1975), 223–4, 249–52.

20 UTA, Ephemera, B81–1058, pamphlet: *University Settlement House*, [1928]; City of Toronto Archives, University Settlement House Collection, SC 24, series B, box 001, Board of Directors of University Settlement Minutes, 1925–34 (10 May 1928).

21 Quoted in Wasteneys, 'A History of the University Settlement,' 156.

22 Ibid., 158–65; UTA, William Tout Sharp, B84-0002/001(08), University Settlement Annual Report, 1946, submitted by Frances Crowther; ibid., B84-0002/001(09), University Settlement Annual Report, 1947, submitted by Mary C. Donaldson.

23 City of Toronto Archives, University Settlement House Collection, SC 24, series B, box 001, Board of Directors of University Settlement Minutes, 1944–50 (28 April 1948).

24 Quoted in Wasteneys, 'A History of the University Settlement,' 177, 317.

25 Wasteneys, 'A History of the University Settlement,' 179–80, 267–8.

26 Stefan Collini, 'Hobhouse, Bosanquet and the State: Philosophical Idealism and Political Argument in England, 1880–1918,' *Past and Present* no. 72 (August 1976), 107; A.B. McKillop, *A Disciplined Intelligence: Critical Inquiry and Canadian Thought in the Victorian Era* (Montreal 1979), 171–203.

27 Meacham, *Toynbee Hall*, 86–129.

28 UTA, Pamphlets, box 6: E.J. Urwick, 'Social Philosophy and Social Work,' in *Training for Social Work in the Department of Social Science, University of Toronto, 1914–1940*, 1940, 52.

Bibliography

Primary Sources

MANUSCRIPT COLLECTIONS

Archives of Ontario:
H.J. Cody Papers, F 980
Department of Education, RG 2

City of Toronto Archives:
Reports, RG 1
University Settlement House Collection, SC 24

Metropolitan Toronto Central Library, Baldwin Room:
S 54, Mary Jennison, 'A History of Canadian Settlements,' 1965
Ethel (Dodds) Parker Papers

National Archives of Canada:
John Joseph Kelso Papers, MG 30, C 97
William Lyon Mackenzie King Papers, MG 26, J 1

Thunder Bay Historical Museum Society:
Biographical File: Cecil King

United Church/Victoria University Archives:
Biographical File: James M. Shaver
Methodist Church (Canada), Toronto Conference, Methodist Union of Toronto,
    84.050C
Young Women's Christian Association, 90.135V

University of Toronto Archives:
Department of Alumni Affairs, A72-0024
William James Ashley, B65-0033
Vincent Wheeler Bladen, B74-0038
Edward Blake, B72-0013
Harry Morris Cassidy, B72-0022
Dorothy W. Eddis, B76-1037
Ephemera. B78-1395. *Some Facts about the University Settlement* [1911]
– B81-1020. Agnes C. McGregor, 'Reminiscences,' TMs [photocopy], 1947
– B81-1058. *University Settlement House* [1928]
– B84-1089. *University of Toronto, Department of Social Service, Special Course in Work with Boys*, n.d.
Examinations. Boxes 014-070, 1880–1938
Department of Graduate Records, A73-0026
Harold Adams Innis, B72-0025
Mossie May Waddington Kirkwood, B74-0020
John Langton Family, B65-0014
Bessie Mabel Scott Lewis, B80-0033
William E. Lingelbach, B73-1124
James Loudon, B72-0031
Department of Political Economy, A65-0005, A69-0007, A76-0025
Office of the President (Henry J. Cody), A68-0006
Office of the President (Robert A. Falconer), A67-0007
Office of the Registrar, A73-0051
Pamphlets. *Letter of Application and Testimonials [of] James Mavor [for the] Lectureship in Political Economy, University College, Liverpool,* [1888]
– *Testimonials in Favour of W.J. Ashley, M.A.: A Candidate for the Drummond Professorship of Political Economy in the University of Oxford,* 1890
– *University of Toronto Young Men's Christian Association, Annual Report,* 1890–91
– Box 6: *Training for Social Work in the Department of Social Science, University of Toronto, 1914–1940,* 1940
– Archibald McKellar MacMechan. *Reminiscences of Toronto University,* n.d.
Ross Family, B83-0031
William Tout Sharp, B84-0002
Social Service Alumni, B89-0004
Faculty of Social Work, A85-0002
Student Christian Movement, B79-0059
United Alumnae Association, B65-0030

University College, A69-0011
University College, Dean of Women, B74-0011
University College Council, A69-0016
Division of University Extension, P78-0055
University Historian, A83-0036
University of Toronto, Board of Governors, A70-0024
University of Toronto, Senate, A68-0012
Waddell Family, B73-0028
Sir Daniel Wilson, B77-1195
M83-0080. *A Brief History of the Student Christian Movement in Canada.* Toronto:
    Student Christian Movement of Canada, 1975
P78-0321. *Toronto University Studies in Political Science.* 1st series, nos. 1–4.
    Toronto: Warwick & Sons, 1889–1895
P78-0712. *The Rebel.* 1917–1920

University of Toronto Library:
William Lyon Mackenzie King Diaries, 1893–1931. Microfiche, manuscript and
    transcript versions. Microfiche produced by University of Toronto Press,
    1973
Agnes C. McGregor, 'Memories,' TMs [photocopy], 1959

University of Toronto, Thomas Fisher Rare Book Library:
John Joseph Kelso Papers, Ms. Coll. 115
James Mavor Papers, Ms. Coll. 119
Toronto Social Welfare Agencies, Ms. Coll. 12

CALENDARS AND REPORTS

London School of Economics and Political Science Calendar. 1913–21
Report of the Commissioners on the Discipline in the University of Toronto. Toronto:
    Warwick Bros. & Rutter, 1895
University of Toronto Calendar. 1915–38
University of Toronto President's Report. 1921–38

NEWSPAPERS AND PERIODICALS

The Rebel (Toronto). 1917–20
Torontonensis (Toronto). 1898–1938
Toynbee Record (London). 1888–1914
The Varsity (Toronto). 1888–1940

BOOKS AND ARTICLES

Addams, Jane. *Twenty Years at Hull-House*. New York: New American Library, 1961
Ames, Herbert Brown. *The City below the Hill*. Toronto: University of Toronto Press, 1972
Ashley, W.J. *What Is Political Science? An Inaugural Lecture Given in the Convocation Hall of the University of Toronto, 9th November, 1888*. Toronto: Rowsell & Hutchison, 1888
– *An Introduction to English Economic History and Theory*. London: Longmans, Green & Co., 1888
– Review of *Arnold Toynbee*, by F.C. Montague. In *Political Science Quarterly* 4, no. 3 (September 1889), 531–4
– 'On the Study of Economic History.' *Quarterly Journal of Economics* 7, no. 2 (January 1893), 3–24
Ashley, W.J., Franklin H. Giddings, Simon N. Patten, and Lester F. Ward. 'Discussion.' *Abstracts in Publications of the American Economic Association* 10, no. 3 (March 1895), 106–17
– *Surveys Historic and Economic*. London: Longmans, Green & Co., 1900
– 'The Present Position of Political Economy.' *Economic Journal* 17, no. 68 (December 1907), 467–89
'As We Grew.' *The Social Worker* 3, no. 10 (August–September 1935), 1–7
Barnett, Henrietta O. *Canon Barnett: His Life, Work, and Friends*. London: John Murray, 1918
Barnett, Samuel A., and Henrietta O. Barnett. *Practicable Socialism: Essays on Social Reform*. London: Longmans, Green & Co., 1888
Brecken, E. 'Religious Life in Oxford.' *Acta Victoriana* 31, no. 7 (April 1908), 457–63
Burnett, Arthur H. 'The Conservation of Citizenship: A Critique on Settlement Service.' *Acta Victoriana* 35, no. 2 (November 1911), 59–62
'Charter Membership List.' *Social Welfare* 9, no. 2 (November 1926), 303
Chown, Alice A. 'The Social Settlement Movement.' *Acta Victoriana* 23, no. 3 (December 1899), 208–12
Cudmore, S.A. 'The Condition of England.' *University of Toronto Monthly* 10, no. 2 (December 1909), 70–8
Dale, J.A. 'The Training of Social Workers.' *Social Welfare* 6, no. 10 (July 1924), 201–2
– 'Social Work's Coming of Age.' *Social Welfare* 9, no. 3 (December 1926), 323–5
Falconer, Robert A. 'Inaugural Address.' *University of Toronto Monthly* 8, no. 1 (November 1907), 6–14
Finlayson, Barbara M. 'Professor Dale.' *Social Welfare* 9, no. 3 (December 1926), 234–5

Fleming, Mae. 'Some Things the Case Worker Desires from the Psychiatrist.' *Social Welfare* 8, no. 8 (June–July 1926), 188–9

Goulding, A.M. 'An University Settlement.' *The Arbor* 1, no. 1 (February 1910), 32–7

Held, Frieda. 'For What Shall We Train Students of Social Work?' *The Social Worker* 4, no. 5 (February 1936), 1–3

Hill, Ruth. 'The Spirit of Case Work as a Philosophy for Life.' *Social Welfare* 8, no. 8 (June–July 1926), 181–4

Hopper, R.W. 'Official Announcement in Respect to the Organization of the Canadian Association of Social Workers.' *Social Welfare* 9, no. 1 (October 1926), 284–6

Innis, Harold A. 'Edward Johns Urwick, 1867–1945.' *Canadian Journal of Economics and Political Science* 11, no. 2 (May 1945), 265–8

– 'The Church in Canada.' In *Essays in Canadian Economic History*, ed. Mary Q. Innis, 383–93. Toronto: University of Toronto Press, 1956

Kelso, J.J. 'Heredity vs. Environment.' *Acta Victoriana* 30, no. 6 (March 1910), 396–8

King, William Lyon Mackenzie. *The Secret of Heroism: A Memoir of Henry Albert Harper*. New York: Fleming H. Revell Co., 1906

Lewis, E.P. 'What the Psychiatrist Can Contribute to Case Work.' *Social Welfare* 8, no. 8 (June–July 1926), 187

Loudon, W.J. *Studies of Student Life*. Vols. 1–5. Toronto: Macmillan, 1923–8

MacIver, R.M. 'Society and State.' *Philosophical Review* 20 (January 1911), 30–45

– 'Society and "the Individual."' *The Sociological Review* 7, no. 1 (January 1914), 58–64

– 'Education and Life.' *Social Welfare* 10, no. 2 (November 1927), 24

– *The Contribution of Sociology to Social Work*. New York: Columbia University Press, 1931

– *Society: A Textbook of Sociology*. New York: Farrar & Rinehart, 1937

– 'Science and Sociology: A Reply to Professor Urwick.' *Canadian Journal of Economics and Political Science* 4, no. 4 (November 1938), 549–51

– *As a Tale That Is Told: The Autobiography of R.M. MacIver*. Chicago: University of Chicago Press, 1968

– *Community: A Sociological Study: Being an Attempt to Set out the Nature and Fundamental Laws of Social Life*. 4th ed. London: Frank Cass & Co., 1970

McGregor, Agnes C. 'Professor Urwick.' *The Social Worker* 13, no. 3 (April 1945), 16

McLean, S.J. 'Social Amelioration and the University Settlement: With Special Reference to Toynbee Hall.' *The Canadian Magazine* 8, no. 6 (April 1897), 469–74

Masterman, C.F.G. *The Condition of England*. London: Methuen, 1909

Mavor, James. *My Windows on the Street of the World*. London: J.M. Dent & Sons, 1923

Milner, Alfred. *Arnold Toynbee: A Reminiscence*. London: Edward Arnold, 1895

Montague, F.C. *Arnold Toynbee*. Baltimore: Johns Hopkins University, 1889

Parker, Ethel Dodds. 'A Code of Ethics for Social Workers.' *Social Welfare* 8, no. 8 (June–July 1926), 196–9
– 'The Origins and Early History of the Presbyterian Settlement Houses.' In *The Social Gospel in Canada*, ed. Richard Allen, 86–121. Ottawa: National Museums of Canada, 1975
Richmond, Mary E. *Social Diagnosis*. New York: Russell Sage Foundation, 1917
– *What Is Social Case Work? An Introductory Description*. New York: Russell Sage Foundation, 1922
'Sara Libby Carson.' *Social Welfare* 11, no. 5 (February 1929), 113
'The Settlement Movement.' *University of Toronto Monthly* 11, no. 2 (December 1910), 34–40
Shaver, J.M. 'The Immigrant in Industry.' *Social Welfare* 3, nos. 10–11 (July–August 1921), 275–7
'In the Slums of "Toronto the Good."' *The Christian Guardian* 80, no. 21 (26 May 1909), 3
'The Social Union Programme.' *Acta Victoriana* 33, no. 4 (January 1910), 292–3
'The Students' Christian Social Union.' *Acta Victoriana* 33, no. 1 (October 1909), 37
Tallents, S.G. 'Toynbee Hall.' *University of Toronto Monthly* 10, no. 4 (February 1910), 200–2
Toynbee, Arnold. *Lectures on the Industrial Revolution in England: Popular Addresses, Notes and Their Fragments*. London: Rivington, 1884
Toynbee, Gertrude. *Reminiscences and Letters of Joseph and Arnold Toynbee*. London: H. Glaisher, 1911
'Universities and the Social Problem.' *University of Toronto Monthly* 15, no. 5 (March 1914), 233–7
'The University Settlement.' *University of Toronto Monthly* 11, no. 4 (February 1911), 112–16
'The University Settlement.' *University of Toronto Monthly* 11, no. 8 (June 1911), 379–81
'University Settlement Movement.' *Acta Victoriana* 21, no. 1 (October 1897), 4–5
Urwick, E.J. 'The Settlement Ideal.' *Charity Organisation Review* (March 1902), 119–27
– 'Sociology and Social Progress.' *Sociological Review* 3, no. 2 (April 1910), 137–49
– *A Philosophy of Social Progress*, 2d ed., rev. London: Methuen, 1920
– 'The Training of Social Workers.' *Social Welfare* 12, no. 8 (May 1930), 176–7
– 'First Principles First.' *Social Welfare* 13, no. 2 (November 1930), 29–30
– 'The Role of Intelligence in the Social Process.' *Canadian Journal of Economics and Political Science* 1, no. 1 (February 1935), 64–76
– 'Is There a Scientific Sociology?' *Canadian Journal of Economics and Political Science* 4, no. 2 (May 1938), 231–40

- *The Values of Life*. Toronto: University of Toronto Press, 1948
Wald, Lillian D. *The House on Henry Street*. New York: Henry Holt & Co., 1915
Ward, Mrs Humphry. *A Writer's Recollections*. London: W. Collins Sons & Co., 1918
- *Marcella*. New York: Penguin Books, 1985
- *Robert Elsmere*. Oxford: Oxford University Press, 1987
Webb, Beatrice. *My Apprenticeship*. New York: Longmans, Green & Co., 1926
'What Is a Social Worker?' *The Social Worker* 4, no. 10 (August–September 1936), 2–7
Woodsworth, J.S. 'Social Work as a Profession.' *Acta Victoriana* 38, no. 6 (March 1914), 292–4

Secondary Sources

THESES

Boutilier, Beverly. 'Gender, Organized Women, and the Politics of Institution Building: Founding the Victorian Order of Nurses for Canada, 1893–1900.' Ph.D. diss., Carleton University, 1993
Bowker, Alan Franklin. 'Truly Useful Men: Maurice Hutton, George Wrong, James Mavor and the University of Toronto, 1880–1927.' Ph.D. diss., University of Toronto, 1975
Irving, Allan. 'A Canadian Fabian: The Life and Work of Harry Cassidy.' Ph.D. diss., University of Toronto, 1982
Wasteneys, Hortense Catherine Fardell. 'A History of the University Settlement of Toronto, 1910–1958: An Exploration of the Social Objectives of the University Settlement and of Their Implementation.' Ph.D. diss., University of Toronto, 1975
Wills, Jacquelyn Gale. 'Efficiency, Feminism and Cooperative Democracy: Origins of the Toronto Social Planning Council, 1918–1957.' Ph.D. diss., University of Toronto, 1989

BOOKS AND ARTICLES

Airhart, Phyllis D. 'Ordering a New Nation and Reordering Protestantism, 1867–1914.' In *The Canadian Protestant Experience, 1760–1990*, ed. George A. Rawlyk, 98–138. Montreal and Kingston: McGill-Queen's University Press, 1990
Alexander, W.J., ed. *The University of Toronto and Its Colleges, 1827–1906*. [Toronto:] The University Library, 1906
Allen, Richard. *The Social Passion: Religion and Social Reform in Canada, 1914–28*. Toronto: University of Toronto Press, 1971
- 'The Background of the Social Gospel in Canada.' In *The Social Gospel in Canada*, ed. Richard Allen, 2–34. Ottawa: National Museums of Canada, 1975.

Alpert, Harry. 'Robert M. MacIver's Contributions to Sociological Theory.' In *Freedom and Control in Modern Society*, ed. Morroe Berger, Theodore Abel, and Charles H. Page, 286–92. New York: D. Van Nostrand Co., 1954

Ashley, Anne. *William James Ashley: A Life*. London: P.S. King & Son, 1932

Ashley, C.A. 'Sir William Ashley and the Rise of Schools of Commerce.' *Commerce Journal*, March 1938, 40–50

Ashton, Rosemary. Introduction to *Robert Elsmere* by Mrs Humphry Ward. Oxford: Oxford University Press, 1987

Bannister, Robert C. *Sociology and Scientism: The American Quest for Objectivity, 1880–1940*. Chapel Hill, NC: University of North Carolina Press, 1987

Barber, Marilyn. 'Nationalism, Nativism and the Social Gospel: The Protestant Church Response to Foreign Immigrants in Western Canada, 1897–1914.' In *The Social Gospel in Canada*, ed. Richard Allen, 186–226. Ottawa: National Museums of Canada, 1975

Bator, Paul Adolphus. '"The Struggle to Raise the Lower Classes": Public Health Reform and the Problem of Poverty in Toronto, 1910 to 1921.' *Journal of Canadian Studies* 14, no. 1 (Spring 1979), 43–9

Berger, Carl. 'Harold Innis: The Search for Limits.' In *The Writing of Canadian History: Aspects of English-Canadian Historical Writing: 1900 to 1970*, 85–111. Toronto: Oxford University Press, 1976

Beveridge, Janet. *An Epic of Clare Market: Birth and Early Days of the London School of Economics*. London: G. Bell & Sons, 1960

Bissell, Claude T., ed. *University College: A Portrait, 1853–1953*. Toronto: University of Toronto Press, 1953

Briggs, Asa, and Anne Macartney. *Toynbee Hall: The First Hundred Years*. London: Routledge & Kegan Paul, 1984

Church, Robert L. 'The Economists Study Society: Sociology at Harvard, 1891–1902.' In *Social Sciences at Harvard, 1860–1920: From Inculcation to the Open Mind*, ed. Paul Buck, 18–90. Cambridge, Mass.: Harvard University Press, 1965

Clark, S.D. 'Sociology in Canada: An Historical Over-view.' *Canadian Journal of Sociology* 1, no. 2 (Summer 1975), 225–34

Collini, Stefan. 'Hobhouse, Bosanquet and the State: Philosophical Idealism and Political Argument in England, 1880–1918.' *Past and Present* no. 72 (August 1976), 86–111

– 'Sociology and Idealism in Britain, 1880–1920.' *Archives européennes de sociologie* 19, no. 1 (1978), 3–50

– *Liberalism and Sociology: L.T. Hobhouse and Political Argument in England, 1880–1914*. Cambridge, England: Cambridge University Press, 1979

Cook, Ramsay. *The Regenerators: Social Criticism in Late Victorian English Canada*. Toronto: University of Toronto Press, 1985

Copp, Terry. *The Anatomy of Poverty: The Condition of the Working Class in Montreal, 1897–1929.* Toronto: McClelland & Stewart, 1974

Craven, Paul. *'An Impartial Umpire': Industrial Relations and the Canadian State, 1900–1911.* Toronto: University of Toronto Press, 1980

Crocker, Ruth Hutchinson. *Social Work and Social Order: The Settlement Movement in Two Industrial Cities, 1889–1930.* Chicago: University of Illinois Press, 1992

Davis, Allen F. *Spearheads for Reform: The Social Settlements and the Progressive Movement, 1890–1914.* Toronto: Oxford University Press, 1967

Dawson, R. MacGregor. *William Lyon Mackenzie King: A Political Biography, 1874–1923.* Toronto: University of Toronto Press, 1958

Deegan, Mary Jo. 'Early Women Sociologists and the American Sociological Society: The Patterns of Exclusion and Participation.' *American Sociologist* 16, no. 1 (February 1981), 14–24

– *Jane Addams and the Men of the Chicago School, 1892–1918.* New Brunswick, NJ: Transaction Books, 1988

Drummond, Ian M. *Political Economy at the University of Toronto: A History of the Department, 1888–1982.* Toronto: University of Toronto Governing Council, 1983

Ehrenreich, John H. *The Altruistic Imagination: A History of Social Work and Social Policy in the United States.* Ithaca, NY: Cornell University Press, 1985

Fitzpatrick, Ellen. *Endless Crusade: Women Social Scientists and Progressive Reform.* New York: Oxford University Press, 1990

Ford, Anne Rochon. *A Path Not Strewn with Roses: One Hundred Years of Women at the University of Toronto, 1884–1984.* Toronto: University of Toronto Press, 1985

Fraser, Brian J. *The Social Uplifters: Presbyterian Progressives and the Social Gospel in Canada, 1875–1915.* Waterloo, Ont.: Wilfrid Laurier University Press, 1988

Gauvreau, Michael. *The Evangelical Century: College and Creed in English Canada from the Great Revival to the Great Depression.* Montreal: McGill-Queen's University Press, 1991

Gelman, Susan. 'The "Feminization" of the High School: Women Secondary School-teachers in Toronto: 1871–1930.' In *Gender and Education in Ontario: An Historical Reader,* ed. Ruby Heap and Alison Prentice, 71–102. Toronto: Canadian Scholars' Press, 1991

Gidney, R.D., and W.P.J. Millar. *Professional Gentlemen: The Professions in Nineteenth-Century Ontario.* Toronto: University of Toronto Press, 1994

Glazer, Penina Migdal, and Miriam Slater. *Unequal Colleagues: The Entrance of Women into the Professions, 1890–1940.* New Brunswick, NJ: Rutgers University Press, 1987

Grant, John Webster. *A Profusion of Spires: Religion in Nineteenth-Century Ontario.* Toronto: University of Toronto Press, 1988

Greenlee, James G. *Sir Robert Falconer: A Biography*. Toronto: University of Toronto Press, 1988

Guest, Dennis. *The Emergence of Social Security in Canada*. Vancouver: University of British Columbia Press, 1985

Hiller, Harry H. *Society and Change: S.D. Clark and the Development of Canadian Sociology*. Toronto: University of Toronto Press, 1982

Jasen, Patricia. '"In Pursuit of Human Values (or Laugh When You Say That)": The Student Critique of the Arts Curriculum in the 1960s.' In *Youth, University and Canadian Society: Essays in the Social History of Higher Education*, ed. Paul Axelrod and John G. Reid, 247–71. Kingston, Ont.: McGill-Queen's University Press, 1989

Jones, Andrew, and Leonard Rutman. *In the Children's Aid: J.J. Kelso and Child Welfare in Ontario*. Toronto: University of Toronto Press, 1981

Kadish, Alon. *Apostle Arnold: The Life and Death of Arnold Toynbee, 1852–1883*. Durham, NC: Duke University Press, 1986

Kealey, Greg, ed. *Canada Investigates Industrialism*. Toronto: University of Toronto Press, 1973

Leiby, James. *A History of Social Welfare and Social Work in the United States*. New York: Columbia University Press, 1978

Lewis, Jane. *Women and Social Action in Victorian and Edwardian England*. Stanford: Stanford University Press, 1991

Lissak, Rivka Shpak. *Pluralism and Progressives: Hull House and the New Immigrants, 1890–1919*. Chicago: University of Chicago Press, 1989

Lubove, Roy. *The Professional Altruist: The Emergence of Social Work as a Career, 1880–1930*. Cambridge, Mass.: Harvard University Press, 1965

MacDougall, Heather. *Activists and Advocates: Toronto's Health Department, 1883–1983*. Toronto: Dundurn Press, 1990

McKillop, A.B. *A Disciplined Intelligence: Critical Inquiry and Canadian Thought in the Victorian Era*. Montreal: McGill-Queen's University Press, 1979

– 'Moralists and Moderns.' *Journal of Canadian Studies* 14, no. 4 (Winter 1979–80), 144–50

McNaught, Kenneth. *A Prophet in Politics: A Biography of J.S. Woodsworth*. Toronto: University of Toronto Press, 1959

McPherson, Kathryn. 'Science and Technique: Nurses' Work in a Canadian Hospital, 1920–1939.' In *Caring and Curing: Historical Perspectives on Women and Healing in Canada*, ed. Dianne Dodd and Deborah Gorham, 71–101. Ottawa: University of Ottawa Press, 1994

Mangan, J.A., and James Walvin, eds. *Manliness and Morality: Middle-class Masculinity in Britain and America, 1800–1940*. Manchester: Manchester University Press, 1987

Marshall, David B. *Secularizing the Faith: Canadian Protestant Clergy and the Crisis of Belief, 1850–1940*. Toronto: University of Toronto Press, 1992

Meacham, Standish. *Toynbee Hall and Social Reform, 1880–1914: The Search for Community*. New Haven, Conn.: Yale University Press, 1987

Mitchinson, Wendy. 'The YWCA and Reform in the Nineteenth Century.' *Histoire sociale / Social History* 12, no.24 (November 1979), 368–84

Muirhead, J.H. 'University of Birmingham: Social Study.' In Anne Ashley, *William James Ashley: A Life*, 105–8. London: P.S. King & Son, 1932

O'Connor, Patricia J. *The Story of Central Neighbourhood House, 1911–1986*. Toronto: Toronto Association of Neighbourhood Services, 1986

Owram, Doug. *The Government Generation: Canadian Intellectuals and the State, 1900–1945*. Toronto: University of Toronto Press, 1986

Palmer, Jean, and Florence Philpott. 'The Story of the Toronto Association of Neighbourhood Services, 1918–1985.' In *The Story of the Toronto Settlement House Movement, 1910–1985*, ed. Patricia J. O'Connor, 51–80. Toronto: Toronto Association of Neighbourhood Services, 1986

Palmieri, Patricia A. 'Here Was Fellowship: A Social Portrait of Academic Women at Wellesley College, 1895–1920.' In *Women Who Taught: Perspectives on the History of Women and Teaching*, ed. Alison Prentice and Marjorie R. Theobald, 233–57. Toronto: University of Toronto Press, 1991

Pedersen, Diana. '"The Call to Service": The YWCA and the Canadian College Woman, 1886–1920.' In *Youth, University and Canadian Society: Essays in the Social History of Higher Education*, ed. Paul Axelrod and John G. Reid, 189–215. Kingston, Ont.: McGill-Queen's University Press, 1989

Pimlott, J.A.R. *Toynbee Hall: Fifty Years of Social Progress, 1884–1934*. London: J.M. Dent & Sons, 1935

Pitsula, James. 'The Emergence of Social Work in Toronto.' *Journal of Canadian Studies* 14, no. 1 (Spring 1979), 35–42

Piva, J. Michael. *The Condition of the Working Class in Toronto, 1900–1921*. Ottawa: University of Ottawa Press, 1979

Poovey, Mary. *Uneven Developments: The Ideological Work of Gender in Mid-Victorian England*. Chicago: University of Chicago Press, 1988

Reaney, James. *The Dismissal: or Twisted Beards and Tangled Whiskers*. Erin, Ont.: Press Porcepic, 1978

Richardson, Douglas. *A Not Unsightly Building: University College and Its History*. Toronto: Mosaic Press, 1990

Richter, Melvin. *The Politics of Conscience: T.H. Green and His Age*. London: Weidenfeld & Nicolson, 1964

Rooke, Patricia T., and R.L. Schnell. *No Bleeding Heart: Charlotte Whitton, a Feminist on the Right*. Vancouver: University of British Columbia Press, 1988

Roper, Michael, and John Tosh, eds. *Manful Assertions: Masculinities in Britain since 1800*. London: Routledge, 1991

Rosenberg, Rosalind. *Beyond Separate Spheres: Intellectual Roots of Modern Feminism*. New Haven, Conn.: Yale University Press, 1982

Ross, Dorothy. *The Origins of American Social Science*. Cambridge, Eng.: Cambridge University Press, 1991

Ross, Murray G. *The Y.M.C.A. in Canada: The Chronicle of a Century*. Toronto: Ryerson Press, 1951

Scott, Joan Wallach. *Gender and the Politics of History*. New York: Columbia University Press, 1988

Shires, Linda M. *Rewriting the Victorians: Theory, History, and the Politics of Gender*. New York: Routledge, 1992

Shore, Marlene. *The Science of Social Redemption: McGill, the Chicago School, and the Origins of Social Research in Canada*. Toronto: University of Toronto Press, 1987

Shortt, S.E.D. *The Search for an Ideal: Six Canadian Intellectuals and Their Convictions in an Age of Transition, 1890–1930*. Toronto: University of Toronto Press, 1976

Smith, Marjorie J. *Professional Education for Social Work in Britain: An Historical Account*. London: George Allen & Unwin, 1965

Soffer, Reba N. *Ethics and Society in England: The Revolution in the Social Sciences, 1870–1914*. Berkeley: University of California Press, 1978

– 'Why Do Disciplines Fail? The Strange Case of British Sociology.' *English Historical Review* 97, no. 385 (October 1982), 767–802

Speisman, Stephen A. 'Munificent Parsons and Municipal Parsimony: Voluntary vs. Public Poor Relief in Nineteenth Century Toronto.' *Ontario History* 65, no.1 (March 1973), 32–49

Strong-Boag, Veronica. *The Parliament of Women: The National Council of Women of Canada, 1893–1929*. Ottawa: National Museum of Man, 1976

Struthers, James. '"Lord give us men": Women and Social Work in English Canada, 1918 to 1953.' *Canadian Historical Association Historical Papers* (1983), 96–112

– *The Limits of Affluence: Welfare in Ontario, 1920–1970*. Toronto: University of Toronto Press, 1994

Sutherland, John. *Mrs. Humphry Ward: Eminent Victorian, Pre-eminent Edwardian*. Oxford: Clarendon Press, 1990

Valverde, Mariana. *The Age of Light, Soap, and Water: Moral Reform in English Canada, 1885–1925*. Toronto: McClelland and Stewart, 1991

Van Die, Marguerite. *An Evangelical Mind: Nathanael Burwash and the Methodist Tradition in Canada, 1839–1918*. Montreal: McGill-Queen's University Press, 1989

Vicinus, Martha. *Independent Women: Work and Community for Single Women, 1850–1920*. Chicago: University of Chicago Press, 1985

Vincent, Andrew, and Raymond Plant. *Philosophy, Politics and Citizenship: The Life and Thought of the British Idealists*. Oxford: Basil Blackwell, 1984

Walden, Keith. 'Respectable Hooligans: Male Toronto College Students Celebrate Hallowe'en, 1884–1910.' *Canadian Historical Review* 68, no. 1 (March 1987), 1–34

– 'Hazes, Hustles, Scraps, and Stunts: Initiations at the University of Toronto, 1880–1925.' In *Youth, University and Canadian Society: Essays in the Social History of Higher Education*, ed. Paul Axelrod and John G. Reid, 94–121. Kingston, Ont.: McGill-Queen's University Press, 1989

Walkowitz, Judith R. *City of Dreadful Delight: Narratives of Sexual Danger in Late-Victorian London*. Chicago: University of Chicago Press, 1992

Wallace, W. Stewart. *A History of the University of Toronto, 1827–1927*. Toronto: University of Toronto Press, 1927

Illustration Credits

University of Toronto Archives: Class executive, *Torontonensis*, 1916; Ashley, B80-1107; Mavor, B85-0018/001P; pamphlet announcing appointment of Ware, B79-0059/035; original Social Service Building, A65-0004 [19.1]; McGregor, A78-0041/14(12); MacIver, A65-0004 [21/37]; Urwick, *Torontonensis*, 1937.

City of Toronto Archives: University Settlement, 1914, (1) DPW 32-305, (2) DPW 32-307; district office, DPW 32-388.

Index